Relationships Rights and Legal Pluralism

I0888345

This interdisciplinary book brings together leading social and legal scholars to tackle the incompatibility of marriage laws with contemporary social reality in Europe. Their critique is based on the assumption that individuals should be able to choose how they organise their close relationships. The contributors emphasise the importance of pluralism of beliefs, values, cultures, and lifestyles and the consequent need for legal recognition to make individuals' private choices valid and respected.

The first part of the book establishes the foundation for the subsequent chapters by exploring the advantages and challenges of focusing on values while accommodating relationship design plurality, the impact of the European Court of Human Rights on the issue, and the transformation of the institution of marriage. The second part presents different legal responses to non-state marriages, particularly religious marriages among Muslim communities, and proposals for reform. The third part of the book features empirical research on the marital experiences of two communities: Muslims and migrants. The chapters concentrate on polygyny among female converts to Islam, the importance of religious knowledge for practising Muslim women in securing rights in their marital relationships, transnational and interreligious marriages, and the impact of acculturative orientation and position in the dual labour market on the choice of life partner among Polish migrant women.

The book will be of interest to academics, researchers, and policymakers working in the areas of human rights law, family law, legal anthropology, law and religion, socio-legal studies, feminism and queer studies, and sociology of family.

Mateusz Stępień is a professor in the Department of Sociology of Law, Jagiellonian University, Poland.

Anna Juzaszek is a PhD candidate in the Department of Sociology of Law and Doctoral School in the Social Sciences, Jagiellonian University, Poland.

Relationships Rights and Legal Pluralism

The Inadequacy of Marriage Laws in Europe

Edited by Mateusz Stępień and Anna Juzaszek

Routledge
Taylor & Francis Group
LONDON AND NEW YORK

First published 2025
by Routledge
4 Park Square, Milton Park, Abingdon, Oxon OX14 4RN

and by Routledge
605 Third Avenue, New York, NY 10158

Routledge is an imprint of the Taylor & Francis Group, an informa business

British Library Cataloguing-in-Publication Data
A catalogue record for this book is available from the British Library

Library of Congress Cataloging-in-Publication Data
Names: Stępień, Mateusz, editor. | Juzaszek, Anna, editor.
Title: Relationships rights and legal pluralism : the inadequacy of marriage laws in Europe / [edited by] Mateusz Stępień, Anna Juzaszek.
Description: Abingdon, Oxon [UK] ; New York, NY : Routledge, 2024. | Includes bibliographical references and index. | Summary: "This interdisciplinary book brings together leading social and legal scholars to tackle the incompatibility of marriage laws with contemporary social reality in Europe. Their critique is based on the assumption that individuals should be able to choose how they organise their close relationships. The contributors emphasise the importance of pluralism of beliefs, values, cultures and lifestyles and the consequent need for legal recognition to make individuals' private choices valid and respected. The first part of the book establishes the foundation for the subsequent chapters by exploring the advantages and challenges of focusing on values while accommodating relationship design plurality, the impact of the European Court of Human Rights on the issue and the transformation of the institution of marriage. The second part presents different legal responses to non-state marriages, particularly religious marriages in Muslim communities, and proposals for reform. The third part of the book features empirical research on the marital experiences of two communities: Muslims and migrants. The chapters concentrate on polygyny among female converts to Islam, the importance of religious knowledge for practicing Muslim women to secure rights in their marital relationships, transnational and interreligious marriages and the impact of acculturative orientation and position in the dual labour market on the choice of life partner among Polish migrant women. The book will be of interest to academics, researchers and policy-makers working in the areas of human rights law, family law, legal anthropology, law and religion, socio-legal studies, feminism and queer studies and sociology of family"— Provided by publisher.
Identifiers: LCCN 2024017024 (print) | LCCN 2024017025 (ebook) | ISBN 9781032741451 (hardback) | ISBN 9781032747637 (paperback) | ISBN 9781003470786 (ebook)
Subjects: LCSH: Marriage law—Europe. | Husband and wife—Europe. | Marriage (Islamic law) | Marriage—Religious aspects—Islam. | Divorce (Islamic law) | Legal polycentricity—Europe.
Classification: LCC KJC1121 .R45 2024 (print) | LCC KJC1121 (ebook) | DDC 346.401/6—dc23/eng/20240416
LC record available at https://lccn.loc.gov/2024017024
LC ebook record available at https://lccn.loc.gov/2024017025

ISBN: 978-1-032-74145-1 (hbk)
ISBN: 978-1-032-74763-7 (pbk)
ISBN: 978-1-003-47078-6 (ebk)

DOI: 10.4324/9781003470786

Typeset in Galliard
by Apex CoVantage, LLC

The research for this publication has been supported by a grant from the Priority Research Area "Heritage" under the Strategic Programme Excellence Initiative at Jagiellonian University.

Contents

Contributors

Amal Alqawasmi

Amal Alqawasmi is a post-doctoral research fellow in the School of Law at the University of Milano-Bicocca. She has been awarded her second PhD in legal sciences, curriculum law and pluralism from the School of Law at the University of Milano–Bicocca, while her first PhD was in jurisprudence and its foundations from The University of Jordan. Her main research interests are family law, religious diversity, comparative legal studies, and human rights.

Anna Juzaszek

Anna Juzaszek obtained her degrees from the Jagiellonian University, Poland: BA in comparative studies of civilizations (2012), MA in law (2014), and MA in sociology (2019). Since 2019, she has been a PhD candidate in the Department of Sociology of Law and Doctoral School in the Social Sciences, Jagiellonian University. Her doctoral thesis focuses on the right to marry and to found a family (Art. 12 of the European Convention on Human Rights). Additionally, she is a principal investigator in the research project "The prohibition of entering into religious-only marriages from the perspective of human rights in Europe" and was a co-investigator in the research project "Let's Empower, Participate and Teach each other to Hype Empathy: Challenging Discourse about Islam and Muslims in Poland". Her main academic interests are empirical legal research, the Muslim minority in India, and human rights, particularly the right to marry and the right to respect for private and family life.

Simran Kalra

Simran Kalra was awarded a PhD in law at Dickson Poon School of Law, King's College London (2023). Her departmentally funded research examined British Muslim women's use of Islamic and state legal ordering in England and identified the plurality of marital unions within the two legal orders. Her work is located at the cusp of legal pluralism and legal consciousness studies. Her research interests include sociology of law, migration, gender, and family relations. She is a lecturer of law at the University of Leicester.

Jan Bazyli Klakla

Jan Bazyli Klakla, PhD in legal sciences and PhD in sociology, both at Jagiellonian University in Cracow. Graduate of law, sociology, and culture studies at the same university and postgraduate studies in international migration at Warsaw University. He works as a social science specialist at the Center for Social and Economic Research in Warsaw and as a postdoc at the Center for Legal Education and Social Theory at the University of Wroclaw. His interests focus on migration, sociology of law, education research, policy analysis, criminology, customary law, green transition, and the methodology of social sciences.

Francesca Miccoli

Francesca Miccoli holds a PhD in political studies from the University of Milan. She graduated in law at the University of Bologna. She is currently a postdoctoral fellow at the University of Basel, working on the research project: "Just Parenthood: The Ethics and Politics of Childrearing in the 21st Century". She is also an adjunct lecturer at the University of Milan, where she teaches "Theories of Equality and Rights" and "Law and Social Change". Her main academic interests are family ethics and politics, legal recognition of unconventional families, especially polyamorous families, and legal feminism. Her current research involves the legal implications of family transformations on family law regimes and socio-legal norms, and the normative implications of parenting and co-parenting, with a specific focus on multi-parenthood, the valorization of intentionality and care to build an ethics of just parenthood, equality between different kinds of families, and gender equality.

Annelies Moors

Annelies Moors is an anthropologist affiliated to the University of Amsterdam. She studied Arabic in Syria and has conducted extensive fieldwork in Palestine and the Netherlands. From 2001–2008 she directed the Muslim Cultural Politics programme at ISIM (the International Institute for the Study of Islam in the Modern World). Engaging with the entanglements of gender, nation, class, and religion, she published widely on Muslim family law; dress, fashion and face-veiling; wearing gold; migrant domestic labor; the politics of marriage; and doing ethnography. She recently held an ERC advanced grant and was a fellow at NIAS (Netherlands Institute for Advanced Studies).

Rehana Parveen

Rehana Parveen is a former family law solicitor and currently an associate professor at Birmingham Law School. She teaches on wide range of modules including family law, decolonising legal concepts, legal skills and methods, and equity and trusts. Her research interests are in investigating the developing relationships between English family law and Islamic family law and how women navigate these interacting frameworks including their use of sharia councils. More recently, she has been exploring how legal concepts and structures may be decolonised to place them within their social, historical, political, and postcolonial context.

Susan Rutten

Susan Rutten is a professor of Islamic family law in a European context at Maastricht University, Faculty of Law, the Netherlands. She has developed long-term research expertise in the area of Islamic family law and family issues amongst ethnic and religious minorities in the Netherlands and Europe. In this field, she regularly coordinates research projects, writes publications, gives lectures and training, acts as an expert, and supervises PhD-theses. More specifically, her research focuses on religious and cultural diversity in the field of marriage (i.a. religious marriages and child marriages); divorce; and issues surrounding children and Islamic family law, including transnational family law and human rights. She is the chair of the Association for the Study of Islamic Law and Law of the Middle East (RIMO) in the Netherlands, a member of the State Committee for Private International Law, a member of the HCCH-Expert Group on Parentage and Surrogacy, and has acted as a substitute Judge at the Court of Appeal (Family Law Chamber) in 's-Hertogenbosch (the Netherlands).

Ibtisam Sadegh

Ibtisam Sadegh is a lecturer at the civil law department at the University of Malta. She completed a PhD at the University of Amsterdam in 2023 on Muslim–Christian couples in Ceuta, the Spanish enclave on the north Moroccan coast. In 2013, she obtained a Doctor of Law (LL.D.) at the University of Malta for her comparative research on religious courts and tribunals in Malta and England and Wales. Her research interests include mixed marriages, religious identities, and minority communities.

Mateusz Stępień

Mateusz Stępień is a professor at the Jagiellonian University, where he combines theoretical work with empirical legal research. He serves as a principal investigator in research projects such as "The Empathy Challenge: The Case of Polish Judges" and "Theory of Legislative Placebo". He has edited volumes including *Bronislaw Malinowski's Concept of Law* (2016) and co-authored the book *Courtroom Power Distance Dynamics* (2021).

Paulina Szydłowska-Klakla

Paulina Szydłowska-Klakla, PhD in psychology. Graduate of psychology and culture studies at Jagiellonian University in Cracow. She defended her thesis about the acculturation experiences of Polish migrant children and their families living in Spain. She works as a psychologist with children and adolescents and as an assistant professor at the Faculty of Psychology in Kraków at the SWPS University.

Pol van de Wiel

Pol van de Wiel is a teacher at the Faculty of Law of Maastricht University. He studied law (BA, 2011) and philosophy at Leiden University, history and political science at the Institut d'études politiques de Paris and political theory at the École des hautes études en sciences sociales in Paris (MA, 2013; mention: very good). In 2023, he obtained his PhD at Radboud University in Nijmegen on the history and transformation of civil marriage in the Netherlands and France. He published on legal professional standards (notably with respect to the Public Prosecutor), political theory and history, and the history of family law. His 2023 dissertation (to be published in Dutch in 2024) follows the trail of civil marriage from its early beginnings through to the present day, guided by the question how the values of freedom and equality, and the processes of secularization and individualization, affected its legal content and social status.

Vanessa Vroon-Najem

Vanessa Vroon-Najem is an anthropologist affiliated with the University of Amsterdam, where she also obtained her PhD. She is specialised in the field of conversion to Islam in the Netherlands and has published about this subject since 2007. Her contribution in this volume is based on her research on how converts to Islam in the Netherlands find a partner and conclude their Islamic and/or civil marriage(s). She has a passion for bridging the gap between academia and public programmes and has curated three museum exhibitions based on her research and made a documentary, titled *Marrying Before Allah – Personal Stories of Converts*, with visual anthropologist Wendy van Wilgenburg. She also works as an educator at Amsterdam Museum and is a member of the board of editors of Amsterdam Museum Journal.

Introduction

Anna Juzaszek and Mateusz Stępień

1. Basic assumptions

Establishing and maintaining close relationships with other people is, for the majority of individuals, one of the most important parts of life. It affects their well-being, identity, sense of security, and happiness, to name but a few. When it comes to the choice of a partner(s), family structure, and the principles on which a given relationship will be based, a variety of preferences are observed in Europe. At the same time, the individual freedom to choose a way of life is considered to be an important characteristic of contemporary European liberal democracies. Therefore, the basic assumption behind this book is that it should be the decision of each person about whom they wish to enter into a relationship with, how they want to structure it, and around what values they want to centre it: love, care, respect, stability, safety, friendship, etc. In other words, individuals should be the ones who determine their relationship design.

To put the aforementioned choice into practice, we need societies in which varying beliefs, different sexual orientations, and numerous cultures are regarded as a value rather than a threat. Consequently, we should take advantage of this plurality rather than pushing only one version of a 'good life' preferably with traditional connotations. This, however, requires a willingness to embrace changes and new ideas, as well as an open-minded attitude. Although the proposed vision may appear to many as utopian, social diversity is already an empirical fact in Europe that cannot simply be ignored. Social changes; postulates of discriminated minorities whose voices have not been heard before; the influx of migrants and their cultures, religions, or habits; the emergence of new religious movements; all introduce a variety of human values, interests, and needs that somehow have to be accommodated.

This pluralisation of social life poses new challenges and raises objections from individuals and groups who value a well-established order, traditions, and culture, as well as those who are afraid of losing their 'way of life'. For this reason, the first reaction is often an attempt to stifle diversity, problematise it, or use old and Eurocentric solutions that are not always well-suited to the new reality. The authors of the book believe this is not the right approach. In their

DOI: 10.4324/9781003470786-1

chapters they demonstrate the injustices that this leads to and ponder more equitable solutions.

2. Marriage, relationships, and family

As indicated at the beginning, this book centres around the variety of relationship designs, focusing on how and with whom adult people choose to spend and share their lives, and why.[1] At the same time, we consider all such relationships to constitute family life, but we do not delve into the subject of defining a family. Given that adult relationships and family in Europe are strongly associated (although not exclusively) with marital status (Palazzo 2021, 4), it is the institution of marriage, including its laws and practices, that is the focal point for the contributors. Nevertheless, using only the term 'marriage' would significantly limit the diversity observed in adult familial relationships (see Chambers and Gracia 2022; Morgan 2011; Swennen 2020) and would contradict the aims and aspirations of this book.

Although many people decide to enter into state-sanctioned marriage and regard this type of arrangement for their close relationship as important and valuable, the number of people cohabiting is increasing (Barlow 2006; Akhtar, Nash, and Probert 2020). Furthermore, there may be close relationships (whether marital or not) that lack the element of cohabitation (Levin and Trost 1999; Haskey and Lewis 2006; Régnier-Loilier 2017). We also observe the phenomenon of marriages that are not concluded and sanctioned according to state law but according to other norms, such as religious (Akhtar 2018b; Bone 2020) and cultural (*Muñoz Díaz v. Spain* 2009), or loosely defined rituals such as humanistic marriages (Probert, Akhtar, and Blake 2023). We will collectively refer to them in the introduction, following one of our contributors – Susan Rutten (2025) in Chapter 5 – as 'non-state marriages' because they are not recognised by state law and therefore not considered as forming a legal marital bond. However, it is important to note that, depending on the country, some marriages solemnised in this way may be recognised by civil law (in most circumstances when meeting additional legal requirements). In such cases, these become state-recognised marriages and are no longer non-state marriages.

Furthermore, the lack of a state-sanctioned marriage between adults living in a close relationship may occur either by choice or because it is impossible to get married according to state rules. The former may be caused by patriarchal and traditional connotations of the marriage institution, not being perceived as something important for emphasising the bond between persons, being seen as just an additional bureaucratic formality, or a result of insufficient awareness of the legal ramifications of not having marital status (Duncan, Barlow, and James 2005; Uddin 2018). The latter may be due to a lack of documentation,

1 Therefore, we don't analyse the issues of children or extended family.

especially in the case of refugees (Akhtar 2018a), the desire to enter into a polyamorous or same-sex relationship (in some countries), or being in another type of relationship that does not qualify as marriage, such as the well-known English case of two cohabiting sisters (***Burden and Burden v. The United Kingdom*** 2008).

The social situation regarding relationship design and the way adults structure their closest family is very complex. However, as we shall see in the book, marriage (as a legal institution) is perceived in Europe in a very rigid and defined way with close connotations to Christian tradition, as a monogamous relationship based on romantic love between people of the opposite sex, and preferably as a lifelong commitment. Furthermore, there is a conviction that this centuries-old institution is sturdy and unalterable (although the assumption of its unchangeability is far from the truth). Therefore, any alterations to this institution or its diminishing importance are often perceived as a threat to the current social order.

3. Recognition by the law

The association of close adult relationships and the family ties they create with the institution of marriage has far-reaching consequences. The most visible one is that in many European countries marriage is the only family arrangement that enjoys full legal protection under state law. Recognition of other family relationships varies between countries and between types of relationship, but they rarely enjoy the same legal status as married couples.

While the contributors do not disregard or ignore important changes, such as same-sex marriages, civil partnerships (and other similar institutions), equalisation of the status of children born in and out of wedlock, recognition of gender-affirming surgery that allows transgender people to marry a person of the opposite sex, and many more, closer examination shows that much more needs to be done if we truly wish to uphold the idea that individuals are free to choose their family structure. The authors believe that this freedom cannot be fully realised if the state only certifies narrowly defined relations, leaving many others outside its scope. Those left behind cannot feel acceptable, equitable, and respected in society. Furthermore, it is not the appropriate way to protect the vulnerable party, if there is any.

How the law is structured in a given society sends a powerful message about what is officially acceptable and desirable. This often has a strong impact on the lives of individuals, especially if their life choices do not fit the path prescribed by the legislator. This impact is not limited to the realm of legal protection but also affects how individuals are perceived by the rest of society. Moreover, legal solutions outside the main marriage laws and rules, such as migration laws and policies, laws connected to accessing the labour market, and other social rights, can also influence relationship choices. Therefore, any legal reform in this regard should ideally draw from extensive research that takes into account various societal groups to avoid undesired infringement on the freedom to choose one's relationship design. Any limitations should be balanced and preceded by careful examination.

4. Aims of the book

The first and basic aim of this book is to present the plurality and complexity of familial relationships, rather than focusing solely on one issue, as is often the case in the literature. While it is not a comprehensive elaboration, as this would be impossible, the book intentionally provides a broad perspective to confirm what has been previously stated, namely that legal reforms must take into account many diverse, and often contradictory, interests and needs. Furthermore, the book is intended to inspire readers originally interested in one of the presented topics to discover that there are others which are closely related.

The second and main aim is to explore how to approach the issue of the plurality of relationship design, particularly from the perspective of the law and public authorities. The contributors examine the status quo and highlight the injustices associated with it. Finally, they propose possible directions for reforms. As there is no single or easy answer in this regard, the authors of this book are free to propose their own ideas and add unique voices to the ongoing discussion.

An analysis of the assumptions underlying the institution of marriage is the third aim. This includes an investigation into the legal regulations, the practices of governmental agencies, court rulings, and the historical context. Such an examination helps us understand how this institution is perceived in Europe, the characteristics attributed to it, and how it is instrumentalised by the state, for example, in migration policies. It is a starting point for discussion: whether there is a need to question the current understanding of marriage, what it protects, what it could protect, and whether there are other ways of looking at it.

The fourth aim is to delve into the experiences of individuals when making their relationship choices. The book examines the driving forces behind their decisions, what was important to them, the obstacles they encountered, and how they describe their experiences. Legal reforms will remain inadequate if those most affected are not given a voice. This is particularly true for women, who are often still the vulnerable party and are the ones whom legal reforms are said to protect. However, their voices are frequently ignored or disregarded, assuming that they lack agency because of their membership in a minority group (e.g., Muslim) or because their choices, such as for example entering into a polygynous marriage, are difficult for the majority to comprehend.

The fifth and final aim, closely connected to the fourth one, is to explore the influence of legal regulations and state actions on relationship choices. The contributors are interested in the potential impact on decisions about who to enter into a relationship with and whether and when to leave a partner. Moreover, certain public policies may negatively affect the overall experience of being in a relationship. Years of efforts to gain recognition, acceptance, and validation can leave their mark on the individuals involved. All of this provides insight into the consequences of legal solutions and may motivate their reconsideration.

To achieve this broad perspective, the book brings together researchers working on various topics such as religious-only marriages, same-sex marriages, polyamorous and polygamous relationships, transnational marriages, and migrant marriages. Additionally, the contributors have diverse academic backgrounds, including law, sociology, anthropology, ethnography, philosophy, history, cultural studies, and psychology. Consequently, the book addresses the issue of relationship design from an intersectional and interdisciplinary point of view, even though the law is at the centre of attention.

This also affects how the authors approach the law in their chapters. The focus is on the interrelation between law and society, not solely on legal rules. The contributors use their experiences from different disciplines to enrich their analysis, making this book a part of research fields such as legal sociology, legal anthropology, and cultural legal studies.

We have combined general approaches with case studies of the actions of international bodies, the laws of specific countries, and the experiences of particular groups. The former includes chapters in which the authors analyse new ways of discussing the plurality of relationship types, historical changes to the marriage institution, and the applicability of legal pluralism in Europe. The latter consists first of chapters dealing with human rights and the adjudications of the European Court of Human Rights (ECtHR) which, at least in principle, can be perceived as a guide for European states on how to approach the issue of marriage and the plurality of relationship designs.

Then, there are chapters on the Netherlands and England and Wales. There is currently a lively discussion in these countries about the topic at hand, especially when it comes to Muslim religious-only marriages, although the planned reform goes in a more general direction. In England and Wales, the latest report from the Law Commission (2022) entitled 'Celebrating Marriages: A New Weddings Law', issued in July 2022, concerns the idea of not making the validity of the marriage dependent on the place of marriage (the place-based approach) but on the marriage officiant (the celebrant-based approach). This, if it is enacted, could result in easier legal recognition of religious or humanistic marriage ceremonies. In the Netherlands, in July 2023, changes in civil law were enacted to facilitate the termination of religious marriages to counter the phenomenon of 'marital captivity'. Spouses are now obliged to cooperate in dissolution and the court may order such a behaviour if one party does not participate (see Chapter 5 by Rutten 2025).

Lastly, we focus on empirical research revolving around two communities: Muslims and migrants. Therefore, there are chapters dedicated to the marital experiences of Muslim women in the Netherlands and England. As they remain a highly problematised minority in Europe, it is crucial to debunk some of the myths and stereotypes that have grown up around them. Finally, there are two chapters on the migrant perspective. The first concerns transnational interreligious couples in Ceuta, and therefore touches upon the issue of migration from outside the European Union (EU). The second refers to intra-EU migration by studying Polish migrant women in Madrid. The juxtaposition of these two chapters gives an interesting perspective. Even though they both focus on the same country, the barriers faced by individuals entering into nationally mixed marriages differ significantly.

5. Structure of the book

The first part of the book provides an introduction to the topic and establishes the foundation for the subsequent chapters. We begin with Chapter 1 by Mateusz Stępień who offers his theoretical propositions on human axiological experiences. He discusses the advantages of focusing on values, as well as the challenges of such an approach, when it comes to accommodating relationship design plurality. Then, we proceed to chapters which focus on the institution of marriage in the European context.

Chapters 2 and 3 are dedicated to human rights. Both authors argue that the human rights framework, when it comes to family relationships, does not support the observed social plurality. On the contrary, it may even impede the potential legal changes in marriage laws by upholding a traditional understanding of marriage and perceiving this legal regime as the most desirable. In the second chapter, Anna Juzaszek centres her analysis on the right to marry and to found a family contained in Article 12 of the European Convention on Human Rights (ECHR). She points out its particular role in maintaining the status quo, while assuming that human rights should commit to value pluralism, and hence, they should be a means to enhance respect and recognition for various lifestyles. Francesca Miccoli then delves into the adjudication of the ECtHR using a queer sociological perspective in the third chapter. Miccoli is particularly interested in how the ECtHR evaluates marriage as opposed to civil partnership and its approach to the idea of various and flexible legal regimes regulating family relationships.

The first part concludes with Chapter 4 by Pol van de Wiel, who presents a historical and philosophical perspective on the transformation of marriage institutions that led to the recognition of same-sex marriage in some European countries. While most of the contributors in the book draw attention to the inadequacies or obsolescence of current marriage laws, Van de Wiel demonstrates that radical transformations are possible in this sphere of social life. This gives hope that the problems discussed in the book may no longer occur in the future, and it serves as a reminder that no social institution is unchangeable.

The second part of the book is devoted to the legal solutions regarding non-state marriages. The section begins with Susan Rutten's Chapter 5, which provides insight into the Dutch legal situation. Rutten outlines how the subject has been approached in the Netherlands, recent reforms, and possible mechanisms for addressing these marriages, including the use of institutional mechanisms in law, general legal concepts, human rights, and the equality principle.

The other two chapters in this part focus predominantly on the topic of religious marriages, especially Muslim marriages. In Chapter 6, Rehana Parveen takes us to England and Wales and discusses the legal arrangements when it comes to these marriages. She points out the Eurocentrism of legal solutions that neglect the plurality of contemporary societies and consequently ignore that Muslims are part of the British society. Parveen suggests that the state should adopt a minimalist approach to marriage laws by shifting the focus away from the specific details of the marriage ceremony that need to be fulfilled for it to have legal effect. Instead, a post ceremony registration process should be implemented. Consequently, this solution would apply not just to the Muslim community.

In Chapter 7 Amal Alqawasmi does not focus on the legal system of any European country. Instead, she approaches the subject from a more general perspective by addressing some of the most common allegations directed at the Muslim community and shows the complexity of the issue. Alqawasmi then ponders how legal pluralism can be applied in this regard and proposes granting recognition and officiality to Muslim family provisions in European jurisdictions.

The third and final part of the book is devoted to empirical research on the marital reality of individuals. In Chapter 8, Vanessa Vroon-Najem and Annelies Moors shed light on the experiences of women who convert to Islam and choose to enter into polygynous marriage. Although these marriages are often portrayed from a negative and simplified perspective, Vroon-Najem and Moors present a more nuanced picture. They explain why women decide to enter into such relationships and discuss both their negative and positive experiences.

In Chapter 9, Simran Kalra explores the importance of religious knowledge and claims to spirituality for practising Muslim women for their marital negotiations. Kalra argues that women are not passive in following religious guidelines. On the contrary, they use Islamic arguments to secure their rights (also legal) in marital relations. However, as the research revealed, gaining religious knowledge is often fraught with difficulties. Therefore, expanding legal awareness or legislating to recognise the nikah in state law might not be sufficient to enhance Muslim women's agency and safeguard their claims in intimate relationships. Instead, there is a need to assist their access to religious education.

Ibtisam Sadegh focuses on transnational and interreligious marriages in Ceuta in Chapter 10. These are perceived as suspicious, especially when they involve one Spanish and one Moroccan spouse, and as possible 'marriages of convenience' by the Ceutan marriage registrar. The reasons are mostly geopolitical in nature as Ceuta sees itself as a gatekeeper to the European Union. The institution of marriage is instrumentalised by the state in its migration policies. All of this influence the lives and experiences of these mixed couples: not just how they feel in Ceuta but also how they speak about their relationship.

Lastly, in Chapter 11, we conclude by looking at Polish migrant women living in Madrid. Jan Bazyli Klakla and Paulina Szydłowska-Klakla consider the potential impact of the acculturative orientation of these women and their position in the dual labour market on their choice of life partner. Consequently, the authors hypothesise that the orientation of the host society and public policies (including legal provisions) related to migrants' access to the labour market in a host country may, in fact, also impact their marital decisions.

6. Conclusion

The topic of marriage, close relationships, and family is intensively discussed in the public sphere on various occasions. Although it may be perceived as a very private matter for individuals, we hope this book shows that this choice is often actively limited by state actions and state law, with its unquestionable power to determine what is considered 'normal' and desirable behaviour. Furthermore, despite visible changes, relationships that fall outside the traditional concept of marriage (influenced by Christianity) are still problematised, stereotyped, and presented as a threat to European values, societies, women, and so on.

It is essential to note that the contributors do not take the position that this sphere should be left outside the state's interest. Being in a close relationship may bring a lot of benefits to the people involved but is also fraught with risks. Embedded in this are dependency and vulnerability, therefore, when there is a change of feelings or bad intentions someone might suffer. In these circumstances, the state apparatus is one of the stronger (although not the only) institutions that can offer protection and lessen the harm. At the same time, we acknowledge there are people who would like to be free from any state influence when it comes to their relationships. Their voices and interests should also be carefully examined and taken into consideration when designing legal solutions. However, it is worth pointing out that a complete invisibility to the law is probably difficult to achieve in today's world.

As previously stated, this book does not provide one comprehensive answer about the legal response to the pluralism of relationship designs in Europe. Rather, it emphasises the complexity of the issue. The authors were free to present their own ideas, and they did not have to agree with one another. Moreover, we do not overestimate the significance of the law. It is not the only tool for empowering people and producing more equality. Probably not even the best one. The law – its use and interpretation – is entangled and dependent on a myriad of things such as culture, religion, worldview, political views, legal awareness, etc. Therefore, the solution to a particular issue may not always lie in legal changes.

Lastly, it is crucial to point out that plurality in the types of relationships is an empirical fact in Europe. Therefore, if we want to uphold the idea of freedom to live one's life in the manner of one's choosing, we need to rethink the assumptions held by European societies and enshrined in European laws surrounding the institution of marriage and other intimate relationships. This does not mean there cannot be limitations on that freedom but only that they should be carefully balanced and better thought through.

Without further ado, hoping we do justice to the thoughts of the contributors to this book, we give them the floor as they will best present their research and ideas. We believe this book will be an inspiring read for researchers from different fields and with various interests when it comes to marriage, relationships, and family.

References

Akhtar, Rajnaara C. 2018a. "The Human Right to Marry: A Refugee's Perspective." *Journal of Social Welfare and Family Law* 40 (2): 262–69.

———. 2018b. "Modern Traditions in Muslim Marriage Practices, Exploring English Narratives." *Oxford Journal of Law and Religion* 7 (3): 427–54.

Akhtar, Rajnaara C., Patrick Nash, and Rebecca Probert. 2020. "Introduction." In *Cohabitation and Religious Marriage: Status, Similarities and Solutions*, edited by Rajnaara C. Akhtar, Patrick Nash, and Rebecca Probert, 1–14. Bristol: Bristol University Press.

Barlow, Anne. 2006. "Cohabitation Law Reform – Messages from Research." *Feminist Legal Studies* 14 (2): 167–80.

Bone, Amra. 2020. "Islamic Marriage and Divorce in the United Kingdom: The Case for a New Paradigm." *Journal of Muslim Minority Affairs* 40 (1): 163–78.

Chambers, Deborah, and Pablo Gracia. 2022. *A Sociology of Family Life: Change and Diversity in Intimate Relations.* 2nd ed. Cambridge, UK; Medford, MA: Polity Press.

Duncan, Simon, Anne Barlow, and Grace James. 2005. "Why Don't They Marry? Cohabitation, Commitment and DIY Marriage." *Child & Family Quarterly* 17 (3): 383–98.

Haskey, John, and Jane Lewis. 2006. "Living-Apart-Together in Britain: Context and Meaning." *International Journal of Law in Context* 2 (1): 37–48.

Law Commission. 2022. *Celebrating Marriage: A New Weddings Law.* London: Crown.

Levin, Irene, and Jan Trost. 1999. "Living Apart Together." *Community, Work & Family* 2 (3): 279–94.

Morgan, David H. J. 2011. *Rethinking Family Practices.* London, UK: Palgrave Macmillan.

Palazzo, Nausica. 2021. *Legal Recognition of Non-Conjugal Families: New Frontiers in Family Law in the US, Canada and Europe.* New York: Hart Publishing.

Probert, Rebecca, Rajnaara C. Akhtar, and Sharon Blake. 2023. *Belief in Marriage: The Evidence for Reforming Weddings Law.* Bristol: Bristol University Press.

Régnier-Loilier, Arnaud. 2017. "Conjugal Outcomes of Different Types of Non-Cohabiting Relationships." In *A Longitudinal Approach to Family Trajectories in France.* INED Population Studies. Vol. 7, edited by Arnaud Régnier-Loilier, 27–50. Cham: Springer International Publishing.

Rutten, Susan. 2025. "Addressing Non-State Marriages in State Law; Responses from the Netherlands." In *Relationships Rights and Legal Pluralism: The Inadequacy of Marriage Laws in Europe*, edited by Mateusz Stępień and Anna Juzaszek. London: Routledge.

Swennen, Frederik. 2020. "Un-Coupling Family Law: The Legal Recognition and Protection of Adult Unions Outside of Conjugal Coupledom." *Feminist Legal Studies* 28 (1): 39–60.

Uddin, Islam. 2018. "Nikah- Only Marriages: Causes, Motivations, and Their Impact on Dispute Resolution and Islamic Divorce Proceedings in England and Wales." *Oxford Journal of Law and Religion* 7 (3): 401–26.

Cited legal cases

Burden and Burden v. The United Kingdom (no. 13378/05, ECtHR, 29 April 2008).

Muñoz Díaz v. Spain (no. 49151/07, ECtHR, 8 December 2009).

I

Theoretical and historical foundations of relationship design, human rights, and pluralism in Europe

1 Value-centered approach to the plurality of types of intimate relationships

Mateusz Stępień

1.1 Introduction

Although the Western liberal world is characterized by hegemony, at least officially, of monogamous opposite-sex civil marriage, de facto pluralism is emerging in the types of intimate relationships that function as the best frameworks for living a 'good life'. This wave of pluralization covers not only same-sex relationships and religious-based intimate bonds but also plenty of mostly care-centered relationship types often established to avoid reproducing cultural and structural features of traditional marriage that are claimed to be discriminatory and unjust.

The changes occurring are driven by diverse factors. Among them are social and economic processes allowing some people to orient themselves around post-material values, as well as cultural changes marked by a preference for the 'idiosyncratic' and authentic elements of relationships. The re-establishment of the importance of religions among some groups (a process to some extent associated with migration) is also mobilizing societal expectations regarding the legal recognition (or not) of the forms of living together prescribed by religions. Interestingly, there are commonalities in argumentation and even common interests between advocates for legal recognition of both religious arrangements and secular unorthodox unions. This adds complexity to the discussion about the forms of relationships that the state should or should not legally recognize and support.

Discussion on the pluralism of types of intimate relationships is mushrooming. Vivid debates oscillate around the legitimized role of the state in licensing and then protecting (and regulating) some types of intimate arrangements (the question about the role of the state; see, e.g., Metz 2010; Chambers 2017). In addition, huge controversy arises around calls for (i) abolishing the existing regimes, mainly marriage, and (ii) developing alternative legal frameworks – often termed 'pluralistic' – within the marriage law that accommodate non-marital relationships (see Aloni 2016). Moreover, there are extensive commentaries both on courts' jurisprudence (e.g., judicial challenges to the so-called traditional marriage; see Rollins 2017) and legislative reforms introduced in some countries, which center on the recognition of certain types of

DOI: 10.4324/9781003470786-3

relationships. Finally, many authors are exploring the philosophical dimension of the issue under consideration. Most arguments are formulated from the liberal, libertarian, feminist, and (new) natural law perspectives. Each of them provides a set of guiding themes and points of reference. However, these voices are largely incomprehensible and incommensurable with each other (see MacIntyre 1989, Ch. XIX). Recognizing the need to move beyond such discourses, as they are infused with ideological assumptions, this chapter explores how we can approach the pluralization of intimate relationships through value-centered lenses.

Notions about marriage and other types of relationships are full of references to values, but most of them are merely ornamental, without any deeper problematization of the axiological dynamic in this sphere. Arguments referring to values are typically aimed at concluding discussions rather than beginning to unpack the networks of complex axiology in which the subject is enmeshed. Moreover, 'value' is often treated as a self-explanatory concept, with a lack of studies demonstrating the complex value dynamics in intimate relationships. Only Elisabeth van Acker (2016, 2017) has provided a comprehensive analysis that focuses on values-related issues of the state policies in this area. While her study has innovative character (especially dwelling on the disconnectedness of relationships' values) and moves from just episodic and ornamental references to values, van Acker's conceptualization of value is flawed (e.g., with an unsophisticated and flat understanding of values and a lack of discussion about value dynamics in the sphere under study). More importantly, van Acker does not offer any, even general, ideas on how taking a value-centered perspective influences one's understanding of the problems associated with approaching the pluralism of types of relationships.

Given the vastness of this debate, there is great scope and need to consider how best to approach de facto pluralism, existing legal regimes, and proposed frameworks. To offer new lenses through which the discussion can be regarded, the chapter utilizes the axiological approach. Placing the complex dynamic of values in society at the heart of the discussion provides fruitful language and conceptual tools to elaborate on the issues. The presented approach also unpacks axiological dynamics (mostly by providing sociologically inspired insights) and tracks the genealogy of actual, empirical (detectable, recognizable), and, to a large extent, inevitable (inherent in the human condition) sites of value pluralism in the subject of interest.

Importantly, rather than offering a particular argument or claim regarding a certain jurisdiction, the chapter instead provides overall insight into what the axiological approach brings to the discussion about approaching the pluralism of types of relationships. In this sense, it presents only an initial exploration into the thinking about approaching the pluralization of relationships, the status of marriage, and other forms of intimate attachments through axiological lenses. As such, the chapter does not map the discussed approaches to values. The employed understanding of value and value dynamics is mainly based on a vast Polish sociological tradition of studying values (e.g., Ossowski [1967] 2000; Pałecki 2013a, 2013b) backed and informed by pragmatism (Dewey 1939) as well as new threads developed in embodied cognitive sciences (Barrett 2023, 41–60).

The first part of the chapter presents the approach to 'value' (and value pluralism) that will be employed in the second part.

1.2 Two initial claims

The argument is based on two starting claims presented here in a nutshell. According to the first, what distinguishes humans from other animals is that we can scan both the material reality and our imaginary worlds and, in doing so, mark and select certain states of affairs that we feel or acknowledge as desirable. Simply, humans valorize and prioritize certain states of affairs (a claim about *homo axiologicus*). Second, what distinguishes humans even more profoundly is that we create, maintain, and upgrade multiple – working on different levels of social organization – tools and toolkits for achieving values. We do so because values call to be protected, expanded, or realized (at least most of them, though not ideational values, which play only aspirational roles and are not actually something we gain). These instruments are highly differentiated (some derive from natural implications, others from cultural dynamics, and most of them from integration of the two) and multi-layered (e.g., there is a difference between the 'flight response' and the establishment of a police force to secure people's safety). To demonstrate the variability among these instruments, one may compare an axe, architecture, and law. Each has a different character (ontological status) and functionality, and they work extremally differently as instruments of achieving values. Moreover, humans living within a given community can (re)create and transform supra-individual, multi-level infrastructure, which stabilizes their achievement of the most crucially desirable states of affairs. Each society needs, to a large extent, non-spontaneous and collectively managed ways of achieving values.

The importance of values does not mean that people are not driven by other determinants. In fact, complete determination of human life by values is impossible. A factor in this is values' inconsistency and conflicts between them. Moreover, social stratification and power structures differentiate who can attain their values and to what extent. The alternative is the total absence of (i) stable ways of translating values into strategies for achieving them, and (ii) further actions for realizing values. The scenario speaks of dehumanization, that is living in extremely unfavorable conditions where life is, in the words of Hobbes, 'nasty, brutish and short'. When humans are completely deprived of the possibility to select and valorize the states of affairs surrounding them, and there is no working social infrastructure aiming to secure and stabilize the processes oriented at gaining, at least, the ultimate values, then something very important is missing.

1.3 Glimpse into the 'axiological world' of an individual

In this approach, values are not fictions or constructs of the researcher, rationalizations of the impression of the subject, or projections imposed on an indifferent world. Values exist in real life – they are phenomena in the world, psychosocial facts. Axiological experiences are empirical; however, attempts to track them generate numerous problems. Moreover, when it comes to the nature of values, one should consider their externalization (including symbolization) or, put differently, how they 'live outside the mind'. This rejects the extreme mentalist claim that values 'reside' only in the minds of subjects (see extensively on this issue: Barrett 2023). While experiencing or recognizing a certain state of affairs as desirable cannot take place without the subject, the latter cannot be in this axiologically active condition all the time. Externalizations help subjects to orient themselves toward certain states of affairs without constantly processing them. Even generic axiological experiences require the formation of tangible externalizations, which, socially shaped and formed, have a feedback effect on subsequent individual experiences.

Setting aside the ongoing discussions, 'value' is understood as a state of affairs (which may be an existing or imagined object, process, relationship, or mental state) that is (non-episodically) felt/experienced as desired or considered/acknowledged to be desired by a given subject. This definition expresses relationism – that is, values do not exist without a subject and an object. Consequently, 'anti-value' is a state of affairs felt (non-episodically) as undesirable or considered/acknowledged (non-episodically) as undesirable by a given subject. Between the two are neutral states. For the sake of convenience, most of the following considerations concern values.

This simple definition is obviously overstatic and does not accentuate the processual nature of values. In fact, 'value' seen as a psychosocial process consists of: (i) a specific, but non-episodic (and, therefore, a repetitive or relatively continuous) type of mental state; (ii) its representation in the mind; (iii) its abstracted or objectified meaning, which is communicable; and (iv) how it is stabilized in a given community, subjected to uniformization and intellectualization, and gains collectively held meaning (often associated with a certain name/word). One should distinguish these modalities, which cover the understanding of value as a process, from mere statements referring to each of the elements of the 'life of value'. As such, values need to be separated from the narrative on them.

Such a simple understanding of value has serious, far-reaching consequences.

Contrary to the Platonic tradition, this approach favors a weak axiological relativism, which means that hypothetically any state of an affair can become a value if a subject experience it or considers it desirable. Why is this weak relativism? For certain fundamental reasons, in all human societies, only some states of affairs are the object of a strong desire by many. Some values retain permanently high positions in most human societies and, in all societies, the set of desirable states of affairs varies little. However, those affairs can be ordered differently, and different toolkits are established for their achievement.

Next, this approach favors the position of axiological individualism, which holds that every human has a unique 'world of values', most simply understood as a dynamic system of scales of values. Behind this lies the recognition, inspired by phenomenology, of the constitutive character of individual experiences. Weak relativism and axiological individualism, however, do not equate with total anti-uniformization of values, understood as a situation in which each person has a completely different 'world of values'. Instead, humans are very similar in this respect. When selecting from an infinite set of potential states of affairs, not only do they choose very similar ones as desirable (though ordering them differently) but they also develop and grow in a cultural environment where they share values and perhaps even deeper axiological structures. Some of the processes behind this are obvious – the social environment simply draws the attention of an individual toward certain things and distracts them from others, subjects them to ready-made assessments, evoking or transforming their axiological reactions. Accordingly, 'relative axiological uniformization', which does not eliminate individualism or axiological relativism, seems the more adequate term.

An individual's inner axiological world is 'moderately' ordered – that is to say, values are placed on scales. People do not develop one universally valid set of hierarchically ordered values and anti-values. Instead, they create several scales of values that are upheld and used in specific contexts (as in the case of 'everyday' and 'festive/sacred time' values). People's scales of values are to some extent inconsistent, and often such uncoherent scales 'split the personality of the individual' (Ossowski [1967] 2000, 100). The world of people's values is not 'geometric'. It does not resemble a pyramid (after all, John Smith does not intentionally reorganize, clarify, order, or refresh his value structures every day). However, plenty of psychosocial processes produce some kind of order to our values (remember that 'value' is a process) or lead us to believe that order exists.

The broad definition previously presented covers different types of values. Moving away from a comprehensive discussion of the typologies of values (see, e.g., Lemos 1995, 34–58), let us consider some of the most important distinctions, which are crucial for understanding the variety of the states of affairs that can be desired or recognized as desirable.

First, there are states of affairs that are individually weighted and embedded in everyday choices (e.g., when one strongly feels it desirable to attend a lecture on a topic that is important to them, rather than go to the cinema and watch a movie starring their favorite actor). Those are close to preferences. Second, there are states of affairs that refer to something beyond people but are dependent on them, often requiring some cooperation between humans to be established (e.g., safety). Third, certain stable conditions of the subject (e.g., happiness, fulfillment, health) often form what is desirable. Fourth, another type of value covers elements of the world, real or imaginary, that are desirable because they embody or even contain desirable states (so-called condensate value). Often, the individual does not experience the variety of states as desirable in a given sphere but refers only to some 'condensate' meanings. To provide an example, most people treat their family as a value, but they refrain from digging into the complex axiological character of this social unit. Five, there are desirable states of affairs that cover standards and general organizing frameworks in certain fields (e.g., equality or autonomy). Here, we move from values as preferences to values as desirable ways of organizing the social realm. They could be called political values. Among them are 'procedural' values that cover how certain things should be processed, done, or approached.

These rudimentary distinctions demonstrate that the set of desirable states of affairs is diverse, which must be acknowledged in order to identify a wise approach to take to comprehend the social and political 'life of values'.

1.4 Tools, toolkits, and infrastructures for attaining values

Moving to the second claim about the toolkits for attaining values, pragmatization is the process of searching for and introducing/applying an 'instrument' aimed at realizing a given value. Pragmatization requires moving from the area of axiological experiences (which are putatively unbounded in scope) to the social and public sphere (where limitations and various requirements exist). The problems and dilemmas associated with the pragmatization of values that are experienced by a multitude of people living together point to the foundations of politics, seen as the collective management of the community. Even the achievement of personal and individual values, not to mention social and collective ones, requires the functioning of a complex social infrastructure (material, imaginative, and normative). If someone at a hypothetical starting point (that is, without any value-attaining instruments), would like to implement individual and collective values, independently of others, then they are going to face serious obstacles. This is because: (i) the cooperation of many peoples and the coordination of many of their tasks (not only the division of tasks) are necessary for the implementation of almost all types of values; (ii) creating tools for achieving values is not easy or obvious, with us often relying on solutions that are present and well-known or have already been tested elsewhere; and (iii) individual axiological experiences are conflicted, with certain incommensurability within the individual's 'world of values'.

Stable tools and toolkits operate at the level of the entire community or within selected areas offering (more or less) standardized 'avenues' for achieving values. These tools are very diverse (recall the differences mentioned before between the axe, architecture, and law). Some are directly related to certain values (the traffic rules), while others form a general framework for attaining various values (for example, most types of intimate relationships allow the parties to attain a broad set of values, which change over time). From this angle, rules form a specific sub-toolkit for attaining values. People often fail to recognize the specific role played by social organizations in attaining values, though these organizations provide a package containing a set of values, embodied in cosmology, with extended infrastructure for their attainment. For example, religions often offer not only toolkits but also, notably, a set of values and systemic justification for them. Furthermore, they generate space for reconfigurations of the values and updates to religion-grounded toolkits. In such ways, most religions install a chain of values (understood as a stabilized network of meanings) for individuals and collectives as well as a large, multi-layered infrastructure for achieving them (based on the cosmological views). Moving to another example, magic – seen as a social system – works differently by providing frames and imaginary justifications for the working of more detailed tools for attaining values (rules, rituals, stratifications, myths). In comparison, modern law is a specific medium, a kind of 'language' – understood in a broad sense – of pragmatization of values established in the political sphere. It provides a standardized layout for value pragmatization and plays a complex, multi-functional role in regard to values and politics (Pałecki 2013b; McIntyre 2021).

Ensuring the functioning of the infrastructure for attaining values maximizes the scope of their achievement by multiple actors (or at least allows many people to realize a large part of their values) poses a challenge. Such a criterion remains only descriptive until we feel or consider that it is desirable to extend the scope of attainment of values by individuals in a given community – then, this state of maximization will become a value in itself (and often part of some worldview or ideology). Regardless, engineering the functioning of the infrastructure so that a large number of people can attain multiple values at the same time, or at least making it putatively possible, is not an easy task.

Several simple general processes explain how it is possible for a large number of people to achieve (at least some of) their values simultaneously. Among the basics is the increasing axiological uniformization (heightening the similarity of individuals' scales of preferences within a given community), which lowers the scope for conflicts between values (within the person and between them) and reduces the coordination demand. Besides that, another process is the simplification of the complex character of an individual's axiological world. Meanwhile, the presence of domination structures (power), on the one hand, limits some people's possibilities of attaining their values in a given society and, on the other hand, stabilizes the working of the social infrastructures that ensure the rest of the people can attain their values. Moreover, politics function as specific machinery aimed at narrowing down the set of values selected to be protected in a given community. Another process is establishing the coordination tools that work for the simultaneous achievement of multiple values. Next, due to various factors, in many cases, people focus on tools and toolkits aimed at achieving certain values instead of referring to and refreshing the values underlying them, which are more important and should be the priority. This can be explained partially by stressing the integrational and sense-making function of orienting toward the 'means'. It is typical for humans to concentrate on preferable ways of achieving values, though we do not constantly refer to our values. Such a strategy provides certain psychical safety and works as a social integration device. However, the picture of value dynamics is even more complex as some means of attaining values are experienced/felt or recognized by the subject as desirable.

1.5 Spheres of pluralism

Given the character of values and the complexity of the individual's 'axiological world', it is easy to conclude that pluralism is unavoidable in this sphere. However, we must question its scope and depth and whether counter-pluralist forces are in motion. In the latter case, although homogenization of values is to some extent unavoidable (and, in general, necessary), the total eradication of pluralism in the field of values is impossible. Even if people were transferred into 'machines' steerable by external orders, slight forms or 'spaces' of pluralism would still exist.

Among the sites where pluralism emerges, the following seem the most fundamental. First, there are differences in an exact set of values that individuals experience/feel or recognize as desirable (horizontal dimension). Moreover, there is a plurality in how those values are organized on individuals' scales (hierarchy of values, relationship between scales of values, number of scales, and their organization). Those two pluralities mean that each individual, to some extent, has an idiosyncratic world of values. Furthermore, differences exist in how strongly collective forces external to individuals define the set of ultimate values and impose their hierarchy in each society. As a result, there is some diversity in how personal and experienced axiological states are structured by social organization. To put it differently, what differs is how deeply and in what spheres the value worlds of individuals are shaped by the social environment. In addition, there are also differences in the tools and toolkits employed on a collective level to attain a set of social values. The same set of values can be secured by various sets of tools, toolkits, and infrastructures. Finally, pluralism also emerges from individual differences in the scope and scale of experiencing/feeling or recognizing these tools, toolkits, and infrastructures as desirable. Some 'instruments' are highly desired and the mere utilization of them is positively valorized by users even to the point, as mentioned later, that sometimes individuals do not take into account what these social vehicles secure and the reason for their functioning (emphasizing 'the means' and forgetting 'the goal').

When collectively considering all of these 'spaces' of pluralism, it seems pertinent to speak of descriptive pluralism in the sphere of values.

1.6 Value-centered interpretation of pluralization of relationship types

A variety of intimate relationships exist, characterized by different scopes and degrees of commitment, shared expectations, and dynamics. A key question is how to respond to such de facto pluralization, especially from the perspective of public authorities. There are many possible ways of approaching this issue. Utilizing a value-centered perspective offers one approach to the problematization of the discussion on marriage and other relationship designs and invigorates the development of ideas concerning this problem. When taking up this perspective, one must move beyond ornamental references to 'value in' and 'values of' marriage and other relationships and instead consider the complex and haphazard dynamics of values in these spheres. This calls for a non-idealistic way of referring to values (as opposed to mere 'decorative' references, which often work as legitimization devices) and exploring the multi-level complexity of values.

We must start from the basics in order to conduct a sounder axiology-based reading of relationship types and how they are approached by the law. As was mentioned, human values need social instruments for their implementation. With this in mind, one can consider the long-lasting relationships between people that take a specific form and structure and are based on norms and social imaginations. Among those are non-episode intimate relationships. Within these relationships, people are connected over a long time horizon and on many different levels. People enter such social forms with different motivations, driven by internal and external forces. Usually, these relationship forms provide frameworks for cooperation and activities including – to various extents – care, affection, and help (by lining up basic rules, obligations, duties, and expectations). These both limit and empower the parties (the former is a condition of the latter). Some forms, for various reasons, are dominant (or popular) in a given society and become an expected template for being together. In general, over the past centuries in Europe, the state had not been directly interested in these relationship forms, leaving them to extra-legal regulators of social life. At some point, monogamous marriage became the only relationship form legally recognized by the state. The *de facto* pluralization that is now taking place should be understood against this background. Such a simple observation provides a starting point for applying value-centered lenses.

In a given community, at a certain place and time, some forms of long-lasting relationships are relatively universally regarded as desirable. In this case, we can talk about a specific 'condensate value' – e.g., marriage, as a relationship form, is experienced as something desirable but not because of specific values that can be (or most often are) implemented within its framework. Instead, it is considered desirable due to the general overtone and positive connotations associated with marriage. In this case, it is a cultural ideal, or an object of aspiration, which is commonly experienced as desirable. In the Western world, when it is said that 'marriage is a value', people often mean just that.

As was described earlier, human axiological experiences not only resonate with the external environment, but the latter also reorganizes and structures an individual's acts of 'experiencing something as desirable'. Subjects do not often monitor their inner life of values, and they very seldom draw a map that classifies their values. As was implied earlier, in normal circumstances, they rarely distinguish between values and tools, toolkits, and infrastructure. Simply put, they do not analyze day-to-day the broad axiological context of their choices. Instead, they simply stick to the tools that are dominant or perceived in that way by their significant others. This creates a situation where people treat a given relationship type as a 'condensate value' without fully grasping the axiological nuances associated with relationship types.

A different situation is one where a given form of intimate relationship is perceived as a tool that serves to achieve certain desirable states of affairs for its individual parties, or people close to them, and also for society. This scenario is supra-individual but also dependent on people's states of affairs as well as so-called 'psychological' values. The list of values that are to be achieved, protected, and multiplied in and by a relationship – for example, marriage – is long and inconsistent and depends on ideological stances. Although at the level of discussion about this subject, the list is highly disputed, the following values are often indicated in this context: love, devotion, companionship, affection, care, (duty, commitment, responsibility, stability, personal happiness, equality, choice, and autonomy), procreation, and family. Judge Henry Floyd, the author of the majority option in an important US case, pinpointed 'intimacy, companionship, emotional support, and security' as values 'provided' by civil marriage (*Bostic v. Schaefer*, No. 14-1167, 4th Cir. 2014). In the landmark *Obergefell v. Hodges* case (576 U.S. 644, 2015), the court listed the following 'ideas' as embodied in marriage: 'love, fidelity, devotion, sacrifice, and family'. Other judgments tell a different story. In a well-known UK-based judgment, marriage was pictured as a means of 'encouraging monogamy', which is aimed at the 'procreation of children and their development and nurture in a family unit' (*Wilkinson v. Kitzinger* [2006] EWHC, 2022 Fam). Clearly, these enumerations of the values embodied by the marriage institution differ markedly. Not only is the list highly contested but there are also different approaches to setting a hierarchy within the proposed set of values, with disputes in this regard and great difficulty in identifying a universal axiological 'core'. Some people distinguish between traditional and progressive values when it comes to marriage, although people will differently assign values as such (especially in the case of the progressive values) (see, e.g., van Acker 2016, 30).

Importantly, when taking this perspective, an emphasis is placed on the forms in which values are realized. Erez Aloni, discussing pluralism in family law, stresses that the dominant approach of having a recognized set of relationship types 'falls short of indication what types of values should be embedded in and distributed by' (2016, 111). If this is the case, the discussion should be supplemented by tracking what values are in real-life contexts. However, it is challenging to identify the internal, embedded values associated with a given form of an intimate relationship.

A simple distinction between (i) a type of relationship as a value and (ii) the values embedded in a given type helps when considering how public authorities do or do not recognize and appreciate certain forms of intimate relationships.

When considering only the cultural, 'condensate value' associated with types of intimate relationships, it is difficult to recognize and approve of other, different, non-dominant forms. However, the situation is different when the emphasis is placed on what values are embedded and inscribed in a given type of relationship. When the point of reference is whether, for example, care, affection, help, and devotion are at the center of the type of relationship, the assessment of non-orthodox forms of relationships looks completely different. Of course, putting at the center or even limiting the desirable values to procreation and starting a family will significantly condition the assessment of relationship types. This leads to the question: what desired states of affairs do we expect lasting intimate relationships should protect and secure? If public authorities considered this, it would surely alter how they approach the management of legally recognized relationship types.

However, the axiological context is more complicated. It is necessary to distinguish between (i) the values embedded in (or inscribed in) a given relationship form due to its structural features (e.g., stability) and (ii) the set of values that can be infused in and implemented within a particular form of relationship by each party or both of them. Referring to the latter, the options are clearly more open and dynamic. The structural properties of relationship types ensure their relative durability and exempt people from making certain decisions while facilitating others, but they also make room for change and dynamics in this respect (e.g., change from material to post-material values; drift from excitement to security; 'romantic' values may be replaced or supplemented by those related to respect or parenting). People enter such long-lasting relationships precisely because they are vehicles that allow for changes and flexibility. As such, relationship forms allow us to absorb various axiological preferences.

Moving on to a higher level of analysis removed from values at the relationship level, it should be noted that (i) legal recognition and protection of various and diverse forms of intimate relationships, (ii) not doing so, or (iii) even doing the opposite is a matter of preference. Each of these states can be desirable for some subjects. Therefore, de facto pluralism itself can be valued as a positive, inspiring call to undertake steps to protect it. Although many details need to be worked out in this regard, valuing pluralism significantly reorients the approach to the topic under consideration. However, even if one recognizes the need to secure pluralism, one can adopt various ways to achieve it (e.g., increasing the options available, introducing an extreme contractual-based type of relationship, creating one broad and inclusive form). Moreover, saying that pluralism is a value requires specification – this is value in itself or there are desired states of affairs related to pluralism seen as an instrument. Accordingly, some point out that it is an intrinsic value and mere recognition of multiplicity is desirable, while others assert that it concerns dignity or political values.

Often, thoughts about valorizing types of intimate relationships and responding to de facto pluralism are based on appeals to abstract political values, which are desirable ways of dealing with first-level values. The focuses are standards, general ways of organizing and approaching values, and tools dedicated to achieving them. In the context of intimate relationships and their regulatory regimes, for example, liberal or libertarian values are often acknowledged. Authors who appeal to the liberal tradition are not unanimous in their ideas; some refer to autonomy, but equality has also been advocated. For many libertarians, the central organizing value is freedom, understood negatively and leaving the issue of intimate relationships to the private sphere. These three exemplary political values provide different criteria for considering how to approach the topic of regulating the types of intimate relationships.

One should also consider another aspect of values in the context of different types of intimate relationships. During the political process in a democracy, values as a kind of experience are transferred into intersubjective goals that form *ratio legis* of legal regulations, in this case, related to recognizing (and protecting) or penalizing certain types of intimate relationships. Through the political process, value experiences are recalibrated and form something more or less intellectually fixed and intersubjective. It is not an easy task to reconstruct the axiological foundations of legal regulations concerning, e.g., the special status of monogamous marriages and the penalization of polygamy in some jurisdictions. When seeking to identify these 'axiological basics', one can refer to legislative materials associated with the introduction of matrimonial laws, which also apply to their constitutional basis. To some extent, it is possible to discover axiological reasons, which are frequently highly intellectualized. Judicial practice, especially in jurisdictions where courts make laws, offers further sources for laying out these grounds, but they are often based on the common understanding of the 'value' of a given type of intimate relationship (close to condensed values). In part, these issues are related to the general process of neutralizing values – flattening, marginalizing, and simplifying the values associated with translating political choices into legal (legislative) decisions. However, detaching the law from values to a large extent provides a way to escape the constant changeability of the sphere of values and its inherent complexity. In this sense, shifting the focus from values to legal norms (which serve them) is a response to problems with the complexity of axiological experiences and the requirements of creating a social (in this case, legal) infrastructure to achieve them. How does this affect the area under consideration? Importantly, it means that one cannot easily identify a coherent set of values that lie behind the legal regulations of one or more forms of intimate relationships. As a further factor in that, despite the regulations devoted to them, some issues are still co-determined by cultural practices, which are not based on reflexive appeals to value dynamics but instead on common unarticulated assumptions and opinions held about what relationship types are desirable and how they should be utilized.

In the case of the political process, it is also true that often those in power, despite the legal arrangements, impose their value orientation – which is usually inscribed into some larger ideological narrative – relevant to marriage and other forms of relationships. Even in a democracy, those who hold political power do not reflect citizens' values but try to change them. Axiological experiences are fragile, and they can quite easily be shaped and adjusted. As was mentioned, the external environment is fundamental to stabilizing individuals' axiological worlds.

1.7 Conclusion

Applying the afore-outlined value-centered perspective to the issue of the plurality of intimate relationship types helps revitalize the discussions and disputes on the topic. Typically, the narratives on relationship types have referred to and used the rhetoric of values but in a way that legitimizes some choices. Often, values in this context are pictured in an idealistic way, as abstract ideals. A more realistic and dynamic approach, which is nuanced and acknowledges both the psychosocial and political dimensions of values and the complexity of the 'axiological world' of the individual, breaks with the idealizing narrative. Moreover, it directs the focus toward the processes that drive discontinuities, neutralizations, ignorance, manipulations, and incoherence in how values interfere with relationship types. Critically, a value-centered perspective, in the form presented in this chapter, does not provide picturesque visions of the role of values in marriage and other relationship types but instead offers a way to deconstruct the plurality of their relevance.

References

Aloni, Erez. 2016. "The Puzzle of Family Law Pluralism." *Harvard Journal of Law & Gender* 39 (2): 317–68.

Barrett, Nathaniel F. 2023. *Enjoyment as Enriched Experience. A Theory of Affect and Its Relation to Consciousness.* Cham: Springer.

Chambers, Clare. 2017. *Against Marriage: An Egalitarian Defense of the Marriage-Free State.* Oxford: Oxford University Press.

Dewey, John. 1939. "Theory of Valuation." *International Encyclopedia of Unified Science* II (4).

Lemos, Ramon. 1995. *The Nature of Value: Axiological Investigations.* Gainesville: University Press of Florida.

MacIntyre, Alasdair. 1989. *Whose Justice? Which Rationality?* Notre Dame: University of Notre Dame.

McIntyre, Kenneth B. 2021. *Nomocratic Pluralism Plural Values, Negative Liberty, and the Rule of Law.* New York: Palgrave Macmillan.

Metz, Tamara. 2010. *Untying the Knot: Marriage, the State, and the Case for Their Divorce.* Princeton: Princeton University Press.

Ossowski, Stanisław. (1967) 2000. *Z zagadnień psychologii społecznej.* Warszawa: PWN.

Pałecki, Krzysztof. 2013a. "An Axiological Explanation of Social Activity." In *Neutralization of Values in Law*, edited by K. Pałecki. Warsaw: Wolter Kluvers.

———. 2013b. "Neutralization of Values in Law – Main Concepts." In *Neutralization of Values in Law*, edited by K. Pałecki. Warsaw: Wolter Kluvers.

Rollins, Joe. 2017. *Legally Straight: Sexuality, Childhood, and the Cultural Value of Marriage.* New York: NYU Press.

van Acker, Elizabeth. 2016. "Disconnected Relationship Values and Marriage Policies in England." *Journal of Social Welfare and Family Law* 38 (1): 36–50.
———. 2017. *Marriage and Values in Public Policy*. New York: Routledge.

Cited legal cases

Bostic v. Schaefer (No. 14-1167, 4th Cir. 2014).
Obergefell v. Hodges (576 U.S. 644, 2015).
Wilkinson v. Kitzinger (2006 EWHC, 2022 Fam).

2 Article 12 of the ECHR

What are the implications of the right to marry for relationship diversity?

Anna Juzaszek

2.1 Introduction

The freedom to choose if and with whom we want to spend and share our life, and what our relationship will look like, should be a fundamental right and the private decision of the people involved in a particular relationship. However, there are many external influences that impact this decision. Our family and friends, the culture and religion in which we were brought up, social norms, etc., all affect how we shape our lives and the relationships we form. The law also plays a significant role.

Legal provisions may send a powerful message about what is acceptable behaviour and what is not (Douglas 2001, 14). The law translates people's everyday experiences into legal relevance and therefore has the power to exclude those who, for various reasons, are deemed undesirable (Smart 1989, 11). Therefore, the law hierarchises people's relationships based on, inter alia, the amount of granted legal significance, with those legally indifferent at the bottom. At the same time, given its legal support, this hierarchisation may seem like the only appropriate way. After all, the law is often perceived as something neutral and objective (Oetken 1991) while, in fact, it is never the case. The shape of the law is a product of particular times, culture, biases, political agendas, etc. Even though it is a truism for many, I believe that the image of law as an impartial entity is still strong in popular imaginaries. The perception of the law as neutral and objective might be particularly powerful and harmful in the case of laws such as human rights due to their status and importance. Thus, my point of departure is to consider the extent and manner in which human rights should intervene in individuals' choices regarding relationships. After all, living this sphere of life entirely free of legal interference is not feasible, nor desirable. Hence, a decision must be made regarding how we want human rights to be understood and executed.

In this chapter, I argue that human rights should commit to value pluralism and embrace social diversity instead of suppressing it. That is to say, when it comes to human rights, we should avoid ignoring human experience, listen to the needs of individuals, and constantly redefine human rights' assumptions to include those who were previously excluded from its framework. This is

DOI: 10.4324/9781003470786-4

particularly important regarding the adjudication of international bodies such as the European Court of Human Rights (ECtHR or the Court) due to their role and authority.

Unfortunately, this is not necessarily observed in the practice of the Court. When it comes to the choice of a partner(s) and the characteristics of a relationship, the official European human rights system disregards social diversity. Even if some changes are occurring, they are very limited in scope and cautious to avoid challenging 1) the perception of marriage as the most appropriate way to be in a relationship and start a family, and 2) the established understanding of this institution as heterosexual and monogamous.

The question remains: Why is this happening? I do not intend to answer this question comprehensively, but I would like to draw attention to Article 12 of the European Convention on Human Rights (ECHR or the Convention), which contains the right to marry and to found a family (Council of Europe 1950). I believe this human right actively promotes a very homogeneous vision of family life based on heteronormativity. This happens for various reasons, ranging from its interpretation in the Court's adjudication to its place in the Convention and its relation to other human rights. In this chapter, I elaborate on some of these reasons and their role in hindering the commitment to value pluralism by the right to marry. In the final part, I briefly consider potential solutions to this situation.

2.2 Value pluralism and human rights

The notion of pluralism is present in the adjudication of ECtHR that openly emphasises its important role in the application and understanding of human rights. In many judicial opinions, the following sentence can be found 'Pluralism, tolerance and broadmindedness are hallmarks of a "democratic society"' (*Leyla Şahin v. Turkey* 2005, para. 108). There is no official definition of pluralism in the European human rights system, but the Court sometimes indicates its understanding of this concept:

> For pluralism is also built on the genuine recognition of, and respect for, diversity and the dynamics of cultural traditions, ethnic and cultural identities, religious beliefs, artistic, literary and socio-economic ideas and concept.
>
> (*Gorzelik and others v. Poland* 2004, para. 92)

Nieuwenhuis (2007) decodes the definition of pluralism from a broader analysis of the case law of the ECtHR and concludes that it is understood as a diversity of opinions, social groups, and values without one dominating the others. This is especially important for minorities, who should not be suppressed by the majority. In this understanding, there is a place for individual and group rights, but it is crucial that individuals must be free to leave a particular association. Pluralism becomes 'both a result of and a condition for the exercise of several rights' (Nieuwenhuis 2007, 374). Consequently, the ECtHR perceives states as protectors and guarantors of pluralism (Nieuwenhuis 2007, 378).

The concept of pluralism is predominantly used in cases concerning free speech, education, freedom of religion, and freedom of association, and the approach to it may vary between cases (Nieuwenhuis 2007). Despite what is said earlier, the ECtHR is also criticised for not truly embracing the declared pluralism in its final conclusions, as seen in some of the cases concerning religious diversity (Calo 2010). The Court also has a negative attitude towards the idea of legal pluralism, for which it has been criticised for the shallowness of its justification and the lack of deeper consideration of the types of legal pluralism (Brems 2017).

There is a lack of theoretical grounding regarding the considerations of the ECtHR on the concept of pluralism. To address this gap and enhance the accuracy of the discussion, I argue that human rights, their usage and understanding, should adhere to and draw from value pluralism and its approach to social diversity. According to this philosophical thought, a multiplicity of objective values exists. They cannot be hierarchically ranked according to a universally adopted measure, often conflict with one another, and there is no ultimate determinant for resolving these conflicts (Polanowska-Sygulska 2003, 185–86). This perception of social reality and human experience should lead, according to I. Berlin, towards an empathetic understanding of different beliefs, values, cultures, forms, and lifestyles (Polanowska-Sygulska 2008, 158). To experience this pluralist world, individuals should have the opportunity to choose from various options regarding the kind of life they wish to pursue and none of these choices, or the absence thereof, should be deemed superior (Yumatle 2015).

After all, every human being has, at least potentially, their own idea of how to lead their life and what it means to make it good. As Griffin (2008, 45) calls it, this is a normative agency, understood as the 'capacity to choose and to pursue our conception of a worthwhile life'. To some extent, although we may share similar approaches in this matter, we often differ, sometimes only in the details but occasionally more fundamentally. For example, many people (but, again, not all) seek love, closeness, and support, but this does not imply everyone will find these in the same type of relationship. Some seek romantic love and sexual attraction, whereas others do not require these to form a strong and intimate bond. Some choose to spend their life with one selected person, while others are open to forming multiple close relationships throughout their life. These are just a few examples of how some people can achieve similar values but in different ways. However, others may not perceive these values as important or prioritise them highly. According to value pluralism, there is no single superior measure by which we could ultimately rank these diverse approaches to life and that is why a space should exist for individual choices (Galston 2004, 5–6).

A deeper philosophical discussion is beyond the scope of this chapter. However, it is crucial to point out that there are various accounts of value pluralism (see: Crowder 2015; Polanowska-Sygulska 2008; Yumatle 2015). In this chapter, I refer only to the basic assumptions which serve as an inspiration for further deliberation. What I derive from value pluralism is that if we agree with the proposed worldview, the only possible way forward is to allow a diversity of human experiences to flourish. As Crowder points out:

> to recognize the plurality of values is to recognize an equal commitment to pursue all of them equally until we have reason to select some rather than others. Pluralists should endorse the pursuit of as many genuine human goods as possible subject to circumstances. A good society will enable its members to pursue the widest possible range of ends subject to good reasons, generated by practical circumstances, for narrowing that range.
> (2015, 553)

One of the steps which should be taken to achieve it is to look closer at the legal provisions since, as mentioned at the beginning, the law has the power to curtail individuals' freedom not only by outright prohibition of particular behaviours but simply by prioritising one way of living over another. Therefore, the law should be designed in such a way that truly allows individuals to freely choose their way of living. This should, at least, be the starting point and basic assumptions when we design, change, and interpret laws.

However, it should be mentioned in advance, and has already been indicated by the cited quote, that the implications of value pluralism should not be understood in absolute terms. There is a place for curbing choices, prohibiting some behaviours, or sacrificing one value for another. What is more, sometimes this will be inevitable and necessary. But these limitations should be the exception and thoroughly scrutinised. It should generally concern those behaviours and practices that are harmful to others. Of course, there is the question of who is judging which behaviour is considered harmful but that is for another discussion. After all, as Galston points out: 'Value pluralism is not relativism. The distinction between good and bad, and between good and evil, is objective and rationally defensible'(2004, 5).

Moreover, we should remember that even thoughtful solutions are not absolute and may require revising. After all, value pluralism, as I understand it, teaches us that there are no definite answers and standards. We will be incorrect many times, and we should, therefore, be prepared to challenge and redefine the adopted solutions. I am interested, in this respect, in the legal field; however, it is a much broader issue.

Therefore, adopting the approach of value pluralism to human rights should lead to their perception as a means to enhance respect and recognition of various lifestyles, whether in terms of differences in religion, dress, type of relationships, partners, or political views. As Heiner Bielefeldt notices:

> rather than making the world uniform, human rights represent the aspiration to empower human beings – on the basis of equal respect and

> equal concern for everyone – to develop and pursue their own specific life plans, to express their most diverse opinions and convictions freely and to generally enjoy respect for their irreplaceable personal biographies.
> (Bielefeldt 2012, 23)

If human rights do not embrace the existing social diversity, they will contribute to further discrimination, injustice, and suffering. After all, as Stępień (2025) points out in Chapter 1, in his approach to the plurality of values, people strive to realise and protect their values. To effectively achieve this, there needs to be some form of social infrastructure that facilitates this process. If this does not function properly or makes it difficult for people to abide by their values, their living conditions may become unbearable.

What is more, a different approach to human rights, their understanding and application, would deny them, in my opinion, their basic *raison d'être* as laws intending to improve the lives of all the people. Their role should be actively promoting a valuable change, not remaining passive and focused on maintaining the established order. Just to clarify this, I am aware it is not possible to allow everyone to live as they want and that building a society often requires choosing between different interests, opinions, values, etc. Therefore, I am only pointing out what the point of departure should be, the vision for which we should strive as much as it is possible.

2.3 The legal response to the variety of relationship designs

Throughout the world, we observe many kinds of relationship practices and forms that constitute for the people in it a family life with its emotional and often economic interdependence. Europe is no exception in this regard. Some of these relationships are based on the institution of civil marriage, while others are based on religious, cultural, or humanistic marriage. Other relationships never go through any kind of ceremony. There are heterosexual, homosexual, or bisexual relationships in monogamous, polygamous, or polyamorous forms. Some people practise sexual exclusivity, while others are more open in this aspect. For some, the sexual component may be absent and undesirable. Some relationships are mainly based on romantic love, others on friendship or the willingness to support and care for each other. The possibilities and variations are countless and difficult to fully describe. Moreover, attempting to accurately depict all the options runs the risk of excluding those we do not know about and have not thought of.

The postulated commitment to value pluralism leads to the conclusion that all of these practices and forms are valuable and deserve equal respect. Andrew Bainham (1995, 2000) emphasises the importance of rejecting any hierarchy of values or forms when it comes to family. For instance, marriage should not be regarded as superior to cohabitation, and this need to be reflected in the legal system. Therefore, we should reconsider the fundamental functions performed by families, which are the true reasons behind their value, and provide legal (but not only) support for them. Limitations should only be placed on practices that are oppressive and harmful.

However, we are still far from achieving these postulates. From a legal perspective, the paradigm of a family is historically based on blood relations and the institution of marriage or adoption (Herring 2014; Herring, Probert, and Gilmore 2015). Nowadays, this narrow and strict understanding is declining, and the legal definition of family is slowly expanding to take into consideration the actual bond between people and their living situation (Herring 2014; Herring, Probert, and Gilmore 2015). For example, the notion of family life contained in Article 8 of the ECHR is understood in broad terms, where the most important question is whether close personal ties exist between people (*Paradiso and Campanelli v. Italy* 2017). However, it would be a mistake to label the ECtHR as widely progressive in this regard (Herring, Probert, and Gilmore 2015). Additionally, many alternative institutions to marriage have emerged throughout Europe, such as civil unions, civil partnerships, or other registration or contractual possibilities for couples (Palazzo 2021).

Without diminishing the significance of the aforementioned changes, I argue that the institution of marriage still carries the most weight in family law in Europe. If two adults who are not related by blood want to ensure they will be recognised as a family by the state and receive the full protection and benefits that come with that status, they have to enter into a civil marriage. In many countries, it is still the main, and often the only, legal option that offers such a range of entitlements, although a registered partnership (often available only for same-sex couples) is becoming more widespread with similar (but not always entirely) legal consequences (Waaldijk et al. 2017). Moreover, if people are married, how they live their lives does not matter; legally, they will be recognised as a family, whilst this may not necessarily be the case for others who live in the same manner but without civil marriage.

The institution of marriage is recognised by the legal system of every European country. Although there are some differences, the core understanding is still very similar and strongly influenced by Christianity (also pointed out in Chapter 6 by Parveen 2025). Traditionally, marriage is understood as the exclusive union of two unrelated adults of the opposite sex who share a household and have sexual intercourse aimed at procreation. Other types of relationships, even if not openly forbidden, often cannot obtain full state recognition even if they want to do so. Consequently, only heterosexual, monogamous couples who are married have full legitimacy in the eyes of the law but also in social perception, which is intertwined with the legal sphere.

The attachment to the aforementioned vision of marriage is well illustrated by the debate on homosexual relationships. Despite the topic being vigorously discussed for many years, currently only 21 European countries offer the possibility of marriage for same-sex couples (Pew Research Center 2023; Musaddique 2024; Gregory 2024). This accounts for less than half of the countries that have signed the ECHR.[1] Therefore, although changes have been observed, they are fairly slow, and the traditional approach remains deeply rooted in the European way of thinking.

Two important issues arise from this: 1) the centrality of marriage in family law, and 2) the narrow approach to who has the right to enter into a marital relationship. Consequently, state intervention in the choice of a life partner is strong and significant. All individuals who do not fit into this well-defined framework are excluded, as Nussbaum points out, from a very important and defining ritual in the human life cycle (Nussbaum 2010, 668). On the other hand, advocating for the opening up of marriage institutions to more types of relationships also poses risks that need to be considered and does not resolve all the issues, which I will expand on at the end of this chapter. It is also not possible to simply leave this sphere of life law-free because

> when the love is absent, or manifests itself in ways society deems inimical, there is a need for legal interventions in family life in order to reveal and punish exploitation, violence and abuse, as well as providing an escape from inequalities, dominance and destructive power imbalances.
>
> (McGlynn 2006, 12)

2.4 Article 12 of the ECHR

When it comes to family life and relationships, there are two important articles in the ECHR: Articles 8 and 12. According to Article 8, 'Everyone has the right to respect for his private and family life, his home and his correspondence' (Council of Europe 1950). Article 12 states 'Men and women of marriageable age have the right to marry and to found a family, according to the national laws governing the exercise of this right' (Council of Europe 1950).

In the jurisprudence of the ECtHR, Article 8 clearly dominates with 2,900[2] judgments issued, juxtaposed with only 35[3] regarding Article 12 (European Court of Human Rights 2021c). Even when compared to other articles of the ECHR, Article 12 is one of the least often examined human rights, with only 11 violations (one solely in conjunction with Article 14 of the ECHR) found by the ECtHR (European Court of Human Rights 2021c). This may seem to imply that there are no issues around the right to marry; however, this is certainly not the case. Some of the reasons for its lesser popularity are most probably its narrow understanding and its relation to Article 8. However, this

1 Today, it is 46 countries. There were 47, but Russia denounced it on 16/03/2022 (entry into force: 16/09/2022) (Council of Europe 2021).

2 As of 24 March 2024, and taking into consideration judgements issued by the Grand Chamber, the Chamber and the Committee.

3 As of 24 March 2024, and taking into consideration judgements issued by the Grand Chamber, the Chamber and the Committee.

does not mean that Article 12 has no impact on the issue of marital and family law. Quite the opposite, as I will argue in this chapter, its mere existence already has a significant influence.

When it comes to the differences between these articles, the former European Commission of Human Rights (the Commission) concluded that Article 12 solely protects the establishment of the family, while Article 8 protects families that already exist (Van der Sloot 2014, 14). However, this distinction has become increasingly blurred over time, and, nowadays, Article 8 has a significant influence on topics such as artificial insemination or sterilisation, which are closely connected to the formation of a family (Van der Sloot 2014, 19).

The reason why the right to marry was considered a human right and included separately in the ECHR and the Universal Declaration of Human Rights (Article 16[4]) was supposedly due to the memories of the Nazis and other fascist regimes which often imposed strict rules on who could be in a relationship with whom and, consequently, who had the right to procreation, for example, by banning racially mixed marriages that were to hinder the creation of a pure Aryan nation (Van der Sloot 2014, 3). Considering that both documents were created in the late 1940s and early 1950s, the atrocities of World War II were still fresh in people's minds. Therefore, there was a strong need to protect freedom in this area of life. Unfortunately, it appears that the final effect of this right has been the opposite.

2.4.1 *The essence*

One of the peculiarities of Article 12 is its concluding words, 'according to the national laws governing the exercise of this right' (Council of Europe 1950). This is the only article in the ECHR where such wording is used. Usually, concrete situations are described that do not contravene particular human right (e.g., Article 2 – the right to life[5]), or there are lists of rules that allow states to limit the right (e.g., Article 8[6]). As asserted by the judgments of the ECtHR,

4

1. 'Men and women of full age, without any limitation due to race, nationality or religion, have the right to marry and to found a family. They are entitled to equal rights as to marriage, during marriage and at its dissolution'.
2. 'Marriage shall be entered into only with the free and full consent of the intending spouses'.
3. 'The family is the natural and fundamental group unit of society and is entitled to protection by society and the State' (United Nations 1948).

5

2. 'Deprivation of life shall not be regarded as inflicted in contravention of this Article when it results from the use of force which is no more than absolutely necessary: (a) in defence of any person from unlawful violence; (b) in order to effect a lawful arrest or to prevent the escape of a person lawfully detained; (c) in action lawfully taken for the purpose of quelling a riot or insurrection' (Council of Europe 1950).

6 'There shall be no interference by a public authority with the exercise of this right except such as is in accordance with the law and is necessary in a democratic society in the interests of national security, public safety or the economic wellbeing of the country, for the prevention of

in case of Article 12, it is the responsibility of each state to determine the procedure and substance of this right (*F. v. Switzerland* 1987; *Christine Goodwin v. the United Kingdom* 2002; *Jaremowicz v. Poland* 2010).

However, this does not mean that the ECtHR relinquished all control over state actions when it comes to marriage laws, nor that states have absolute freedom in this regard. According to the ECtHR, state intervention in this area of social life cannot impair 'the very essence of the right' (*Schalk and Kopf v. Austria* 2010, para. 49). Thus, there exists a line that a state cannot cross while imposing limitations and procedural conditions on exercising the right to marry.

The Commission, and later the ECtHR, emphasised that the wording of Article 12, and the lack of possible limitations contained in it, means that a state cannot restrict the right encapsulated in Article 12 (it was even called *an absolute right* by the Commission) as much as it can with the right contained in Article 8 (*X. v. United Kingdom* 1975; *Frasik v. Poland* 2010). However, in reality, the situation appears quite different, mainly due to the understanding of the essence of the right to marry.

The jurisprudence of the ECtHR provides the only indication on this subject. As will be demonstrated, the ECtHR's understanding of marriage aligns with a traditional, narrow, and conservative approach. It strongly upholds heteronormativity and mononormativity. Even though the ECtHR introduced the living instrument doctrine in the 1970s (Letsas 2013, 109), which means that the interpretation of the ECHR should consider present-day conditions and is not immutable, little has changed regarding the characteristics attributed to the institution of marriage. The ECtHR still considers it to be, above all, a lasting, monogamous relationship between two people of the opposite sex.

The preference for stability is manifested by the fact that the right to divorce and, consequently, the right to remarry are not guaranteed by Article 12. However, their application may be protected under Article 12 if a particular state introduces them in its national laws (European Court of Human Rights 2021b). Therefore, countries can choose to grant the possibility of divorce to their citizens and determine the conditions. This sometimes leads to quite extreme situations. For example, in the case of *Babiarz v. Poland* (2017), the Polish courts refused to grant a divorce to Mr Babiarz due to the objection of the spouse who was not responsible for the breakdown of the marriage. According to the ECtHR, there was no violation of Article 12, even though Mr Babiarz had been in a different committed relationship with another woman for 11 years and had a child with her. One of the reasons given for this decision was the belief that reaching a different conclusion would result in a situation where anyone could obtain a divorce simply because they decided to leave their partner and enter into a new relationship.

disorder or crime, for the protection of health or morals, or for the protection of the rights and freedoms of others' (Council of Europe 1950).

While this may appear to be a valid concern, it raises the question: Can we compel individuals to remain legally bound when the relationship has effectively ended (which was not disputed in this case), and what is the purpose of doing so? I believe there are better ways to protect and support an abandoned individual, such as providing alimony or dividing property, rather than preserving a marriage that no longer exists in reality. Furthermore, this approach made it impossible to fully acknowledge the existence of the ongoing second relationship. Therefore, in this particular case, the preservation of marital stability was deemed more important than recognising the factual change in someone's life.

In this decision, one can observe the influence of the Christian tradition with its notion of the indissolubility of marriage and a hesitance towards the concept of serial monogamy. Non-monogamous relationships are not even considered under Article 12. In 1992, there was a case, *Bibi v. United Kingdom* (1992), brought under Article 8, which concerned the denial of entry to the United Kingdom for the second wife of the applicant. In this case, the Commission stated that 'preservation of the Christian based monogamous culture' (*Bibi v. United Kingdom* 1992) is a legitimate aim.

Regarding the heterosexual nature of marriage, the ECtHR stated in *Rees v. The United Kingdom* (1986, para. 49) that Article 12 'refers to the traditional marriage between persons of opposite biological sex', and this line of case law remains unchanged to this day. One of the main arguments supporting this assertion is the wording of Article 12: 'Men and women . . .' instead of *everyone* despite the fact that this phrase was used mainly to emphasise gender equality not the heterosexuality of marriage (see Johnson and Falcetta 2020, 94). However, in the case of *Schalk and Kopf v. Austria* (2010, para. 61), the ECtHR slightly altered its stance, stating that 'the Court would no longer consider that the right to marry enshrined in Article 12 must in all circumstances be limited to marriage between two persons of the opposite sex'. Nevertheless, this does not signify a revolutionary statement, as the essence of the right to marry continues to encompass only heterosexual marriage. However, if a European state decides to grant this right to same-sex couples, they would be protected under Article 12. This approach mirrors the solution found in the case of divorce and remarriage. Furthermore, the heteronormativity of the right to marry and the institution of marriage is further reinforced by the ECtHR's approach to other forms of registered partnerships beyond marriage. In a case such as *Vallianatos and Others v. Greece* (2013), where this alternative form was exclusively reserved for different-sex couples, the Court left no doubt that this constituted unjustified discrimination (Shahid 2017, 187). Although the ECtHR does not explicitly state that, by definition, marriage can only be a heterosexual institution, its rulings demonstrate a clear preference for heteronormativity (for more see Shahid 2017; Johnson and Falcetta 2020; Chapter 3 by Miccoli 2025).

Lastly, procreation has been considered a primary function of marriage for some time, as evidenced by the adoption of a biological test in cases involving transgender people who went through gender-affirming surgery. They were unable to marry individuals of the opposite sex because there was no possibility of procreation (Van der Sloot 2014, 6–8). However, this line of reasoning could not be upheld indefinitely, as it fails to account for the fact that not all heterosexual cisgender couples can or desire to have children, yet they are still permitted to marry (*Christine Goodwin v. the United Kingdom* 2002). While this shift in adjudication was significant for some, there are many transgender people who do not want to or cannot undergo a surgery. Furthermore, the traditional image of marriage as a union between two individuals of the opposite sex remains unchanged.

2.4.2 Tradition

The topic of the essence of Article 12 and its application in accordance with national laws is intertwined with the issue of tradition and the concept of 'traditional marriage'. The ECtHR explicitly emphasised in the case of *F. v. Switzerland* (1987, para. 33) that the field of marriage is particularly closely tied to 'the cultural and historical traditions of each society and its deep-rooted ideas about the family unit'. As a result, European countries may have divergent marriage laws, and a country deviating from others does not necessarily constitute a violation of the ECHR. Respect for tradition was deemed more significant than the living instrument doctrine and the European consensus. However, in this particular case, which pertained to a temporary prohibition on remarriage, the ECtHR found a violation of Article 12 due to the disproportionate nature of the measure in relation to the pursued aim, while the importance of tradition remained unquestioned.

This reasoning has also been affirmed in more recent cases (*Schalk and Kopf v. Austria* 2010; *Hämäläinen v. Finland* 2014; *Chapin and Charpentier v. France* 2016). Consequently, it provides the Court with an argument for refraining from intervention and granting a broad margin of appreciation to European states in matters of marriage. This approach aligns with the subsidiary role of the ECtHR, in which the Court is responsible for guaranteeing only a minimum standard of human rights recognition rather than striving for a maximum standard (Gerards 2018, 496). Thus, it is a wider issue when it comes to the European human rights system, which seems to be particularly strong when Article 12 is considered.

The issue of culture and tradition is complex. It would be a mistake to disregard its importance and ignore it when it comes to shaping the law. However, it cannot serve as an excuse for disregarding the needs of a significant number of individuals who have strayed from the socially designated path. Traditions tend to reflect majority preferences, particularly when it comes to determining what should be legally protected and publicly endorsed in a democratic society (Brown 1993, 205). Moreover, as Kim Forde-Mazrui (2011) points out, tradition possesses features that should make us cautious when using it as a justifiable basis for legal provisions, such as speculative utility, rhetorical appeal, and manipulability.

The answer is not to dismiss tradition, as it holds significant value for many individuals. Rather, the questions that need to be asked are: What other values do we sacrifice in return, and do we genuinely make it impossible to adhere to tradition for those who want to if we choose an alternative approach? In the context of marriage laws, the objective is not to eradicate traditional forms of relationships. Many people will continue to opt for lifelong heterosexual monogamous relationships with procreation as one of their primary purposes. The crucial point is to publicly acknowledge that individuals may have different preferences in this matter without asserting that only one option is valuable (or more valuable) and to provide equal legal recognition for these diverse choices.

2.4.3 Institution

It is noticeable in the adjudication of the ECtHR concerning Article 12 that the type of bond between people, how they live, whether they depend on each other, their needs, and their social reality are of little importance. The discussion centres around the institution of marriage: What it means, its characteristics, and how important it is for the culture and tradition of each society. While these are valid points, it seems that instead of concentrating mainly on individuals, the emphasis is placed on the institution and its shape.

This has far-reaching consequences. Firstly, Article 12 is used as a guarantor of the existence of the institution of marriage in the meaning described earlier. Thus, it hinders changes; although not completely, but to a noticeable degree. It might not be such an issue if it were not for the exclusionary and narrow understanding of marriage in the adjudication of the ECtHR, and, associated with this, its insufficiency in protecting the rights of all individuals. Moreover, it is at least disturbing that the human rights framework is more preoccupied with protecting the intact structure of the institution, rather than the well-being of people. The dissenting opinion of Judges Pejchal and Wojtyczek in *Orlandi and Others v. Italy* (2017) serves as an example. Their argument is that extending the right to marry to same-sex couples cannot be realised because that would change the meaning of the term ‘marriage’, without actually explaining why that would be a negative thing (Gonzalez-Salzberg 2019, 137).

Secondly, it also reinforces the approach that in order to protect individuals in relationships and secure their rights, as well as obligations, there is a need for a clear and strictly defined institution (or institutions) provided by law. Consequently, as Valeria Coscini (2020) points out, the entire discourse is focused on the structure of the relationship rather than on the self-expression of the people involved. Therefore, acquiring rights is dependent on fitting into a predefined relationship form, rather than on the actual experiences and needs of the individuals. Additionally, a variety of relationship institutions designed for different relationship structures may lead to their hierarchisation, as already observed in the practice of the ECtHR (see Chapter 3 by Miccoli 2025). This threat is particularly significant when only one of those institutions is guaranteed as a human right. Finally, with the predefined frameworks into which individual experience needs to fit, there is a risk that many will find they do not. This is mainly because those frameworks will likely be prepared by the majority who often may not understand or accept the needs of a minority.

2.4.4 *Symbolic meaning*

I argue there is also a symbolic meaning to the existence of Article 12 of the ECHR. By excluding the right to marry and to found a family as a separate provision, it conveys a powerful message: marriage is of greater importance than other aspects of familial life and any other types of relationships. Consequently, it requires stronger and special protection, as well as additional attention, and care. This message is particularly potent considering the existence of Article 8 of the ECHR. After all, it can be argued that what is safeguarded under Article 12 could easily be protected under Article 8.

The terms 'family life' and 'private life' used in Article 8 are very broad concepts. As mentioned earlier, the most crucial aspect for family life is the presence of a close personal bond. Regarding private life, the ECtHR acknowledges it is impossible to provide an exhaustive definition and emphasises that it encompasses aspects related to physicality as well as identity (European Court of Human Rights 2021a). This broad understanding of both family and private life allows them to be more adaptable to the changing social reality, and in theory, it is easier to apply them to a variety of relationship designs and experiences. Still, it was decided that the right to marry requires separate protection.

The special significance of placing marriage separately in Article 12 was even confirmed by the ECtHR in its decision of inadmissibility: 'indeed, it [marriage – AJ] is singled out for special treatment under Article 12 of the Convention' (*Courten v. United Kingdom* 2008). This argument was used to justify the differential entitlement of rights between married heterosexual couples and unmarried homosexual couples because, according to the ECtHR, they cannot be considered to be in analogous situations (Gonzalez-Salzberg 2019, 102).

Taking it a step further, Article 12 may create the impression that being a family without marriage is regarded as inferior to being a family founded on a couple's marital status. Although Article 12 encompasses two rights: the right to marry and the right to found a family, they are treated as a single right in which founding a family is connected to the institution of marriage, even though it appears that this was not the intention of the drafters of the Convention (Van der Sloot 2014, 13; European Court of Human Rights 2021b). Furthermore, in another decision of inadmissibility (*Manenc v. France* 2010), the ECtHR stated that the distinction between married couples and those in civil partnerships serves a legitimate purpose, namely, the protection of families based on marriage. Therefore, the marital institution is considered by the ECtHR as the most valuable and appropriate way of starting a family.

Consequently, the mere existence of Article 12 and its connection with Article 8 holds a tremendous symbolic meaning. It communicates much more than just that the ability to marry and to found a family is important to people (after all, it is a human right). Marriage has become a special institution, while all other family arrangements and relationship designs, even if accepted, are less desirable and, as a result, less worthy of state recognition and legal protection (Gonzalez-Salzberg 2019, 103). This not only applies to same-sex, polyamorous, or non-conjugal relationships but also to couples who, despite generally conforming to the heteronormative model, choose not to marry (at least not according to civil law), such as many people living in cohabitation, religious-only marriages, or humanistic marriages. Therefore, Article 12 sets out a hierarchy of ways of building close intimate familial relationships by placing marriage on a pedestal. Marriage understood in a very rigid way.

2.5 Does Article 12 commit to value pluralism?

Returning to the fundamental premise of this chapter, the purpose of human rights is to enable individuals to lead their own version of a fulfilling life without promoting any specific path and to be able to adhere to the values they espouse. It is challenging, to say the least, to characterise the impact of Article 12 in such a way.

Firstly, its understanding is limited to a very narrow vision of relationships and family life. Therefore, some people are, by the very definition of the right, outside its scope, even though, as a human right, it should be available to everyone. However, the right to marry is granted only to individuals with specific sexual preferences and identities who wish to structure their emotional life in an approved state manner, meaning heterosexual, monogamous couples who want to go through a civil marriage. Whenever the ECtHR finds a violation of Article 12, the case concerns this type of relationship. Only in some of the cases concerning transexuals, the ECtHR slightly expanded this vision.

Secondly, its connection to tradition in the ECtHR adjudication also plays a significant role. Tradition tends to be majoritarian, and its shape is often controlled by those in positions of power. Deviations are often defined in terms of a threat to society and the established order. Article 12 became a right of European states to determine the shape of the institution of marriage and only secondarily a right of individuals to be able to marry. This goes against the very idea of human rights, which were supposed to first and foremost protect all individuals against excessively arbitrary actions by states.

Consequently, European states have a wide margin of appreciation in the realm of marital issues. They can open it up to a broader group of people, but they are not obliged to do so. If they do not disproportionately hinder the right to marry for heterosexual monogamous couples, then the ECtHR will not intervene (at least not on the basis of Article 12). Hence, individuals may use Article 12 to safeguard their rights, only if they possess 'the suitable' preferences when it comes to relationship design, as well as 'the proper' sexual and gender identity.

Thirdly, Article 12 focuses on the protection of the institution rather than the protection of individuals. It is less important to provide as many individuals as possible with access to the rights reserved for married couples than maintaining the traditional structure of the marriage institution (at least in how Article 12 is understood in the adjudication of the ECtHR). It does not matter that the connection and bond visible in non-traditional types of relationships, as well as the problems, issues, needs, and struggles, are the same or similar to what is observed in heterosexual and monogamous married relationships. Or at least there is no deeper and critical consideration in this regard.

Lastly, the mere existence of the right to marry as a separate right sends a very powerful message about what type of relationship is the most desirable. All others, even if tolerated or legally recognised through a different institution, are deemed inferior. It provides arguments and support to those who are against changes. Therefore, it is the human rights framework that actively contributes to maintaining the status quo.

In light of this, the right to marry does not commit to value pluralism and even hinders it. Therefore, it does not fulfil one of its roles which I consider fundamental for the human rights system. The activity of the ECtHR on this matter does not increase the number of people who can live in accordance with their values, implement them, and thus strive to achieve a happy life without discrimination. On the contrary, Article 12 and its understanding promote only one vision of a relationship as the most valuable option. It excludes many human experiences and proposes a very homogeneous vision of society. Moreover, the exclusionary application of this right is poorly justified without a deeper reconsideration of its impact on the well-being of individuals. One may wonder whether we can call it a human right after all, at least in its current interpretation.

The main issue with the exclusionary character of the right to marry is that being married is not just a statement by a couple that they are in a close and intimate relationship. Apart from social recognition, there are many legal rights and obligations that come with this institution. It grants people privileges, simplifies administrative duties, provides protection in the event of the death of one person or separation, etc. Therefore, by restricting access to the married status, we may also restrict the enjoyment of other human rights, such as equality, identity, and dignity (Vundamati 2021, 234).

2.6 Conclusions

One might ask what the solution to the outlined problem is. When only considering the ECHR and the adjudication of the Court, I see three possibilities.

However, I am aware that each is difficult to achieve, has limitations, and it is hard to predict the consequences.

The most extreme solution would be to revoke Article 12. This would, to some extent, deprive marriage of its special status in the European human rights framework. The topic of relationships would then be solely dealt with by Article 8, and hopefully, it would lead to greater equality. After all, the most significant changes in the discussed topic are introduced through the right to respect for private and family life, not the right to marry and to found a family (see especially the case of *Fedotova and others v. Russia* 2023). However, the removal of a human right may set a dangerous precedent. Moreover, it may have different outcomes than expected. We cannot be sure how it would affect future adjudications under Article 8 concerning family laws and non-heteronormative relationships. Additionally, although I argue that Article 12 does more harm than good when it comes to the transformation of family laws, it cannot be ruled out that it actually has some empowering impact on those who are excluded from the marriage institution. They can argue that if the right to marry is considered to be a human right, then we should strive towards granting this right practically, not only formally, to as many people as possible.

Another solution would be to postulate a change in the understanding of what is the essence of the right to marry to make it more open to other types of relationships. However, the phrase 'to marry' directly relates to the institution of marriage, the understanding of which is dominated by conservatives in Europe and controlled by the legal orders of European countries. Consequently, even a small change in marital laws goes through a huge and lengthy debate, as seen in the case of, for example, same-sex marriages. Moreover, there are postulates to remove the marriage institution from state law (Chambers 2013; Metz 2010). One reason is its oppressiveness to women, homosexuals, and those who choose not to marry, as well as its patriarchal and sexist origins (Chambers 2013). Another reason is its incompatibility with the basic values of a liberal state: equality and liberty, as its privileges the marital (in the state's understanding) family while we observe a flourishing diversity in this regard (Metz 2010). There are also arguments that opening the marriage institution to, for example, same-sex couples may do more harm than good by assimilating them into the mainstream and depriving them of their uniqueness (Ettelbrick 1989). Therefore, we have to ask ourselves the question: Do we want to save the institution of marriage by modernising it and remaining with a system in which it is crucial to fit into a state-designed institution to acquire rights?

The third solution, towards which I am leaning, would be a change in the wording of Article 12 to remove the marriage connotation but at the same time underline the right to some form of legal recognition of an intimate or close relationship. The point of departure for me is what is written by Grigolo (2003), who distinguishes two sexual rights: 1) the right to choose sexual activity and sexual identity, and 2) the right to establish relationships and family life in accordance with this choice. The first right highlights a more private sphere in which we should be able to live according to our preferences, whatever they might be, as long as everyone involved fully consents to it. However, as Grigolo rightly points out, this is not enough, and this choice also needs recognition in the public sphere. Therefore, reformulation of Article 12 could, firstly, distance itself from the marriage institution and, secondly, emphasise the second sexual right distinguished by Grigolo.[7]

In this chapter, there is no space to ponder on what this new wording of Article 12 should be. Nevertheless, there are several crucial points to consider. Legislation should transition towards prioritising the actual living situation of people, the existing bond between them, and their needs. Legal provisions should not be exclusively tethered to institutional aspects such as marriage or civil unions but should move towards a more universal system that accommodates various forms of relationships, regardless of how someone decides to formalise it (if at all).

Furthermore, there should be a more profound assessment of why individuals in marital unions are entitled to specific rights guaranteed by the law. After all, these rights are not simply attributed due to someone being in a state-prescribed institution but because of the assumption that people who choose to marry are in a particular living situation: they form a family, are the closest people to each other, share their lives and struggles, depend on and support each other, and so forth. Therefore, relationships that satisfy these characteristics, regardless of formalisation through civil marriage or similar institutions, deserve the same legal recognition.

Ultimately, access to legal rights should depend on how people actually live their lives without passing a value judgement on individual choices. By adopting such an approach, we may hope to encompass a wide array of diverse partnerships, family units, and relationships within the realm of legal recognition.

References

Bainham, Andrew. 1995. "Family Law in a Pluralistic Society." *Journal of Law and Society* 22 (2): 234–49.

———. 2000. "Family Rights in the Next Millennium." *Current Legal Problems* 53 (1): 471–94.

Bielefeldt, Heiner. 2012. "Freedom of Religion or Belief – A Human Right Under Pressure." *Oxford Journal of Law and Religion* 1 (1): 15–35.

Brems, Eva. 2017. "Legal Pluralism as a Human Right and/or as a Human Rights Violation." In *Human Rights Encounter Legal Pluralism*, edited by Eva Brems, Giselle Corradi, and Mark Goodale, 17–36. Oxford: Hart Publishing.

Brown, Rebecca L. 1993. "Tradition and Insight." *The Yale Law Journal* 103 (1): 177–222.

Calo, Zachary R. 2010. "Pluralism, Secularism and the European Court of Human Rights." *Journal of Law and Religion* 26 (1): 261–80.

7 Although for Grigolo (2003), both of these sexual rights can be safeguarded by Article 8.

Chambers, Clare. 2013. "VII – The Marriage-Free State." In *Proceedings of the Aristotelian Society*. Vol. 113 (pt. 2), 123–43. Oxford: Oxford University Press.

Coscini, Valeria. 2020. "Relationships as a Form of Self-Expression in Regional and International Human Rights Jurisprudence." *Griffith Law Review* 29 (3): 351–73.

Council of Europe. 1950. "European Convention on Human Rights." Accessed March 25, 2024. https://www.echr.coe.int/documents/d/echr/convention_ENG.

———. 2021. "Impact in 47 Countries." Accessed November 29, 2023. www.coe.int/en/web/human-rights-convention/impact-in-47-countries?fbclid=IwAR3969VZaGySbWxr5IyzAgbk4vTV1fuh6j2f0daHombMPNK2Yz1eIE4sp2w/.

Crowder, George. 2015. "Value Pluralism, Diversity and Liberalism." *Ethical Theory and Moral Practice* 18 (3): 549–64.

Douglas, Gillian. 2001. *An Introduction to Family Law*. Oxford: Oxford University Press.

Ettelbrick, Paula. 1989. "Since When is Marriage a Path to Liberation?" *Out/Look* 1 (1): 14–17. Reprinted in *Same-Sex Marriage: Pro and Con*, edited by Andrew Sullivan, 118–24. New York: Vintage Books, 2009.

European Court of Human Rights. 2021a. "Guide on Article 8 of the European Convention on Human Rights." *Prepared by the Registry*. Accessed March 25, 2024. https://www.echr.coe.int/documents/d/echr/guide_art_8_eng.

———. 2021b. "Guide on Article 12 of the European Convention on Human Rights." *Prepared by the Registry*. Accessed March 25, 2024. https://www.echr.coe.int/documents/d/echr/Guide_Art_12_ENG.

———. 2021c. "HUDOC Database." Accessed November 29, 2023. https://hudoc.echr.coe.int/eng#{%22documentcollectionid2%22:[%22GRANDCHAMBER%22,%22CHAMBER%22]}.

Forde-Mazrui, Kim. 2011. "Tradition as Justification: The Case of Opposite-Sex Marriage." *The University of Chicago Law Review* 78 (1): 281–343.

Galston, William A. 2004. *Liberal Pluralism: The Implications of Value Pluralism for Political Theory and Practice*. Cambridge: Cambridge University Press.

Gerards, Janneke. 2018. "Margin of Appreciation and Incrementalism in the Case Law of the European Court of Human Rights." *Human Rights Law Review* 18 (3): 495–515.

Gonzalez-Salzberg, Damian A. 2019. *Sexuality and Transsexuality Under the European Convention on Human Rights: A Queer Reading of Human Rights Law*. London: Bloomsbury Publishing.

Gregory, James. 2024. "Greece Legalises Same-Sex Marriage." *BBC*. Accessed March 25, 2024. https://www.bbc.com/news/world-europe-68310126.

Griffin, James. 2008. *On Human Rights*. Oxford: Oxford University Press.

Grigolo, Michele. 2003. "Sexualities and the ECHR: Introducing the Universal Sexual Legal Subject." *European Journal of International Law* 14 (5): 1023–44.

Herring, Jonathan. 2014. *Family Law: A Very Short Introduction*. Oxford: Oxford University Press.

Herring, Jonathan, Rebecca Probert, and Stephen Gilmore. 2015. *Great Debates in Family Law*. London: Bloomsbury Publishing.

Johnson, Paul, and Silvia Falcetta. 2020. "Same-Sex Marriage and Article 12 of the European Convention on Human Rights." In *Research Handbook on Gender, Sexuality and the Law*, edited by Chris Ashford and Alexander Maine. Cheltenham: Edward Elgar Publishing.

Letsas, George. 2013. "The ECHR as a Living Instrument: Its Meaning and Legitimacy." In *Constituting Europe: The European Court of Human Rights in a National, European and Global Context*, edited by Andreas Føllesdal, Birgit Peters, and Geir Ulfstein, 106–41. Cambridge: Cambridge University Press.

McGlynn, Clare. 2006. *Families and the European Union: Law, Politics and Pluralism*. Cambridge: Cambridge University Press.

Metz, Tamara. 2010. *Untying the Knot: Marriage, the State, and the Case for their Divorce*. Princeton: Princeton University Press.

Miccoli, Francesca. 2025. "Resisting Family Diversity? A Queer Perspective on the European Court of Human Rights Attitudes Towards Heteronormativity and Legal Pluralism in Family Regimes." In *Relationships Rights and Legal Pluralism: The Inadequacy of Marriage Laws in Europe*, edited by Mateusz Stępień and Anna Juzaszek. London: Routledge.

Musaddique, Shafi. 2024. "This Article Is More Than 2 Months Old Same-Sex Couples Able to Marry in Estonia from New Year's Day." *The Guardian*. Accessed March 25, 2024. https://www.theguardian.com/world/2024/jan/01/same-sex-couples-able-to-marry-in-estonia-from-new-years-day.

Nieuwenhuis, Aernout. 2007. "The Concept of Pluralism in the Case Law of the ECtHR." *European Constitutional Law Review* 3 (3): 367–84.

Nussbaum, Martha C. 2010. "A Right to Marry?" *California Law Review* 98 (3): 667–96.

Oetken, J. Paul. 1991 "Form and Substance in Critical Legal Studies." *Yale Law Journal* 100 (8): 2209–37.

Palazzo, Nausica. 2021. *Legal Recognition of Non-conjugal Families: New Frontiers in Family Law in the US, Canada and Europe*. London: Bloomsbury Publishing.

Parveen, Rehana. 2025. "A Study of Muslim Marriage (and Divorce) Practices in England & Wales: Making a Case for Reform." In *Relationships Rights and Legal Pluralism: The Inadequacy of Marriage Laws in Europe*, edited by Mateusz Stępień and Anna Juzaszek. London: Routledge.

Pew Research Center. 2023. "Gay Marriage Around the World." Accessed November 29, 2023. www.pewresearch.org/religion/fact-sheet/gay-marriage-around-the-world/.

Polanowska-Sygulska, Beata. 2003. "Tragiczność i pluralizm wartości w filozofii Isaiaha Berlina." *Przegląd Polityczny* 64 (1): 217–43.

———. 2008. *Pluralizm wartości i jego implikacje w filozofii prawa*. Kraków: Księgarnia Akademicka.

Shahid, Masuma. 2017. "The Right to Same-Sex Marriage: Assessing the European Court of Human Rights' Consensus-Based Analysis in Recent Judgments Concerning Equal Marriage Rights." *Erasmus Law Review* 10 (3): 184–95.

Smart, Carol. 1989. *Feminism and the Power of Law*. London: Routledge.

Stępień, Mateusz. 2025. "Value-Centered Approach to the Plurality of Types of Intimate Relationships." In *Relationships Rights and Legal Pluralism: The Inadequacy of Marriage Laws in Europe*, edited by Mateusz Stępień and Anna Juzaszek. London: Routledge.

United Nations. 1948. "Universal Declaration of Human Rights." Accessed March 25, 2024. https://www.un.org/en/about-us/universal-declaration-of-human-rights.

Van der Sloot, Bart. 2014. *Between Fact and Fiction: An Analysis of the Case-Law on Article 12 of the European Convention on Human Rights*, 1–24. Accessed December 1, 2023. www.ivir.nl/publicaties/download/1561.pdf.

Vundamati, Rajyalakshmi. 2021. "Right to Marry and Found Family: A Most Challenged Human Right in Post Modern Era." *Indian Journal of International Law* 59 (1–4): 229–55.

Waaldijk, Kees, Natalie Nikolina, Giuseppe Zago, and Daniel Damonzé, eds. 2017. *The Laws and Families Database – Aspects of Legal Family Formats for Same-sex and Different-sex Couples*. Paris: INED. Accessed November 29, 2023. www.LawsAndFamilies.eu.

Yumatle, Carla. 2015. "Pluralism." In *The Encyclopedia of Political Thought*, edited by Michael T. Gibbons, 2820–26. Chichester: Wiley Blackwell.

Cited legal cases

Babiarz v. Poland (no. 1955/10, ECtHR, 10 January 2017).
Bibi v. United Kingdom (no. 19628/92, ECmHR, 29 June 1992).
Chapin and Charpentier v. France (no. 40183/07, ECtHR, 9 June 2016).
Christine Goodwin v. the United Kingdom (no. 28957/95, ECtHR, 11 July 2002).
Courten v. United Kingdom (no. 4479/06, ECtHR, 4 November 2008).
F. v. Switzerland (no. 11329/85, ECtHR, 18 December 1987).
Fedotova and others v. Russia (nos. 40792/10, 30538/14 and 43439/14, ECtHR, 17 January 2023).
Frasik v. Poland (no. 22933/02, ECtHR, 5 January 2010).
Gorzelik and others v. Poland (no. 44158/98, ECtHR, 17 February 2004).
Hämäläinen v. Finland (no. 37359/09, ECtHR, 16 July 2014).
Jaremowicz v. Poland (no. 24023/03, ECtHR, 5 January 2010).
Leyla Şahin v. Turkey (no. 44774/98, ECtHR, 10 November 2005).
Manenc v. France (no. 66686/09, ECtHR, 21 September 2010).
Orlandi and Others v. Italy (nos. 26431/12; 26742/12; 44057/12 and 60088/12, ECtHR, 14 December 2017).
Paradiso and Campanelli v. Italy (no. 25358/12, ECtHR, 24 January 2017).
Rees v. The United Kingdom (no. 9532/81, ECtHR, 17 October 1986).
Schalk and Kopf v. Austria (no. 30141/04, ECtHR, 24 June 2010).
Vallianatos and Others v. Greece (nos. 29381/09 and 32684/09, ECtHR, 7 November 2013).
X. v. United Kingdom (no. 6564/74, ECmHR, 21 May 1975).

3 Resisting family diversity? A queer perspective on the European Court of Human Rights attitudes towards heteronormativity and legal pluralism in family regimes

Francesca Miccoli

3.1 Introduction

Western societies are undoubtedly witnessing a shift towards family pluralism, which challenges traditional norms in family relationships. The so-called 'new' families are potentially queer (Stacey 1996), as they subvert the state-sanctioned way of 'doing family' (Palazzo 2018). To comprehensively understand this non-normative turn in intimate and family relationships, I argue that a queer socio-legal perspective (Roseneil 2000; Budgeon and Roseneil 2004; Romero 2009) should be adopted. By 'queer' I mean a methodological approach rather than a substantive concept, involving a non-normative inquiry into social norms and behaviours, laws, and political and legal institutions. In essence, a queer socio-legal methodology 'is oppositional or at odds with – and thus in relation to – that which is normal or dominant. The term "queer", then, refers to relational scholarship that postures itself somehow against or at variance with the normative' (Romero 2009, 195). While a queer socio-legal approach need not focus exclusively on gender and sexuality, I contend that in studies of gender and sexuality, including unconventional family relationships, a queer perspective is the most desirable posture to adopt for a twofold reason.

On the one hand, a queer sociological perspective acknowledges, values, and takes seriously the importance of non-traditional ways of living, allowing them a central place in social change analysis. Within the family domain, it focuses on social norms, such as heteronormativity, and how these are enforced or challenged by individuals. Since, in turn, social transformation prompts fundamental questions about the law's role in regulating new ways of living, including new ways of 'doing family', a queer approach should be extended to legal theory as well. This approach casts a gaze on how laws and political and legal institutions perpetuate or disrupt traditional norms. I suggest that queer legal theory also aligns with a pluralistic attitude that involves implementing legal reforms that recognise and value diverse intimate relationships through a plurality of flexible non-marital regimes. From this perspective, traditional heterosexual monogamous marriage is no longer the sole (or the most desirable) legal regime to regulate family relationships.

DOI: 10.4324/9781003470786-5

In practical terms, 'queering' socio-legal analyses of family relationships involve two main aspects. Firstly, it requires acknowledging the social norms that shape family relationships, particularly heteronormativity, and examining how these norms are being challenged and reshaped by unconventional forms of family. Secondly, it entails, on the one hand, a critical deconstruction of socio-legal norms about family, in order to show how these norms are socially constructed and historically contingent. On the other hand, it involves analysing the legal changes emerging in response to the evolving landscape of intimacy in contemporary societies, notably, whether legal changes are keeping pace with social transformations, and evaluating the degree to which courts and policymakers are responding to the needs and interests of non-conventional family structures, including same-sex couples, non-biological parents, and non-dyadic partnerships. In essence, a queer perspective entails determining whether institutions are effectively recognising and accommodating the diverse forms of family that are emerging through a plurality of flexible legal regimes, thus adapting and evolving in line with these changes, or whether they are resistant to the subversion of traditional social and legal norms.

Accordingly, this work aims to evaluate the 'judicial standpoint' (Johnson 2011) of the European Court of Human Rights (ECtHR) concerning unconventional family relationships, by assessing the ECtHR's approach to heteronormativity and legal pluralism, from a queer socio-legal perspective. The chapter is structured as follows. Firstly, the evolution in family relationships towards pluralism and non-normativity will be presented briefly, followed by an assessment of the key relevance of the ECtHR's 'judicial standpoint' in the legal domain of family. Secondly, the existing literature on heteronormativity and the ECtHR (Johnson 2011, 2012, 2015; Falcetta 2015; Viggiani 2015; Johnson and Falcetta 2020) will be reconsidered in the light of a more recent case: *Ratzenböck and Seydl v. Austria*, in order to argue that the ECtHR has not yet departed from a heteronormative approach to family relationships. Subsequently, it will be contended that the ECtHR's ruling in *Ratzenböck and Seydl* is also significant since it highlights the limited capacity of the ECtHR to adopt a pluralistic viewpoint (Palazzo 2022). Ultimately, the lack of litigation concerning multi-partner relationships and the scarcity of disputes involving members of non-conjugal families will be remarked upon. This dearth of legal cases complicates efforts to comprehensively appraise the ECtHR's stance towards other entrenched conventional norms in family relationships, such as mononormativity and amatonormativity. Nonetheless, tentative conjectures regarding the possible resolution of disputes involving these alternative forms of family relationships will be offered, drawing on the aforementioned discussions on heteronormativity and legal pluralism.

3.2 Increasing family diversity and the role of the ECtHR

Nowadays, most European societies are experiencing a significant paradigm shift in their approach to family relationships. This has resulted in an increasingly pluralistic outlook towards the concept of family, challenging the traditional nuclear family model. This model, which has been dominant since the latter half of the 20th century, is characterised by its conjugal, heterosexual, monogamous, and romantic nature. As a result, crucial questions have emerged about the adequacy of the available family regimes to safeguard the rights of new families and their suitability to confer status, rights, and benefits to non-traditional family relationships. Such a transformation prompts key questions about the rights of new families and the suitability of the available family regimes to protect those rights. Moreover, the significance of marriage as the sole and preferred regime for conferring such status has also been questioned.

The first kinds of non-marital families that became visible, widespread, and socially accepted resembled the traditional family in their main pillars, despite not being sanctioned by the state. Stepfamilies and cohabitations were mostly heterosexual, conjugal, and monogamous kinds of family relationships, thus making them easier to accept socially and legally regulate. Accordingly, divorcing and re-marrying have been made legal in most European countries, and second-parent adoption has been established as a legal remedy for adopting one's partner's child. Cohabitees have been granted the possibility of opting-in to certain legal benefits and duties, and a de facto family life has been conceded some forms of legal regulation, along the same lines as marital regimes. The ECtHR also moved from the mere protection of the traditional marital family

> to protecting other *de facto* family situations, including those of unmarried cohabiting couples, grandparents and grandchildren, uncles and nephews, siblings, single fathers and the children conceived when the mother and the father cohabited, as well as divorced father and child.
>
> (Caballero 2004)

More disruptive challenges to the conventional notion of the family came from the rise of new forms of parenthood, the demand for the legal recognition of same-sex families, and the increasing visibility of other kinds of subversive ways of 'doing family'. In the first place, advances in reproductive technology have led to non-traditional forms of parenthood, potentially involving a multiplication of parents, such as situations where the gamete donor and/or surrogate mother remain involved in the child's life after birth. Additionally, the focus on social rather than biological parenthood is facilitating the emergence of multi-parenting within extended, multigenerational and stepfamilies, as well as 'poly-parenting' arrangements (Pallotta-Chiarolli, Sheff, and Mountford 2020).

Challenges to the traditional notions of biological and gestational parenthood raised new claims for the legal regulation of diverse 'vertical' family ties between adults and children. While many European countries have allowed for same-sex parenthood, some still refuse to confer any legal status on the non-biological parent. Same-sex adoption, procreation through a donor's gametes, and surrogacy are not always legally sanctioned throughout Europe. No international instrument recognises a right to adopt. Consequently, the ECtHR has been referred to several times to settle disputes involving *status filiations* and the right to adopt for same-sex couples and gay or lesbian single parents.

When it comes to non-marital 'horizontal' family relationships between adults, there are various degrees of subversiveness, each corresponding to a different level of resistance towards social acceptance and legal regulation. According to the classification developed elsewhere (Miccoli 2022), 'unconventional' non-marital families lack at least one alleged feature of the traditional nuclear family, making them potentially queer in nature as they resist and subvert the traditional state-sanctioned way of doing family. Examples of such unconventional horizontal family ties include not only same-sex families but also less visible family forms such as non-dyadic conjugal families (e.g., polyamorous ones), as well as dyadic and non-dyadic non-conjugal families.

Of these, same-sex families are the most visible, widespread, and socially accepted unconventional family form. Nowadays, most European countries[1] legally recognise same-sex unions, whether in the form of same-sex marriage or registered partnerships. Yet despite being legally recognised, same-sex families remain 'unconventional' as they challenge heteronormativity, a powerful traditional norm in family relationships. A focus on the path towards legal recognition for same-sex relationships is crucial to advancing provisions for other unconventional families to be recognised by the law. Same-sex unions, particularly domestic partnerships, may pave the way for more flexible ways to regulate a plurality of diverse family relationships.

However, as I shall point out later in this chapter, widespread legal recognition of same-sex unions does not necessarily imply the defeat of heteronormativity. This shall be clear in analysing ECtHR rulings concerning the legal recognition of same-sex marriage and the extension of domestic partnership to different-sex couples. As a matter of fact, the ECtHR displays resistance towards subverting traditional family norms, posing a significant obstacle to the legal recognition of queer families other than same-sex ones in the ECtHR's jurisprudence. In other words, as long as the heterosexual norm remains powerful and entrenched, it is unlikely that other family norms, such as mononormativity and amatonormativity,[2] will be challenged in the near future. Those norms are respectively enshrined in polyamorous and

1 According to the Human Rights Campaign Foundation, same-sex marriage is currently recognized in 18 European states: Austria, Belgium, Denmark, Finland, France, Germany, Iceland, Ireland, Luxembourg, Malta, the Netherlands, Norway, Portugal, Slovenia, Spain, Sweden, Switzerland, and the United Kingdom (Human Rights Campaign n.d.). European countries which instead recognise only civil unions include Croatia, Cyprus, Czech Republic, Estonia, Greece, Hungary, Italy, Latvia, Liechtenstein, Monaco, Montenegro, and San Marino.

2 The meaning of these terms will be explained in detail in the section headed Legal pluralism and queer families.

non-conjugal families, which are perceived as even less conventional and conforming than same-sex ones. These kinds of families do not currently benefit from any legal protection in Europe or elsewhere in Western countries.

All the aforementioned ways of 'doing family', from more conventional non-marital families, new forms of parenthood, and unconventional families, show an increasing pluralism in family relationships and a queer disposition in challenging traditional norms. The increasing pluralism and subversion of family relationships in Western societies has significant implications for social policy, family law, and cultural attitudes towards family life. To effectively address these challenges and implications, I propose the adoption of a queer socio-legal perspective that aligns with a pluralistic approach. This approach entails abandoning the normativity that privileges certain types of relationships over others and fostering a more inclusive and diverse understanding of family. Such a paradigm shift involves questioning and challenging the entrenched norms and assumptions about what constitutes a 'proper' or 'normal' family while recognising the legitimacy and value of diverse family structures.

This theoretical framework should then be translated into practical political and legal actions aimed at ensuring the effective protection of the rights of individuals in non-traditional families. To this end, it is crucial to develop new policies and legal frameworks that acknowledge and support the diversity of family relationships. This includes advancing culturally sensitive and inclusive services that meet the needs of a broad range of family structures as well as ensuring legal protections and benefits for non-traditional families. The failure of policymakers to provide the necessary legal mechanisms to safeguard these families results in uncertainty regarding the rights and responsibilities of family members. This uncertainty can only be addressed on a case-by-case basis through litigation before national and international courts.

Because the protection of the rights of unconventional families is often left to the discretion of the courts, the aim of this work is to assess the prevailing attitude of the ECtHR in settling litigations concerning family relationships for a twofold reason. On the one hand, according to the *Guide on the Case-Law of the European Convention of Human Rights: Rights of LGBTI Persons*:

> The Court's judgements and decisions serve not only to decide those cases brought before the Court but, more generally, to elucidate, safeguard and develop the rules instituted by the Convention, thereby contributing to the observance by the States of the engagements undertaken by them as Contracting Parties.
>
> (European Court of Human Rights 2022)

In other words, ECtHR case law purports to have a de facto *erga omnes* effect (Helfer and Voeten 2014, 78) for all the European contracting states whose legal regimes, in turn, should reflect the principles and values endorsed by the

European Convention on Human Rights (the Convention or ECHR) and upheld by the ECtHR in its judgements.[3] Despite the ECtHR's ruling exerting a variable degree of influence and the orientation of national policies, empirical studies proved that 'IC [International Courts] judgments can help overcome domestic opposition to policy change under particular institutional and political circumstances' (Helfer and Voeten 2014, 79). More specifically, Helfer and Voeten found that 'an ECtHR judgment against one nation increases the likelihood that all CoE [Council of Europe] countries will adopt the same pro-LGBT policy' (2014, 80).

On the other hand, the analysis of ECtHR case law on same-sex unions proves to be enlightening if one endorses an anti-formalist legal perspective and acknowledges the creative action of judges, who translate socio-cultural perspectives and norms into legal terms (Falcetta 2015). Norms in family relationships are integral to the ECtHR's reasoning and, as Johnson notes: 'judicial "ways of thinking" about heteronormativity are vitally important in both the reproduction and disruption of heteronormative law' because 'judicial standpoints that are critical of heteronormativity reflect social, rather than personal, "points of view"' (2011, 349). One may presume that judges tend to exercise their discretion following their private interests, particularly when evaluating sensitive moral cases and, hence, are charged with 'judicial activism' (Kmiec 2004). However, Johnson's analysis reveals that 'judicial standpoints' are, in fact, key to deciding the judgement, but also that such standpoints reflect 'public, rather than private, interests' (2011, 354). To put it differently, 'judicial standpoints' in sensitive moral matters typically resonate with the community's perceptions of social rules and political values (Dworkin 1963), rather than with personal opinions.

Thus, the analysis of the ECtHR's 'judicial standpoint' towards traditional norms in family relationships and legal pluralism in family regimes may accurately reflect the current state of social perceptions of non-conventional family relationships. In turn, as I argue elsewhere (Miccoli 2021), the degree of social acceptance is likely to influence future opportunities for legal recognition. Hence, the next step is to evaluate whether the ECtHR upholds a queer socio-legal perspective and a legal-pluralistic approach when addressing disputes related to non-marital family structures.

3 International courts, including the ECtHR, do not have the authority to enforce their decisions. Furthermore, rulings are formally binding only *inter partes*, even if courts often assert the *erga omnes* effect of their decisions. Despite the ECtHR having asserted the *erga omnes* effects of its judgements since the 1970s, this is not considered by all state members as a binding requirement. In general terms, the *erga omnes* effect of international courts' case law is highly contested both from a political and legal perspective (Helfer and Voeten 2014). This is not to say that international courts do not often exert power to influence actors to implement their judgements.

3.3 Heteronormativity in the ECtHR case law

A queer sociological perspective offers an inclusive understanding of diverse family structures that defy traditional norms, recognising their social significance. According to Budgeon and Roseneil:

> Making sociology queerer means allowing lesbians, gay men, bisexuals and all those whose lives transgress heteronormative assumptions a place in our analyses, and then theorising from their lives. This needs to be linked to casting a gaze on relationship normativities, which allows us to register not just assumptions about the gender of intimate sexual partners, but also expectations within the heterosexual relationship order – or what might be called, heterorelationality – of co-residence, romantic love, monogamy and the primacy of the conjugal couple.
>
> (2004, 129)

In other words, making sociology 'queerer' means acknowledging the existence of traditional norms in intimate and family relationships, analysing how these norms act as regulatory practices for individuals and societies (Roseneil 2000), and deconstructing the norms through a critical analysis of their origins, functions, and social meaning. In addition, I suggest that making socio-legal studies 'queerer' also entails recognising the legal and institutional standpoints towards traditional norms in family relationships. Institutions, such as judges and policymakers, may either contribute to the reproduction of normativity or help subvert it, by promoting fair and non-oppressive legal regimes and, in turn, social orders (Falcetta 2015). In upholding a queer socio-legal approach to the ECtHR case law, this study aims to cast a gaze on the ECtHR's 'judicial standpoint' (Johnson 2011) concerning traditional norms in family relationships. Depending on the case, the ECtHR has shown the potential to be a vehicle of change or, more frequently, a vessel for maintaining the status quo.

Arguably, one of the most deeply rooted and powerful traditional norms in family relationships that the ECtHR case law must be evaluated against is heteronormativity. Heteronormativity entails the presumption that heterosexual relationships are the 'normal' or 'natural' form of intimacy, thereby establishing a hierarchy that privileges them over non-heterosexual relationships (Warner 1991). As Berlant and Warner explain, heteronormativity encompasses 'the institutions, structures of understanding, and practical orientations that make heterosexuality seem not only coherent . . . but also privileged' (1998, 548). Drawing on Falcetta's work (2015), this paper argues that the ECtHR upholds heteronormativity in rulings where the entitlement to rights enshrined in the ECHR is curtailed on the basis of sexual orientation. Specifically, when the ECtHR dismisses claims of discriminatory treatment or endorses the legitimacy of differentiated legal treatment for same-sex and different-sex couples (Falcetta 2015, 28).

Same-sex unions are typically regulated either through marriage or non-marital statuses, such as civil unions and domestic partnerships. In a few cases, both legal regimes coexist, notably in jurisdictions where those schemes are independent of partners' gender.[4] More often, non-marital statuses, available for same-sex couples only, have been repealed by marriage once the latter has been extended regardless of the partners' gender (Palazzo 2022). In the academic literature, it is the widely held view that not only the denial of legal recognition to same-sex couples but also the establishment of 'separate but equal regimes' harms their dignity and creates a second-class citizen status. Macedo (2015) argues that excluding same-sex couples from legal recognition violates the principle of equal citizenship, while Sullivan (1989) contends that such exclusion perpetuates a sense of inferiority and social stigma. At the same time, queer theorists have been mostly critical of the push for same-sex marriage as the ultimate goal of LGBTQ+ activism, highlighting the risk of assimilationism and normalisation. Redding (2010) argues that same-sex marriage reinforces the notion of monogamous, nuclear family structures as the ideal and fails to challenge the heteronormative assumptions underlying them. Similarly, Ettelbrick (1997) critiques the idea that marriage equality is the sole or even primary goal of queer activism, contending that social and legal validation of certain kinds of intimate relationships perpetuates a distinction between moral and immoral ways of living.

However, there are also queer perspectives that see the legal recognition of same-sex marriage as a means of potentially subverting heteronormativity. For example, Warner (2002) argues that same-sex marriage challenges the gendered hierarchy of traditional marriage and could contribute to the destabilisation of normative gender roles. Similarly, Halperin (2003) suggests that same-sex marriage has the potential to disrupt the idea that procreation is the primary purpose of marriage, opening up possibilities for non-reproductive forms of intimacy and kinship. Despite my suspicion towards marriage and preference for more flexible legal schemes, I am sympathetic to the view that legal recognition of same-sex marriage – as long as different-sex marriage is in place – can help subvert heteronormativity by disrupting heterosexual privilege, special status, and hierarchy in the legal regimes that govern family relationships. Extending same-sex marriage to same-sex couples potentially entails a politics of resignification, an inner transformation of a traditional heterosexual institution. Therefore, I argue that any failed attempt to extend marriage to same-sex couples perpetuates heteronormativity.

Maintaining this view, then, I suggest that most ECtHR case law in the matter of same-sex unions follows a heteronormative approach. The ECtHR failed to recognise the equal right of same-sex couples to marry, thereby endorsing a hierarchical attitude towards different kinds of family relationships.

4 See, for instance, *cohabitation légale* in Belgium, *Pacte civile de solidarité* in France, and registered partnerships in the Netherlands.

Nonetheless, it is important to acknowledge the ECtHR's significant role in promoting LGBTQ+ rights in Europe, and some of its rulings may even be seen as eschewing heteronormativity in supporting same-sex couples' rights. Due to the vast and intricate nature of ECtHR jurisprudence on LGBTQ+ rights, it cannot be thoroughly addressed here. Yet it is noteworthy that the ECtHR's attitude towards heteronormativity does not follow a linear trajectory (Johnson 2011). To give a few examples, Johnson identified a non-heteronormative approach to same-sex kinship in *E. B. v. France* (2008),[5] which, according to the author: 'challenges the heteronormative structures of kinship that are imagined to be essential for the social, psychological and moral development of a child' (2012, 62). Nevertheless, authors such as Ammaturo (2014) argue that ECtHR case law concerning same-sex kindship and adoption rather demonstrates inconsistency, if we consider the ECtHR's swift change over a period of six years in cases concerning adoption for LGB single individuals[6] and its non-linear jurisprudence on second-parent adoption.[7] The ECtHR's jurisprudence on the parental rights of LGB persons is not the central topic of this chapter. Yet it seems to me that, although lately there appears to be a growing trend in recognising same-sex parenthood in light of the best interests of the child and the protection of family life,[8] the ECtHR still fails to question heteronormative assumptions in the regulation of kinship.

Johnson (2015) also identified a non-heteronormative attitude in two litigations concerning same-sex de facto marital cohabitations, namely, *Karner v. Austria* (2003) and *Kozak v. Poland* (2010). Here, the ECtHR granted the surviving partner of same-sex couples a similar entitlement to that of unmarried different-sex couples, specifically, the right to succeed the deceased partner's tenancy agreement. Johnson argues that although the couples were unmarried, the rights and benefits addressed by the cases were strongly linked to marriage, and thus, both cases may be interpreted as a step towards 'undoing the symbolic and material heteronormativity of law relating to marriage' (2015, 67). However, when it comes to litigation directly involving marriage and non-marital statuses, a prevailing heteronormative standpoint is typically displayed.

5 *E. B. v. France* was not directly concerned with same-sex adoption. Here, the ECtHR upheld a violation of Article 8, taken in conjunction with Article 14, for the alleged discrimination on the basis of sexual orientation suffered by the applicant in the process of adopting a child as a single (lesbian) woman.

6 From *Fretté v. France* (2002), to *E. B. v. France* (2008).

7 In *Gas & Dubois v. France* (2012) the ECtHR dismissed the allegation of a violation of Article 8 taken in conjunction with Article 14 in the case concerning a refusal to concede second-parent adoption (only available to married couples), despite recognising the existence of family life between the litigants. In 2013, the ECtHR revised its own decision in *X and Others v. Austria* (2013) and ascertained a violation of the Convention, foregrounding that the couple was discriminated against in comparison with non-married heterosexual couples.

8 See, among others: *X and Others v. Austria* (2013) and, most recently, *D. B. and Others v. Switzerland* (2022).

On the one hand, the ECtHR has made crucial contributions in enhancing the protection of same-sex unions under Article 8 (the right to private and family life), sometimes taken in conjunction with Article 14 (the prohibition of discrimination) of the ECHR. Notably, in landmark cases such as *Vallianatos and Others v. Greece* (2013) and *Oliari and Others v. Italy* (2015), the ECtHR conceded a violation of same-sex partners' right to respect for family life in the absence of any legal scheme of regulation available to same-sex relationships. On the other hand, heteronormativity is shown in the ECtHR consolidated jurisprudence denying the right to same-sex marriage, where its interpretation of Article 12 – namely, the right to marry – has reinforced a heteronormative understanding of marriage itself (Johnson and Falcetta 2020). The ECtHR's interpretation of Article 12 has consistently maintained that states are not obliged to provide access to marriage for same-sex couples. *Schalk and Kopf v. Austria* (2010) is a pivotal case in this regard. In the first place, the ECtHR rejected the plaintiff's argument regarding the wording of Article 12.[9] According to the ECtHR, the reference to 'men and women' should be taken as reflecting the 'traditional sense' of marriage as 'the union between partners of different sex' (*Schalk and Kopf v. Austria* 2010, paras. 57–58). The second argument for rejecting the applicants' claim was based on the purported lack of European consensus regarding same-sex marriage.[10] According to Johnson and Falcetta (2020), in *Schalk and Kopf* the ECtHR fell short of protecting same-sex individuals' rights, rather privileging a conservative interpretation preserving tradition, in so far as it stressed the 'deep-rooted social and cultural connotations' (*Schalk and Kopf v. Austria* 2010, para. 62) of marriage in Europe. I argue this could be read as a heteronormative stance, failing to challenge traditional norms in family relationships.

It should be noted that not all scholars share the view that *Schalk and Kopf v. Austria* (2010) reflects a clear-cut heteronormative attitude. For instance, Viggiani (2015) suggests that the reference to Article 8, which entails family as well as private life, in *Schalk and Kopf* was a significant development in the ECtHR's jurisprudence. Prior to *Schalk and Kopf*, any case concerning violations of LGB family rights based on sexual orientation had been decided based solely on Article 8 with reference to private life, and not family life (see, among others, *E. B. v. France* 2008). From *Schalk and Kopf* onwards, the ECtHR started to hold that the relationship of a cohabiting same-sex couple living in a stable de facto relationship falls within the notion of family life (*Schalk*

9 'Men and women of marriageable age have the right to marry and to found a family, according to the national laws governing the exercise of this right.'

10 This is not the place for a case-by-case analysis of European policies and laws disciplining same-sex unions and parenting and for the assessment of their heteronormative stance. It is only worth mentioning that throughout Europe there has been increasing favour for the legal regulation of same-sex relationships by the means of same-sex marriage. It will be interesting to assess future evolutions of the ECtHR's discretion since it is becoming harder to claim there is not a widespread consensus towards same-sex marriage.

and Kopf v. Austria 2010, para. 94). Furthermore, there is an advance in the jurisprudence on same-sex marriage when the ECtHR stated that, in the light of socio-legal developments, it cannot be said that 'the right to marry enshrined in Article 12 must *in all circumstances* [italics – FM] be limited to marriage between two persons of the opposite sex' (*Schalk and Kopf v. Austria* 2010, para. 61). However, I am inclined to interpret the case as reinforcing heteronormativity by emphasising that, in the ECtHR's view, while marriage need not *necessarily* be limited to heterosexual couples, the broad margin of appreciation accorded to states implies that it may often be so.

Ultimately, in the case of *Oliari and Others v. Italy* (2015), the ECtHR found a violation of the applicant's right to family life (Article 8) due to the lack of any legal remedy that sanctions same-sex relationships. However, the ECtHR declared the complaint regarding the inability to marry, raised under Article 12, inadmissible. This was based on the fact that, in the five years since *Schalk and Kopf*, there had been an insufficient change in states' perspectives on same-sex marriage. While *Oliari and Others* can be considered a significant achievement in the recognition of same-sex relationships, since it condemned policy falling short of satisfying the core needs and interests of couples in a stable committed relationship (*Oliari and Others v. Italy* 2015, para. 169), it also reinforces a heteronormative conception of marriage by legitimising a differential legal regime and not recognising the discrimination in the denial of the right to same-sex marriage. This bespeaks a hierarchical conception of legal regimes and, in turn, a hierarchy among different kinds of families, where legally sanctioned same-sex unions are perceived as less valuable than married heterosexual couples.

It is important to emphasise that the existing body of literature examining the ECtHR's approach to heteronormativity predominantly focuses on cases lodged by same-sex couples unable to access same-sex marriage or non-marital statuses, which are exclusively available to different-sex partners. However, it is worth noting that there is an additional case that has been overlooked, wherein the ECtHR displayed a heteronormative stance: *Ratzenböck and Seydl v. Austria* (2017). Here, for the first time, the ECtHR settled litigation concerning a differentiated legal treatment adversely affecting heterosexual couples who were unable to access Austrian domestic partnerships, which were exclusively available to same-sex couples. Remarkably, the ECtHR dismissed the complaints raised by the heterosexual plaintiffs. The applicants argued that they experienced discrimination based on sexual orientation, invoking Article 14 in conjunction with Article 8 of the ECHR. They contended that 'marriage was not a suitable option for them, as it was substantially different from a registered partnership. In their view, a registered partnership was in many ways more modern and "lighter" than marriage' (*Ratzenböck and Seydl v. Austria* 2017, para. 9).

While the ECtHR deemed the application admissible, it ultimately rejected the applicants' claim, providing concise justifications. A clear-cut heteronormative posture can be first traced within the Austrian Government's motivation for excluding different-sex couples from civil partnerships, stressing the aim of 'supporting and promoting the traditional family model and the full development opportunities of the traditional family as safeguarded by Article 12 of the Convention' (*Ratzenböck and Seydl v. Austria* 2017, para. 25). Subsequently, the ECtHR stated that 'the applicants, as a different-sex couple, have access to marriage. This satisfies . . . their principal need for legal recognition. They have not argued for a more specific need' (*Ratzenböck and Seydl v. Austria* 2017, para. 41). I concur with Palazzo who argues that in dismissing the applicants' claim, the ECtHR appears to have internalised the perspective that 'registered partnerships are an inferior regime compared to marriage' (2022, 46). The ECtHR implicitly questions why different-sex couples would seek the legal remedy of a domestic partnership when they are already entitled to marriage. This subtly suggests that marriage bestows a higher legal, social, and moral status compared to a domestic partnership. When viewed in conjunction with the consolidated jurisprudence that denies the right of same-sex couples to marry, it becomes evident that the ECtHR's jurisprudence upholds the heterosexual norm within family relationships rather than challenging it.

To summarise, the ECtHR has undoubtedly played a role in advancing the rights of same-sex couples in cases where no legal protection was previously available. However, the ECtHR also dismissed claims of discrimination from both same- and different-sex couples lamenting their inability to access, respectively, marriage and non-marital statuses, thereby legitimising differential legal treatment based on the type of family relationship. Additionally, the ECtHR's consolidated jurisprudence has denied the existence of a right to same-sex marriage, and its reasoning in *Ratzenböck and Seydl v. Austria* (2017) revealed its hierarchical understanding of marital and non-marital legal regimes. Based on these considerations, it can be concluded that the ECtHR's case law overall reinforces heteronormativity.

In fact, the existence of separate legal regimes for different types of families, coupled with the belief that one of these legal regimes holds hierarchical superiority over the others, perpetuates a hierarchy among these diverse family forms. Within this social and legal context where marriage is still perceived as the most esteemed institution, the differential legal treatment of same-sex couples and their exclusion from marriage reflects the notion that heterosexual relationships are the norm and the most desirable, resulting in the highest legal, moral, and social status, as well as exclusive legal benefits. Consequently, a 'separate but equal' regime of this nature portrays gays and lesbians as second-class citizens, and the ECtHR appears to have upheld, or at least not challenged, this view thus far.

3.4 Legal pluralism and queer families

If we acknowledge that a 'separate but equal' regime, where traditional heterosexual marriage is considered morally and legally superior, is detrimental to the rights of LGB individuals within a heteronormative framework, the question arises of how we can ensure equal rights and dignity for same-sex relationships. The most straightforward answer is to extend marriage to same-sex couples, thereby granting them the same rights as heterosexual couples. I maintain that as long as (heterosexual) marriage is in place, same-sex marriage should also be legitimate. However, I argue that this may not be the most desirable solution from a queer socio-legal perspective, for two main reasons. Firstly, extending marriage to same-sex couples runs the risk of assimilating same-sex families into a traditional family model and normalising them. This may undermine the unique experiences and identities of queer families. Additionally, it fails to address the needs of other subversive family forms, such as non-monogamous and non-conjugal families, which may require different, more flexible legal frameworks. Therefore, I propose that instead of simply extending marriage, we should explore the concept of 'queering family law' as a valuable opportunity to protect the rights of unconventional families while avoiding their assimilation into a normative family model.

As already mentioned, queer legal theory refers to a critical, oppositional, non-normative methodological perspective on law and legal institutions. From a queer legal perspective, it is crucial to analyse whether laws, policymakers, and courts – including the ECtHR – uphold or, rather, challenge norms concerning sexuality, intimacy, and gender. Furthermore, embracing the idea of 'queering the law', I advocate for a pluralistic approach for a twofold reason. First, legal pluralism recognises that heteronormativity itself may serve as a proper regulatory framework that needs to be challenged. This view builds on Harding's attempt to bring together the concepts of heteronormativity and legal pluralism to shed light on the legal understandings of 'family'. Harding suggested a 'nuanced understanding of heteronormativity as an example of a plural legal framework' (2011; cited in Harding 2014, 183). This insight draws on Tamanaha's approach to legal pluralism, according to which: 'law is whatever people identify and treat through their social practices as "law"' (2000, 313; cited in Harding 2014). If heteronormativity is experienced as a compulsory practice, a coercive norm, and a social expectation, then it can be regarded as a proper regulatory framework. As a result, heteronormativity triggers LGB individuals' struggle to enter marriage, and this, in turn, contributes to strengthening a one-size-fits-all normative state-sanctioned model of relationships (Croce 2015).

Secondly, endorsing legal pluralism also involves offering a plurality of flexible legal remedies available to all the different family forms. If a queer legal approach takes seriously the increasing diversity of family relationships, it also acknowledges that different family forms require tailored legal regulations that address their unique needs and configurations. Legal pluralism provides the most suitable framework to address these challenges by offering specific and diverse legal frameworks that recognise and protect non-traditional families (Redding 2010). Through this legal-pluralistic viewpoint, one should value the plurality of legal regimes *per se* (Palazzo 2022).

These two approaches to legal pluralism are interrelated. On the one hand, if one admits it is legitimate to pursue different lifestyles and values, norms in family relationships such as heteronormativity are challenged, and the latter may lose its grip as a compulsory regulatory framework of intimacy and sexuality. On the other hand: 'the plurality of legal regimes is a way to mirror the plurality of ways in which individuals arrange their family relationships and the beliefs that constitute the groundwork on which these relationships stand' (Palazzo 2022, 47). Thus, the role of legal pluralism is crucial in reflecting different needs, arrangements, and values within family relationships. With this methodological and theoretical framework in place, the ultimate aim of this work is to assess whether the ECtHR upholds a pluralistic approach in its legal regimes concerning family relationships.

The case of *Ratzenböck and Seydl v. Austria* (2017) is significant not only for its insights into the ECtHR's stance on heteronormativity but also for evaluating the ECtHR's perspective on legal pluralism. Preliminarily, it should be noted that – as the ECtHR also emphasised – there is no widespread consensus in Europe regarding non-marital statuses for different-sex couples. At the time of the *Ratzenböck and Seydl* case in 2017, only eight states provided alternatives to marriage for different-sex couples. Historically, non-marital statuses were primarily introduced to address the lack of legal protection for same-sex relationships, to the extent that these legal frameworks were often repealed once same-sex marriage became available. This highlights a heteronormative understanding of family law regimes in Europe, establishing a hierarchy between marriage (at the top) and other legal regimes that become unnecessary when marriage is an option.

However, there is a growing trend in Europe, as identified by Palazzo (2022), of heterosexual couples seeking legal recognition through means other than marriage. These couples, whether explicitly or not, demonstrate a certain degree of resistance to traditional marital relationships, resisting normative regimes and practices. According to Palazzo, examples of such couples include those less concerned with fidelity or traditional sexual practices, less attached to the ideal of permanence, more interested in material benefits than symbolic ones, or those choosing not to have children (2022, 20). For these couples, marriage may be problematic due to its patriarchal and religious roots, as well as the values, social expectations, formality, and rigidity associated with it. These motivations were explicitly articulated in the *R (on the application of Steinfeld and Keidan) v. Secretary of State for International Development* (2018) case, where a heterosexual couple successfully sought access to the civil partnership law in the United Kingdom by expressing their genuine objection to marriage based on identity.

Compared to marriage, non-marital statuses not only carry fewer traditional values and expectations but are also more flexible and 'lighter', as emphasised by the applicants in *Ratzenböck and Seydl v. Austria* (2017). If non-marital statuses may be more suitable for heterosexuals eschewing traditional marital values, the same holds true for any other family structure that subverts social norms. In other words, I concur with Palazzo's argument that 'non-marital statuses can promote a more pluralistic model of relationship recognition, and . . . offer legal protection to families that eschew the paradigm of the traditional marital family' (2022, 4). Therefore, when the ECtHR in *Ratzenböck and Seydl v. Austria* (2017) denies the right to a different-sex domestic partnership, it overlooks the significance of the choice between marriage and domestic partnership, while it is evident that, from a queer socio-legal perspective, a choice of legal regimes *does* matter, for both same-sex and different-sex couples, as well as for any different family configuration enshrining different values and lifestyles. Choice matters if one

> acknowledge[s] that nowadays it is legitimate to pursue different lifestyles and values. Put differently, the plurality of legal regimes is a way to mirror the plurality of ways in which individuals arrange their family relationships and the beliefs that constitute the groundwork on which these relationships stand.
>
> (Palazzo 2022, 47)

Consequently, the ECtHR not only upholds a heteronormative viewpoint on family relationships, as argued earlier, but also fails to adopt a legal-pluralistic approach. It either does not challenge heteronormativity as a regulatory framework or overlooks the importance of the diverse legal regimes that regulate family relationships, including non-traditional heterosexual relationships in this particular case. The ECtHR's decision in *Ratzenböck and Seydl v. Austria* (2017) ultimately reflects the limited potential for a more inclusive and diverse approach to family law that challenges even more radical norms than heteronormativity.

Indeed, in addition to heteronormativity, other influential traditional norms exist in family relationships, namely homonormativity, mononormativity, and amatonormativity. Homonormativity (Duggan 2002) refers to the normalisation and hierarchisation of certain forms of same-sex relationships, typically privileging the gay or lesbian, cisgender, middle-class, white, monogamous, married couple. Homonormativity entails a more or less subtle validation of heterosexual norms such as marriage, monogamy, and procreation, thereby perpetuating a stigma against queer families that differ from same-sex monogamous conjugal relationships.

The case law of the ECtHR on same-sex relationships has already exhibited homonormativity (Ammaturo 2014). Landmark judgements like *Schalk and Kopf v. Austria* (2010), *Vallianatos and Others v. Greece* (2013), and *Oliari and Others v. Italy* (2015) recognised the right to family life for homosexuals, but they consistently invoked criteria such as cohabitation, stability, and long-term commitment to justify an analogy with different-sex relationships and the need for legal regulation (Croce 2018). The *Schalk and Kopf v. Austria* (2010) case is particularly significant in this regard. The ECtHR declared that 'same-sex couples are just as capable as different-sex couples of entering into stable, committed relationships. Consequently, they are in a relevantly similar situation to a different-sex couple as regards their need for legal recognition and protection of their relationship' (*Schalk and Kopf v. Austria* 2010, para. 99). Accordingly, the ECtHR only sanctioned 'respectable' dyadic monogamous conjugal same-sex unions, in so far as they are conceived ***just like*** heterosexual ones (Ruskola 2005). This posture does not legitimise all kinds of relationships but only certain ones, disregarding more subversive forms of intimacy that challenge the norms of monogamy and romanticism. Once again, a queer socio-legal perspective enables us to recognise the normalising influence exerted by legal recognition when it fails to embrace pluralism and diversity in family relationships (Croce 2018).

To conclude, this analysis is pivotal to foreseeing the future of potential claims coming from applicants involved in non-conjugal and multi-partner relationships. Also in this case, adopting a queer and legal-pluralistic theoretical framework would emphasise the key value of diversity and pluralism not only in family relationships but also in legal regimes regulating family relationships. Assessing the ECtHR's stance on mononormativity and amatonormativity is more challenging due to the limited litigation concerning non-monogamous and non-conjugal relationships. Mononormativity is a term coined by Pieper and Bauer (2005) to refer to 'the forms of power which help establish the monogamous couple bond as an idealised and normative model' (Gusmano and Motterle 2019, 352). In other words, monogamy is usually considered the norm in intimate relationships, and this is a powerful assumption, for every relationship that deviates from this alleged norm is stigmatised and marginalised. Amatonormativity is a term coined by Brake which means that 'a central, exclusive, amorous relationship is normal for humans, is a universally shared goal, and that such a relationship is normative, in that it should be aimed at in preference to other relationship types' (2012, 89).

Those norms are respectively enshrined in polyamorous and non-conjugal families, which are perceived as even less conventional and conforming than same-sex ones. These kinds of families do not currently benefit from any legal protection in Europe or elsewhere in Western countries. Concerning polyamorous relationships, there is a complete lack of ligation before the ECtHR. Their scarce visibility, let alone social acceptance, makes it hard to consider any path for any kind of legal recognition in the short run. Regarding non-conjugal relationships, the case of ***Burden v. the United Kingdom*** (2008) already went in the direction of remarking that 'the relationship between siblings is qualitatively of a different nature to that between married couples and homosexual civil partners under the United Kingdom's Civil Partnership Act' (***Burden v. the United Kingdom*** 2008, para. 62).[11] The ECtHR's rejection of the

11 The case involved two cohabiting sisters, lamenting discrimination based on the circumstance that 'when the first of them died, the survivor would be required to pay inheritance tax on the dead sister's share of the family home, whereas the survivor of a married couple or a homosexual relationship registered under the Civil Partnership Act 2004 would be exempt from paying inheritance tax in these circumstances' (***Burden v. the United Kingdom*** 2008, para. 62).

analogy with conjugal families reflects a powerful amatonormative narrative, where romantic relationships are placed at the top of the hierarchy of significant relationships. Therefore, in light of the current legal framework, the ECtHR's attitudes toward heteronormativity and the shortcomings of pluralism contribute to narrowing the possibility for systematic legal recognition of non-conjugal families as well.

3.5 Conclusion

The existence of various subversive queer family forms that defy normativity necessitates the adoption of a queer socio-legal approach, which takes seriously the existence of all non-normative family relationships. This approach involves examining whether political and legal institutions promote traditional norms such as heteronormativity, homonormativity, mononormativity, and amatonormativity. A queer socio-legal approach is also closely linked to legal pluralism, acknowledging the benefits of having plural legal regimes *per se*. This includes choosing between different legal frameworks and tailoring relationships according to diverse needs, values, and lifestyles. Unfortunately, the ECtHR has failed to adopt such an approach so far. A queer socio-legal analysis of the ECtHR's jurisprudence reveals its endorsement of a heteronormative view and its rejection of a legal-pluralist perspective.

The case of *Ratzenböck and Seydl v. Austria* (2017) was particularly significant in assessing these converging attitudes. The ECtHR's consolidated jurisprudence that dismisses claims for the right to same-sex marriage, along with the subtle preference for marriage over non-marital statuses evident in the *Ratzenböck and Seydl* case, are clear indications of a heteronormative approach. Furthermore, by denying a different-sex couple the possibility of accessing a domestic partnership, the ECtHR disregarded the intrinsic value of a plurality of non-marital regimes. This highlights its failure to recognise the existence and needs of other types of unconventional families, which may not conform to the traditional image of same-sex cohabiting committed monogamous couples, not displaying the same 'respectability'.

Consequently, at present, the ECtHR seems to be unequipped to afford legal recognition to subversive, queer families, including non-traditional heterosexual and homosexual couples as well as polyamorous and non-conjugal relationships. This demonstrates a concerning disregard for the importance of embracing family diversity and challenging traditional norms. As a result, individuals within these unorthodox family structures are left vulnerable and unprotected, while the subversive attitudes of less conventional heterosexual families are overlooked when their claims for access to more flexible forms of regulation are rejected.

However, queer families do exist. Starting from heterosexuals eschewing traditional marital norms, they are seeking (or they will soon seek) legal protection. Hence, from a queer socio-legal perspective, the ideal solution is not to uphold heteronormative prescriptions of family relationships and family law but rather to acknowledge the differences between families and accommodate their diverse needs through flexible and plural legal regimes tailored to individuals' interests and needs. If this project fails, the tension towards normalisation prevails over the desirable goal of extending protection to vulnerable members of all diverse family configurations (Croce 2018). In conclusion, legal pluralism is key because, if a 'separate but equal' regime violates the dignity of same-sex couples, then we should advocate many different 'separate but better' (Redding 2010) regimes. Given the current circumstances and the prevailing attitude of the ECtHR, achieving such a goal in the short term seems highly challenging. However, as Johnson (2012) demonstrated, the ECtHR's jurisprudence regarding LGBT+ rights has proven to be anything but linear. Therefore, surprises cannot be ruled out.

References

Ammaturo, Francesca R. 2014. "The Right to a Privilege? Homonormativity and the Recognition of Same-Sex Couples in Europe." *Social & Legal Studies* 23 (2): 175–94.

Berlant, L, and Michael Warner. 1998. "Sex in Public." *Critical Inquiry* 24 (2): 547–66.

Brake, Elizabeth. 2012. *Minimizing Marriage: Marriage, Morality and the Law*. Oxford: Oxford University Press.

Budgeon, Shelley, and Sasha Roseneil. 2004. "Editors' Introduction: Beyond the Conventional Family." *Current Sociology* 52 (2): 127–34.

Caballero, Susana Sanz. 2004. "Unmarried Cohabiting Couples Before the European Court of Human Rights: Parity with Marriage?" *The Columbia Journal of European Law* 11 (1): 152–66.

Croce, Mariano. 2015. "Secularization, Legal Pluralism, and the Question of Rela tionship-Recognition Regimes." *The European Legacy* 20 (2): 151–65.

———. 2018. "Desiring What the Law Desires: A Semiotic View on the Normalization of Homosexual Sexuality." *Law, Culture and the Humanities* 14 (3): 402–19.

Duggan, Lisa. 2002. *The New Homonormativity: The Sexual Politics of Neoliberalism*. Durham: Duke University Press.

Dworkin, Ronald. 1963. "Judicial Discretion." *The Journal of Philosophy* 60 (21): 624–38.

Ettelbrick, Paula. 1997. "Since When is Marriage a Path to Liberation?" In *Same-Sex Marriage, Pro and Con. A Reader*, edited by Andrew Sullivan and Joseph Landau, 118–24. New York: Vintage Books.

European Court of Human Rights. 2022. "Guide on the Case-Law of the European Convention on Human Rights: Rights of LGBTI Persons." *Prepared by the Registry*. Accessed November 18, 2023. https://ks.echr.coe.int/documents/d/echr-ks/guide_lgbti_rights_eng.

Falcetta, Silvia. 2015. "L'eteronormatività nell'operato della Corte Europea dei diritti umani: luci e ombre in materia di riconoscimento giuridico delle coppie formate da persone dello stesso sesso." *AboutGender* 4 (7): 19–41.

Gusmano, Beatrice, and Tatiana Motterle. 2019. "The Micropolitics of Choice in Italy: How the Law Affects Lesbian and Bisexual Women's Daily Life." *Journal of Lesbian Studies* 23 (3): 336–56.

Halperin, David M. 2003. *What Do Gay Men Want? An Essay on Sex, Risk, and Subjectivity*. Ann Arbor: University of Michigan Press.

Harding, Rosie. 2011. *Regulating Sexuality. Legal Consciousness in Lesbian and Gay Lives*. New York: Routledge.

———. 2014. "(Re)inscribing the Heteronormative Family. Same-Sex Relationships and Parenting 'After Equality'." In *After Legal Equality. Family, Sex, Kinship*, edited by Robert Leckey, 181–200. New York: Routledge.

Helfer, Laurence R., and Erik Voeten. 2014. "International Courts as Agents of Legal Change: Evidence from LGBT Rights in Europe." *International Organizations* 68 (1): 77–110.

Human Rights Campaign. n.d. "Marriage Equality Around the World." Accessed November 18, 2023. www.hrc.org/resources/marriage-equality-around-the-world.

Johnson, Paul. 2011. "Challenging the Heteronormativity of Marriage: The Role of Judicial Interpretation and Authority." *Social & Legal Studies* 20 (3): 349–67.

———. 2012. "Heteronormativity and the European Court of Human Rights." *Law Critique* 23: 43–66.

———. 2015. "Marriage, Heteronormativity, and the European Court of Human Rights: A Reappraisal." *International Journal of Law, Policy and The Family* 29: 56–77.

Johnson, Paul, and Silvia Falcetta. 2020. "Same-Sex Marriage and Article 12 of the European Convention on Human Rights." In *Research Handbook on Gender, Sexuality and the Law*, edited by Chris Ashford and Alexander Maine, 91–103. Cheltenham: Edward Elgar Publishing.

Kmiec, Keenan D. 2004. "The Origin and Current Meanings of 'Judicial Activism'." *California Law Review* 92 (5): 1441–77.

Macedo, Stephen. 2015. *Just Married: Same-Sex Couples, Monogamy & the Future of Marriage*. Princeton: Princeton University Press.

Miccoli, Francesca. 2021. "Legal Recognition of Polyamory: Notes on Its Feasibility." *Whatever. A Transdisciplinary Journal of Queer Theories and Studies* 4: 357–80.

———. 2022. "Should All Families be Treated Equally by Law? In Support of Equal Dignity and Legal Recognition of Unconventional Families." *Biblioteca della Libertà* LVII (235): 73–104.

Palazzo, Nausica. 2018. "The Strange Pairing: Building Alliances Between Queer Activists and Conservative Groups to Recognize New Families." *Michigan Journal of Gender and Law* 25 (2): 161–237.

———. 2022. "Marriage Apostates: Why Heterosexuals Seek Same-Sex Registered Partnership." *Columbia Journal of Gender and Law* 42 (1): 186–258.

Pallotta-Chiarolli, Maria, Elisabeth Sheff, and Ruby Mountford. 2020. "Polyamorous Parenting in Contemporary Research: Developements and Future Directions." In *LGBTQ-Parent Families. Innovations in Research and Implications for Practice*, edited by Abbie E. Goldberg and Katherine R. Allen, 171–84. Cham: Springer.

Pieper, Marianne, and Robin Bauer. 2005. "Polyamory und mono-normativität." In *More than One Love: Polyamoros Relationships*, edited by L. Méritt, T. Bührmann, and N. Schefzig, 59–69. Berlin: Orlanda.

Redding, Jeffrey A. 2010. "Dignity, Legal Pluralism, and Same-Sex Marriage." *Brooklyn Law Review* 75 (3): 791–863.

Romero, Adam P. 2009. "Methodological descriptions: "Feminist" and "Queer" Legal Theories." In *Feminist and Queer Legal Theory. Intimate Encounters, Uncomfortable Conversations*, edited by Martha Albertson Fineman, Jack E. Jackson, and Adam P. Romero, 179–99. Farnham: Ashgate Publishing.

Roseneil, Sasha. 2000. "Queer Frameworks and Queer Tendencies: Towards an Understanding of Postmodern Transformations of Sexuality." *Sociological Research Online* 5 (3).

Ruskola, Teemu. 2005. "Gay Rights versus Queer Theory: What is Left of Sodomy After Lawrence v. Texas?" *Social Text* 23 (3–4): 84–85.

Stacey, Judith. 1996. *In the Name of the Family: Rethinking Family Values in the Post-Modern Age*. Boston, MA: Beacon Press.
Sullivan, Andrew. 1989. "Here Comes The Groom. A (Conservative) Case For Gay Marriage." *New Republic*, August 28.
Tamanaha, Brian Z. 2000. "A Non-Essentialist Version of Legal Pluralism." *Journal of Law and Society* 27 (2): 296–321.
Viggiani, Giacomo. 2015. "La resilienza dell'eteronormativita nell'interpretazione degli artt. 8 e 12 della Convenzione europea dei diritti umani." *Materiali per una storia della cultura giuridica* XLV (1): 85–102.
Warner, Michael. 1991. "Introduction: Fear of a Queer Planet." *Social Text* 29: 3–17.
———. 2002. "Publics and Counterpublics." *Public Culture* 14 (1): 49–90.

Cited legal cases

Burden v. the United Kingdom [GC] (no. 13378/05, ECtHR, 29 April 2008).
D. B. and Others v. Switzerland (no. 58252/15 and 58817/15, ECtHR, 22 November 2022).
E. B. v. France (no. 43546/02, ECtHR, 22 January 2008).
Fretté v. France (no. 36515/97, ECtHR, 26 February 2002).
Gas & Dubois v. France (no. 25951/08, ECtHR, 15 March 2012).
Karner v. Austria (no. 40016/98, ECtHR, 24 July 2003).
Kozak v. Poland (no. 13102/02, ECtHR, 2 March 2010).
Oliari and Others v. Italy (no. 18766/11 and 36030/11, ECtHR, 21 July 2015).
R (on the application of Steinfeld and Keidan) v. Secretary of State for International Development, [2017] EWCA Civ 81 (Supreme Court of the United Kingdom, 27 June 2018).
Ratzenböck and Seydl v. Austria (no. 28475/12, ECtHR, 26 October 2017).
Schalk and Kopf v. Austria (no. 30141/04, ECtHR, 24 June 2010).
Vallianatos and Others v. Greece [GC] (no. 29381/09 and 32684/09, ECtHR, 7 November 2013).
X and Others v. Austria [GC] (no. 19010/07, ECtHR, 19 February 2013).

4 The transformation of marriage

A historical interpretation of a triple change

Pol van de Wiel

4.1 Introduction

It is clear that the social place of the marital union has drastically altered compared to earlier times, but we can easily fail to notice what has changed exactly and the meaning of this. Few will dispute that the movement that started in the 1960s has had important consequences for the until then dominant position of marriage in society: starting and giving shape to relationships has increasingly become the domain of individual choice and conscience. It is quite a revolution. Slowly but surely, freedom has become the norm in that sphere: one can be joined in matrimony, but it is no less legitimate to live as an unmarried couple, whether or not cohabitating and with children. What the French family law expert Jean Carbonnier saw as a noticeable change in 1978 has become self-evident: 'The family is henceforth based on the couple . . . there can thus exist a family that has not first been celebrated, non-religious celebration at the town hall included, but solely based on affection' (Carbonnier 2014, 92). According to Carbonnier, this new fact is, to a great extent, due to the breakthrough of the values of freedom and equality.

This development may be common knowledge, but how does the 'opening' up of marriage for persons of the same sex – which has become reality in 36 countries worldwide since the turn of the century, especially in Western Europe (Italy is the only exception), the United States (US) and a large part of Latin America – relate to it? What is striking, anyhow, about the phenomenon of 'gay marriage' is that the institution became the centre of public interest, and the subject of often fierce political debate. 'The case for same-sex marriage can't be made on nonjudgmental grounds. It depends on a certain conception of the telos of marriage – its purpose or point', Michael Sandel wrote in *Justice* (2009), when the discussion on same-sex marriage raged heavily in many American states (Sandel 2010, 253). But now that the issue seems settled on the aforementioned continents and getting married has become an option there for gay couples as well, the question remains whether the state of affairs and the meaning of marriage have really changed. Did the debates show a revival of the institution, or do they rather fit into the general tendency that citizens wish to organise their relationships as they please? The

DOI: 10.4324/9781003470786-6

latter development has, in any case, not been stopped. There seems to exist an unbridgeable gap between the centrality and the obviousness of marriage in former times and its elective, optional character today. No misconceptions: people keep getting married; for everybody who takes the step it is a big day, and tying the knot has tangible legal effects. But the place of marriage in society is clearly different from before.

How to understand this situation and what is its genesis? Let us return for a moment to the recent occasion to reflect on this topic. No justification of 'gay marriage' is without an idea on the point of marriage, wrote Sandel. I take up that incitement, but in another direction and in another way than he had in mind. My goal is to lay out a non-normative, *historical* interpretation – in two parts – of the metamorphosis that the institution has undergone in the past decades. With such an approach, I join the work of authors like Pierre Rosanvallon, Caroline Sörgjerd and Irène Théry. The first mentioned stated in his inaugural lecture at the Collège de France in 2002 with respect to democracy that democracy not so much *has* a history, but *is* a history, where the point is to 'retrace the long genealogy of contemporary political questions in order to make them thoroughly intelligible. . . . History conceived in this way is the *active laboratory* that created our present and not simply its background' (Rosanvallon 2006, 38–39). Sörgjerd and Théry have, in different ways, traced the history of modern marriage and its law and symbolism, respectively focused on Sweden and France, and, importantly, examined the meaning of the institution today in the light of that history (Sörgjerd 2012; Théry 2013). Théry, in a retrospective of the French opening up of marriage for same-sex partners, says:

> What most lacked in the debates about the *mariage pour tous* is shared knowledge of at least the tenor of the transformations of marriage and the family. What is the collective, legal and social history that has led from the obvious situation, in 1792, that the newly created *mariage civil* could only be the union between a man and a woman, to the idea that marriage could or even had to become the union between two men or two women as well?
>
> (2016, 20)[1]

In my PhD research[2] and in this chapter, I focus on the legal, political and social history of civil marriage in France and the Netherlands, but their

1 See also Théry's 2016, ch. 2, and Théry 2022, ch. 2 and 3, that brings together her earlier writings on the history of the *mariage civil.*

2 The thesis (Dutch title: *Zo zijn we niet meer getrouwd. De transformatie van het burgerlijk huwelijk in Nederland en Frankrijk*) was defended at Radboud University Nijmegen in November 2023.

developments show important similarities with those in other countries in Europe.

Following Théry's question, there are good reasons indeed to take the starting point for such a history as not the aforementioned 1960s but as roughly 175 years earlier. This seems a big step back in time, but it can clear up the view about what has been going on for well over half a century. Comparing and contrasting the current situation with what preceded it is a method copied from the way in which the political philosopher Claude Lefort has examined modern democracy: '[Its] singularity only becomes fully apparent if we recall the nature of the monarchical system of the Ancien Regime. . . . This model reveals the revolutionary and unprecedented feature of democracy' (Lefort 1988, 16–17). As traditional, hierarchical and 'religiously embedded' family law prior to the 1960s may seem to us – the husband's marital authority; the legal incapacity of the married woman; divorce only based on the fault principle; a sharp distinction between legitimate and illegitimate children; and, in penal law, criminalisation of homosexuality – it is important to observe that the primacy of the institution of marriage has been in the hands of the state since the 19th century. This did not come about spontaneously; it had to be prised out of the grip of the churches. And this happened after the French example, which was conceived in a period that, like the 1960s, formed a clear break with what preceded it.

I therefore proceed in two parts. In the first one (I), from around 1800 up to around 1960, secularised marriage is 'invented' and remains the self-evident framework for sexuality and procreation. The values of equality and freedom, that play a leading part in the political revolutions from the end of the 18th century onwards, are latent in this first part and do not fully blossom with regard to the spheres of marriage and the family. This will be shown via a look at three elements of marriage law that are indicators of the extent of the hierarchy incorporated in the institution: the legal relationship between the spouses, divorce law and the position of illegitimate children (Chloros 1978, pref.). The second part (II) sketches a 'transformation', that is to say how marriage law, but just as much the social *place* of marriage, undergoes a fundamental and permanent metamorphosis. Through legal reforms in the 1970s, the values of freedom and equality are cautiously admitted into family law. But meanwhile, and fully unexpectedly, a revolution is taking place through which those values break through socially, depriving marriage of its monopoly of sexual relationships and procreation. These developments will lead to two important amendments of the law, one silent, the other unmistakable: around the turn of the century, in many countries on the continent the legal-terminological distinction between legitimate and illegitimate parentage is abolished, and in the 21st century, more and more countries introduce what the Netherlands modifies first in 2000–2001: 'A marriage can be concluded by two *persons* [italics -PvdW] of different or of the same sex' (Dutch Civil Code 1992, Art. 1:30). The legal redefinition makes a slumbering transformation explicit.

4.2 Methodological questions

What is central here, but not exclusively, is legal history. A historical reconstruction of only marriage law will not directly lead to the idea of a 'transformation'. A broader scope is required. Marriage has a legal side, but another side as well: *Say Yes to the Dress*, a tendency among French young people of ever more extensive, expressive and personal marriage announcements, preparations and weddings (Maillochon 2016), a *Guide pratique du mariage homo . . .* (Océanerosemarie 2013). These are random recent cultural phenomena that show that marriage also has a 'symbolic' side. When hearing phrases like 'I've fallen in love with a married man', 'Will you marry me?' or 'Let me introduce you to my husband John', few will immediately think of marriage law. Most people will first of all associate 'marriage' with the fact that the union is concluded festively and concerns an exclusive love bond. Beyond any legal question, the notion thus plays a role in our world. Why is it useful to distinguish this dimension from law?

Specific to marriage, one would say nowadays, is the combination of a 'legal package' and a recognisable – linked to an 'immemorial tradition' – public recognition. But not so long ago, it would be strange to speak of the symbolic side of the institution apart from marriage law. The opposition in earlier times was (civil) law as distinct from *religion*. And long after the state appropriates marriage law, matrimony continues to be part of a religious culture where it self-evidently forms the imperative framework for sexuality and procreation, and where the religious celebration is deemed more important than the civil one. It is true, however, that the legal side of the union was subject to criticism since the end of the 19th century. 'Progressive' reformers (liberals, feminists, socialists) denounced the legal marital relations. It is important to note that what was at stake was marriage *law*, not marriage itself. In the 1970s, a reform process finished whereby the inequalities (almost) disappeared from marriage law, and a union could be dissolved by mutual consent. But since the aforementioned religious culture was, at the same time, crumbling, the 'matrimonial constellation' as such then changed: marriage lost its monopoly of relationships and procreation. The substantial and lasting decrease of the relative number of marriages that set in during the 1970s and, a little later, the similar increase in the number of extramarital births confirm this fact. Is a couple's choice not to get married related more to the symbolic side – a step that is considered as 'traditional', 'bourgeois' or simply 'unnecessary' – or to the 'heavy' common legal character of the institution? One can suppose that the former aspect is decisive, whereas the package of marriage rights is apparently not judged indispensable.

At the close of his lecture 'Science as a Vocation' (1917), the sociologist Max Weber made an unmistakable point: there is an unbridgeable tension between the value spheres of modern science and what he calls 'religious salvation', but it is valid just as well for our 'world of meaning' instead:

> Our age is characterised by rationalisation and intellectualisation, and above all, by the disenchantment of the world. Its resulting fate is that

> precisely the ultimate and most sublime values have withdrawn from public life. They have retreated . . . into the fraternal feelings of personal relations between individuals.
>
> (2004, 29–30)

It is a central observation for the movement with regards to marriage outlined earlier, and the tendency will only intensify half a century after Weber's observation and onwards. It would nevertheless be a mistake to think that due to the fading of the religious setting of the institution, 'only law' remains. The question of 'gay marriage' shows that. It is about equal rights (succession rights, taxes, rent protection, social security, etc.), but certainly about symbolic recognition as well – it turns out that when the equal rights are (almost) attained by a registered partnership, the claim to marriage does not abate. This dimension, unreducible to law, is indeed recognised during the Dutch same-sex marriage reform in 1999–2000: 'a certain symbolic and emotional value' belongs to the institution, and although it is about 'granting equal rights', the result is that the 'symbolics' become accessible for gay couples as well. Something similar can be read and heard during the French reform in 2012–2013: it is true that the partnership *Pacte civil de solidarité* has neared marriage via legislation, but it does not sufficiently meet the desire for equal rights – marriage 'as an institution . . . with its whole symbolic connotation' does (Dutch Lower House 1999, 3; 2000, 4–5; Dutch Senate 2000, 15–656, 672; Assemblée nationale 2012, 7, 9–10, 20–22; Journal officiel de la République française 2013, 470 and 491). Understandably so: even in a non-religious context, it is undeniable that something happens during the celebration of a marriage. The *symbolic authority* of such a ceremony causes that there is a before and an after.[3]

But, before returning to these contemporary questions, let us first rewind to earlier times when the relation between marriage and religion was subject to important changes.

4.3 Secularisation and civil order

'The law considers marriage only as a civil contract'. With these words, stated in Article 7 of the French Constitution of 1791, a groundbreaking new principle appeared. It will be put into effect by two laws a year later – one on civil record-keeping and one on divorce – and the *mariage civil* will be maintained in the Civil Code, promulgated in 1804 by Napoleon Bonaparte. The French marriage laws between 1789 and 1804 are of broader interest because it is instructive to see what happens when the individual rights of freedom and equality enter into the 'most natural' realm of all, the family and marriage. The early and unprecedentedly liberal legislation with respect to divorce (1792)

3 See for this term: Moyaert 1994, 45–51.

and the equality of legitimate and illegitimate children (1793) – withdrawn again soon afterwards – only 'returns' in Europe and the United States from the 1970s onwards. The great innovation in the field of marriage rules is then also theorised by writers like Olympe de Gouges (Gouges 2018), Mary Wollstonecraft (Wollstonecraft 2004), Theodor von Hippel (Hippel 1979; Hippel 1994) and more radically a little later by the utopist Charles Fourier (Fourier 1996), who all welcome the new principles of reason, equality and freedom. However, a sharp reaction soon follows. This 'backlash against family innovations' leads to the realisation of the secular but morally particularly conservative Civil Code (Desan 2004, ch. 7–8). The civil orders and thus the marriage orders on the continent are in large part grafted onto the system that was conceived and adopted around 1800 in France. When we create a 19th century European chronology of the moments that establish civil marriage, equally for all citizens, or at least create the choice between civil marriage and a religious marriage with civil effects – by which the primacy of the state is no less expressed – then the order is Belgium (1796), the Netherlands (1809), England and Wales (1837), Norway (1845), Denmark (1851), Sweden (1863), Italy and Romania (1865), Austria (1868), Spain (1870), Switzerland (1874–1875), Germany (1875), Hungary (1894). This covers the secularisation of the *form* of the wedding ceremony; what happened to the *content* of marriage law?

It is important to recall the broader historical context here. From the second half of the 18th century, a new political and social division emerges: the opposition between the private and public spheres. They become two sharply separated worlds with their own logic and laws. This can be seen in the ideas of the philosophers Jean-Jacques Rousseau (Rousseau 1979), Johan Gottlieb Fichte (Fichte 2000) and Georg Wilhelm Friedrich Hegel (Hegel 2008), who agree on two points: all three situate marriage in the private sphere of the family, at a clear distance from the political state, and, secondly, they think that a strict hierarchy is necessary in that private sphere, on the basis of gender distinction and gender relations considered *natural*. Importantly, these authors do not ground their ideas in any traditional theology, to which they are opposed, but on reason, morality and nature. Despite the national diversity, it is possible to outline a common set of similar principles in the 19th century legal systems – the French (1804) and the Dutch Civil Code (1838), but in other codifications as well (Antokolskaia 2006, para. 10.2). Following the three aforementioned indicators: legal equality between the spouses is unconceivable; the husband is the head of the family; and the wife lacks the legal capacity to act, marriage acts thus as a 'selection mechanism' to the public sphere, in which the husband is to represent the family. Divorce – if it exists at all in the legal order, which is not the case in France (between 1816 and 1884), Italy, Spain, Portugal and Malta – is almost everywhere grounded on the fault principle, which means practically that it can only be obtained in the case of adultery. And thirdly, illegitimate children are fundamentally social and legal pariahs who have no family and cannot inherit.

However, from the last three decades of the 19th century onwards, this matrimonial universe will be questioned. Two signs of the contestation that then commences are the publication in 1869 of John Stuart Mill's *The Subjection of Women*, soon translated into other languages and influencing women's movements in several countries; and in 1872, the French writer Alexandre Dumas *fils* gives political meaning to the word 'feminism' for the first time, which was a medical term until then; he uses the neologism *les féministes* to designate those who say that 'all bad things come from the fact that people do not want to recognise that woman is equal to man' (1872, 91–92). Apart from the so-called first wave feminists, liberals and socialists challenge *l'ordre établi*. They do so in the name of equality and, to a lesser extent, freedom. The difficulty in obtaining a divorce is denounced; the dire position of illegitimate children is called into question; more equality between husband and wife is laid claim to. In the first half of the 20th century, some 'radical pioneers' like Alfred Naquet (1908), Léon Blum (2021) and Victor Margueritte (2015) in France; Marie Stopes (2004) in the United Kingdom, and Wibaut-Van Berlekom and Wibaut (1932) in the Netherlands dare to imagine a sexually freer future separate from the framework of marriage, but their pleas remain marginal. It is important to note that, setting aside individual cases, the consensus consists of the desire for reform of aspects of marriage *law*, not marriage as such. Two world wars work as a leveller between the sexes, as does women's suffrage obtained in many countries after World War I. But by the first years after World War II, only equality between spouses has been achieved, not the relaxing of divorce rules, nor a fundamental improvement in the position of illegitimate children.

4.4 Transformation

In the 1960s, many things happen quickly after and at the same time as each other. We should mention here the appearance of the contraceptive pill; secularisation in society, especially among the young; the sexual revolution; second-wave feminism and individualisation. These are anything but isolated phenomena. During the development of and discussions about 'the pill' in the first half of the 1960s, the idea settled that it is up to the spouses themselves to decide whether and when they wish to have children. This individualisation is, of course, also secularisation: religious authorities become more liberal or simply lose their grip on an area of human life over which they could formerly assert their influence. This may already be a significant step, but simultaneously or just a little later, the changing norms in the sphere of love and sexuality go further. In the first place, sexuality is not limited anymore to the frame of marriage, but, on the contrary, becomes an autonomous domain of human behaviour and expression. Marriage loses its symbolic 'monopoly' of it. And also love and relationships gain a more independent status, separate from the 'objective' institution. Secondly, the idea emerges that marriage is a 'stiff', 'bourgeois' or even hypocritical institution that draws a veil over tensions, problems and inequalities. This criticism has not disappeared from the culture since. This does obviously not mean, on the contrary, that choosing marriage is henceforth not possible anymore. But since romantic love and sentiment become, more sharply than before, the basis of relationships, the big shift is that getting married indeed becomes a *choice*, an *option*, a *possibility* for a couple – and not any longer the self-evident and binding *norm*. People start to see matrimony as a relation between two people, less as an institution.

It is important, however, to observe that the effects of these shifts have an incubation period of years or even a decade. At the beginning of the 1970s, matrimony seems to flourish as never before, as is shown by the discourse during the introduction of divorce by mutual consent in Dutch Lower House (1971) and French (1975) legislation and the equalisation of legitimate and illegitimate children in France (1971–1972). The ministers of Justice of both countries admit that yes, these are liberalisations of marriage law, but they assure that, in any case, the improvement in the position of natural children will not make marriage less attractive, and not much use will be made of the relaxed possibility of divorce (Dutch Lower House 1971, 65–3371, 65–3373; Journal officiel de la République française 1971, 4273; 1975, 3299). They could not be more wrong. From the 1970s onwards, we see clear changes in three marital statistics: the relative number of marriages (per 1,000 habitants) starts to decrease, the percentage of divorces begins to grow, and thirdly, and perhaps most importantly, the percentage of live births outside wedlock starts to increase. To their amazement, demographers start noticing these trends around 1980, and in the beginning of the 1990s two sociologists make two important and fundamental observations: Anthony Giddens (1992, ch. 4) notes that marriage is less and less the distinguishing category for love and sexuality, but on the contrary *relationships*, while his French colleague Irène Théry (1993, intr.) gives the following content to a process that she calls *le démariage*: whether to marry or not has become a subjective experience, choosing it or breaking the bond is a matter of individual conscience. It turns out that what they describe is a continuous, ongoing process: whereas the percentage of extramarital births is below 10% almost everywhere in Europe (except the Nordic countries) at the end of the 1970s, by the year 2000 in the Netherlands this is around 25% and in France around 40%, and at the end of the 2010s, respectively more than 50% and more than 60%. And it is a European phenomenon: apart from a few exceptions, the part of live births outside marriage everywhere is at least a third, more often almost half or already more than half – the EU average being around 42% in 2016–2020 (Jacobs 2023).[4] Against the background of these numbers, it does not seem illogical that increasingly the need is felt to not only equalise the rights of 'legitimate' and 'illegitimate' children – the tendency that becomes the norm after the

4 In Ukraine, Poland, Greece, Switzerland, Serbia, Croatia and Lithuania, the percentage is below 30%.

European Court of Human Rights (ECHR) landmark case *Marckx v. Belgium* (1979, especially paras. 36–65) – but to call into question those hierarchical designations as such. From the end of the 1980s onwards, the distinction between legitimate and illegitimate parentage is removed from the family law terminology in Belgium, England and Wales, Germany, the Netherlands and France. Hence, marriage is no longer the linchpin of parentage and of parentage *law* – instead these have been put on their own 'pedestal'.

Same-sex marriage also springs from the movement that started in the 1960s, which as a slogan would read *my private life is my business*. This principle unleashes a veritable revolution as to the way in which not only marriage is seen, but, more broadly, love, sexuality and gender relations; it is not limited to the traditional married couple and its internal relations, but on the contrary it takes away the exclusive legitimacy of that bond. Not only is it up to a woman and a man how they wish to give shape to their relationship, but this can henceforth also consist of two men, two women or more people. The French philosopher Olivier Roy recently identified this aspect of the 1960s as an anthropological paradigm shift that breaks with the until then dominant 'secularised Christian' values and with the idea of a 'natural order' between the sexes (2019, ch. 5). This, again, is a process over years, but part of it is that the self-evident and tacitly assumed norm that a man and a woman are naturally inclined to one another gradually makes way for the acceptance of other inclinations. This emancipation movement leads to the call for some legal recognition of same-sex couples (in the second half of the 1980s), and also to the claim for 'access' to the institution of marriage (first seriously made in the Netherlands, West Germany, Belgium and the United States in 1989). The latter claim is then politically marginal, but a step-by-step process starts. It notably goes from the introduction of a *registreret partnerskab* in Denmark in 1989 to similar steps in other European countries in the 1990s, habituation to an 'absurd' or even 'ridiculous' idea that obtains a parliamentary majority in the Netherlands in the second half of the 1990s and is first made a reality by the second Kok cabinet in 2000–2001, gradually followed in the following decades by 35 countries until now. Every social and political context is specific, but two crucial factors are, in general, the acceptance of homosexuality and the growing ability to see not only a partnership but also marriage as separate from discussions about 'vertical' parentage relations – hence, conceiving matrimony first and foremost horizontally as a bond between two persons. Conspicuously, this process shows significant turnarounds in many countries, where what is 'absolutely out of order' at a given moment, can be adopted with huge majorities and gain ample social approval less than a decade later.

Are we heading towards a European consensus on the subject, or rather a division? As of 2023, only two countries (Slovenia and Estonia) not belonging to Western Europe in 1989 have taken the step. The ECHR reiterates in 2014–2016 what it established in the 2010 case of *Schalk and Kopf v. Austria*: none of Articles 8, 12 or 14 of the European Convention on Human Rights, alone nor combined, imposes an obligation on member states to grant same-sex couples access to marriage. However, the Court considers that in the absence of marriage, these couples have a particular interest in obtaining the option of entering into a form of civil union or registered partnership since this would be the most appropriate way in which they could have their relationship recognised and which would guarantee them the relevant protection; furthermore, such partnerships have an intrinsic value irrespective of their legal effects, and this recognition would bring a sense of legitimacy to same-sex couples (*Schalk and Kopf v. Austria* 2010, paras. 57–58, 60–64, 101, 107–8, 110; European Court of Human Rights 2022, 25–27, 38–39; *Hämäläinen v. Finland* 2014, para. 96; *Oliari et al v. Italy* 2015, paras. 174, 192–93; *Chapin and Charpentier v. France* 2016, paras. 37–39). Between 1991 and 2020, a number of Central and Eastern European countries constitutionalised that marriage is the union between a man and a woman. These steps show, of course, that the *idea* of same-sex marriage also circulates there. They are not necessarily the expression of a decreased acceptance of the LGBT community since there is often an internationally organised political movement against 'foreign influence' behind it. Nevertheless, opening up marriage seems unthinkable there in the near future (Wikipedia 2023; Mos 2020).

4.5 Conclusions

According to the *Oxford English Dictionary*, 'transformation' means 'the action of changing in form, shape, or appearance'. This is what has been central here with regards to the institution of marriage. The movement that has been going on for decades does *not*, in my opinion, lead to its end, 'abolition' or 'privatisation'. This idea, often propagated in the name of a truly liberal, strictly secularised state and antidiscrimination, has popped up and been defended every now and then in the past decades, but it has been implemented nowhere.[5] It is remarkable that almost all pleas in favour of abolition recognise the *legal* value and necessity of marriage and consequently want to offer citizens the possibility of a 'neutral, strictly practical-legal' partnership. It is true that the traditional and *Christian* symbolism that apparently also sticks to civil marriage would then disappear. But it is a fundamental legal reform – as was observed by the French government in the *mariage pour tous* bill in 2012 – and is the game worth the candle? For how important is the 'abolition desire' really (Assemblée nationale 2012, 21–22)? I think that the possible advantages of abolition for reasons of principle are outweighed by the obvious legal value and the *remaining* symbolic force of the institution.

5 A selection from Dutch, Anglo-Saxon and French pleas to that effect: Verlegh, Maarseveen, and Korthuis 1984; Kinsley 2003; Maillard 2004; Chaumier 2004; Birnbaum 2004; Metz 2010; Chambers 2017; Huijer 2018, ch. 16; Balen 2021.

In a similar vein, there is another idea that to my mind will not become reality soon. After the opening up of marriage for persons of the same sex, there still exists liberal criticism on marriage law. It concerns its 'restrictive' aspects (comprising only two persons, in principle concluded for life, legal privileges going with it) and indicates how it should be 'relaxed' and 'minimised'.[6] Marriage law reforms in France and the Netherlands in the past decades have indeed gone in the direction of relaxation and individualisation.[7] But even though legally sanctioned polygamy cannot be excluded on principle, it is a fact that pleas for it do not cause the same dynamics at all as the idea of same-sex marriage did earlier. Apparently, principles are not yet a truly socially and politically supported *claim*.

So what *are* the implications of the transformation? An allegory can help us distinguish a triple metamorphosis. The political philosopher Claude Lefort has given a supplement to the idea that the Ancien Regime represented its unity and its identity to itself as that of a body. According to Lefort, the modern democratic revolution bursts out when the body of the king is destroyed, his head falls off and the 'corporeality of the social is dissolved'. That event has three consequences: the 'disincorporation' of individuals (who become countable entities, for example, in elections), and the appearance of social division on the one hand and, on the other, a set of distinctions that is constitutive of the political order (state vs. civil society, the independent spheres of power, law and knowledge) (Lefort 1986, 302–3). Specifically, the autonomy of law is bound up with 'the impossibility of establishing its essence': 'it is always dependent upon a debate as to its foundations, and as to the legitimacy of what has been established and of what ought to be established' (Lefort 1988, 18).

Similarly, the transformation of the marital union reveals three fundamental new characteristics that were formerly interwoven in a self-evident way. In all three, marriage is understood as a horizontal bond. Firstly, the institution has, henceforth, a facultative status and increasingly has to tolerate other, socially equally accepted forms of relationship beside it, extra-legal (often the factual living together of *two* persons, but not necessarily so) or legal rivals (a symbolically and/or legally 'lighter' partnership, or a cohabitation contract) (Riele and Stückradt 2019, 7; StatLine 2023a; Insee 2023a, 2023b). French family law professors state that marriage, partnership and factual cohabitation grow towards one another and increasingly resemble each other as three *statuts du*

6 Hoogen 2010; Ternaux 2012; Cate 2013; Smits 2016; for the American context, see Brake 2012, 2016. The literature on polygamy and polyamory is obviously much more extensive but almost always passes over legal aspects, and exactly these are central here.

7 The Dutch Civil Code (1992) with amendments of 1 July 1992, 31 May 2001 and 24 April 2017 that respectively facilitates and advances the possibility of divorce, removes the obligation for spouses and registered partners to live together, and reduces the community of property; the French Law on Divorce (2004) of 24 May 2004 and the French Law on the Modernization of Justice in the 21st Century (2016) of 18 November 2016 that facilitate divorce.

couple (Malaurie and Fulchiron 2020, 275–76; Leroyer 2022, 295–96). Secondly, marriage is no longer the linchpin of parentage law, which now stands 'on its own socle'. In the Netherlands, marriage has shared its effects on parentage law with the *geregistreerd partnerschap* since 2014, whereas the *présomption de paternité* in France remains marriage's prerogative, but anyhow the meaning of this effect has changed. From the moment that the privileged link between marriage and parentage law is cut by the removal of the legal terms 'legitimate/illegitimate', and moreover marriage is decreasingly the framework in which procreation takes place (less than half of the births in France since 2006, in the Netherlands since 2016), the paternity presumption can hardly be seen any more as the 'core' on which a system is built; it is rather a simple effect of marriage (Boer, Kolkman, and Salomons 2016, no. 10 and 52; Théry 2022, 189–93).[8] In both cases, the unity of one normative model makes way for a pluralism of possibilities. Breaking the link between marriage and parentage law is of course, thirdly, also connected with the institution's redefinition, that became reality after a debate on the legitimacy of something obvious (the sex difference). The consequence: whereas marriage had already ceased to be the only structure that connects the different generations, its exclusive characteristic is neither the junction of the sexes anymore.

References

Antokolskaia, Masha. 2006. *Harmonisation of Family Law in Europe: A Historical Perspective. A Tale of Two Millennia.* Antwerp; Oxford: Intersentia.

Assemblée nationale. 2012. "Projet de loi nr. 344." Accessed November 7, 2012.

Balen, Saskia van. 2021. "Schaf het burgerlijk huwelijk af." *Trouw*, March 18.

Birnbaum, Jean. 2004. "Jacques Derrida: 'Je suis en guerre contre moi-même'." *Le Monde* 19 August.

Blum, Léon. (1907) 2021. *Du mariage.* Paris: Bouquin (Pocket).

Boer, J., J. D. Kolkman, and F. R. Salomons. 2016. *Mr. C. Assers Handleiding tot beoefening van het Nederlands Burgerlijk Recht. 1. Personen- en familierecht. Deel II. Huwelijk, geregistreerd partnerschap en ongehuwd samenleven.* 19th ed. Deventer: Kluwer.

Brake, Elizabeth. 2012. *Minimizing Marriage. Marriage, Morality and the Law.* New York: Oxford University Press.

———, ed. 2016. *After Marriage. Rethinking Marital Relationships.* New York: Oxford University Press.

Carbonnier, Jean. (1978) 2014. "À chacun sa famille, à chacun son droit." In idem, *Essais sur les lois*, 91–97. Paris: LGDJ.

Cate, Roxane ten. 2013. "De ratio van het polygamieverbod." *Nederlands Juristenblad*, September 27, 2250–54.

8 If the *geregistreerd partnerschap* counts as marriage, the percentage of extramarital births stabilises in the Netherlands from 2007 until 2022 at between 40% and 45% (see StatLine 2023b; Insee 2023b). Other European countries where more children are born outside than inside marriage are the United Kingdom, Belgium, Sweden, Portugal, Bulgaria, Denmark, Norway and Slovenia (see Statista 2023).

Chambers, Clare. 2017. *Against Marriage. An Egalitarian Defence of the Marriage-Free State*. Oxford: Oxford University Press.
Chapin and Charpentier v. France (no. 40183/07, ECtHR, 9 June 2016).
Chaumier, Serge. 2004. "À quoi sert le mariage?" *Libération*, August 6.
Chloros, A. G. 1978. *The Reform of Family Law in Europe. (The Equality of the Spouses – Divorce – Illegitimate Children)*. Deventer: Kluwer.
Desan, Suzanne. 2004. *The Family on Trial in Revolutionary France*. Berkeley; Los Angeles; London: University of California Press.
Dumas fils, Alexandre. 1872. *L'homme-femme. Réponse à M. Henri d'Ideville*. Paris: Michel Lévy frères.
Dutch Civil Code. 1992.
Dutch Lower House. 1971. "Proceedings of the Dutch Lower House, 1970–1971." 16 March, 1971, pp. 65-3373 and 65-3371.
———. 1999. "Documents of the Dutch Lower House, 1998–1999, 26672, nr. 3." 8 July, 1999, p. 3.
———. 2000. "Documents of the Dutch Lower House, 2000–2001, 26672, nr. 92a." 27 November, 2000, pp. 4–5.
Dutch Senate. 2000. "Proceedings of the Dutch Senate, 2000–2001." 19 December, 2000, pp. 15-656 and 15-672.
European Court of Human Rights. 2022. "Guide on the Case-Law of the European Convention on Human Rights: Rights of LGBTI Persons." Prepared by the Registry. Accessed November 24, 2023. https://ks.echr.coe.int/documents/d/echr-ks/guide_lgbti_rights_eng.
Fichte, Johan Gottlieb. (1796–1797) 2000. *Foundations of Natural Right According to the Principles of the Wissenschaftlehre*. Translated by Michael Baur. Cambridge: Cambridge University Press.
Fourier, Charles. (1808) 1996. *The Theory of the Four Movements*. Translated by Ian Patterson. Cambridge: Cambridge University Press.
French Law on Divorce. 2004. LOI n° 2004-439 du 26 mai 2004 relative au divorce.
French Law on the Modernization of Justice in the 21st Century. 2016. LOI n° 2016-1547 du 26 novembre 2016 de modernisation de la justice du XXIe siècle.
Giddens, Anthony. 1992. *The Transformation of Intimacy. Sexuality, Love and Eroticism in Modern Societies*. Cambridge: Polity Press.
Gouges, Olympe de. (1791) 2018. *The Declaration of the Rights of Women*. Translated by Alayne Pullen. London: Octopus.
Hämäläinen v. Finland (no. 37359/09, ECtHR, 16 July 2014).
Hegel, Georg Wilhelm Friedrich. (1820–1821) 2008. *Outlines of the Philosophy of Right*. Translated by T. M. Knox. Oxford: Oxford University Press.
Hippel, Thedor von. (1792) 1979. *On Improving the Status of Women*. Translated by Timothy F. Sellner. Detroit: Wayne University Press.
———. (1794) 1994. *On Marriage*. Translated by Timothy F. Sellner. Detroit: Wayne University Press.
Hoogen, E. J. A. van den. 2010. "Bi-, poly- of toch maar gewoon monogaam huwelijk?" *Tijdschrift voor Familie- en Jeugdrecht*, April, 86–92.
Huijer, Marli. 2018. *Beminnen. Nieuw licht op seksuele vrijheid*. Amsterdam: Boom.
Insee. 2023a. Accessed August 28, 2023. www.insee.fr/fr/statistiques/2381498.
———. 2023b. Accessed August 28, 2023. www.insee.fr/fr/statistiques/2381394.
Jacobs, Frank. 2023. "In These 11 European Countries, Births Out of Wedlock are in the Majority." *Big Think*. Accessed November 24, 2023. https://bigthink.com/strange-maps/births-out-of-wedlock-europe-us/.
Journal officiel de la République française. 1971. "Assemblée nationale, session of 5 October 1971." p. 4273.
———. 1975. "Assemblée nationale, session of 28 May 1975." p. 3299.

———. 2013. "Assemblée nationale, session of 29 January 2013." pp. 470 and 491.
Kinsley, Michael. 2003. "Abolish Marriage." *The Washington Post*, July 3.
Lefort, Claude. (1979) 1986. "The Image of Body and Totalitarianism." In idem, *The Political Forms of Modern Society*, translated by John B. Thompson, 292–306. Cambridge: MIT Press.
———. (1983) 1988."The Question of Democracy." In idem, *Democracy and Political Theory*, translated by David Macey, 7–20. Cambridge: Polity Press.
Leroyer, Anne-Marie. 2022. *Droit de la famille*. Paris: Presses universitaires de France.
Maillard, Jean de. 2004. "Suppression!." *Le Monde*, May 28.
Maillochon, Florence. 2016. *La passion du mariage*. Paris: Presses universitaires de France.
Malaurie, Philippe, and Hugues Fulchiron. 2020. *Droit de la famille*. 7th ed. Paris: LGDJ.
Marckx v. Belgium (no. 6833/74, ECtHR, 13 June 1979).
Margueritte, Victor. (1922) 2015. *The Bacheloresse*. Translated by Brian Stableford. Los Angeles: Black Coat Press.
Metz, Tamara. 2010. *Untying the Knot. Marriage, the State, and the Case for Their Divorce*. Princeton; Oxford: Oxford University Press.
Mos, Martijn. 2020. "The Anticipatory Politics of Homophobia: Explaining Constitutional Bans on Same-Sex Marriage in Post-Communist Europe." *East European Politics* 395–416.
Moyaert, Paul. 1994. *Ethiek en sublimatie. Over* De ethiek van de psychoanalyse *van Jacques Lacan*. Nijmegen: SUN.
Naquet, Alfred. 1908. *Vers l'union libre*. Paris: Félix Juven.
Océanerosemarie. 2013. *Le guide pratique du mariage homo*. Paris: La Martinière.
Oliari et al v. Italy (no. 18766/11 and 36030/11, ECtHR, 21 July 2015).
Riele, Saskia Te, and Katharina Stückradt. 2019. *Ruim twintig jaar geregistreerd partnerschap*. The Hague: CBS.
Rosanvallon, Pierre. (2002) 2006. "Inaugural Lecture, Collège de France." In idem, *Democracy Past and Future*, edited by Samuel Moyn, 31–58. New York: Columbia University Press.
Rousseau, Jean-Jacques. (1762) 1979. *Emile or on Education*. Translated by Allan Bloom. New York: Basic Books.
Roy, Olivier. 2019. *Is Europe Christian?* Translated by Cynthia Schoch. London: Hurst & Co.
Sandel, Michael. (2009) 2010. *Justice. What is the Right Thing to Do?* London: Penguin.
Schalk and Kopf v. Austria (no. 30141/04, ECtHR, 24 June 2010).
Smits, J. M. 2016. "Tot de dood ons scheidt? Pleidooi voor een tijdelijk huwelijk." *Weekblad voor Privaatrecht, Notariaat en Registratie* 7127 (November 18): 935–37.
Sörgjerd, Caroline. 2012. *Reconstructing Marriage. The Legal Status of Relationships in a Changing Society*. Cambridge; Antwerp; Portland: Intersentia.
Statista. 2023. Accessed May 9, 2023. www.statista.com/statistics/294571/live-births-in-england-wales-uk-by-age-and-marital-status-of-mother/.
StatLine. 2023a. Accessed August 28, 2023. https://opendata.cbs.nl/#/CBS/nl/navigatieScherm/zoeken?searchKeywords=huwen%20en%20partnerschapsregistraties;%20kerncijfers%E2%80%99.
———. 2023b. Accessed August 28, 2023. https://opendata.cbs.nl/statline/#/CBS/nl/navigatieScherm/zoeken?searchKeywords=%22geboorte%20gehuwd%22.
Stopes, Marie. (1918) 2004. *Married Love*. Oxford: Oxford University Press.
Ternaux, Catherine. 2012. *La polygamie, pourquoi pas?* Paris: Grasset.
Théry, Irène. 1993. *Le démariage. Justice et vie privée*. Paris: Odile Jacob.
———. 2013. " 'Ouverture' ou 'redefinition' du mariage civil?" In *Mariage de même sexe et filiation*, edited by Irène Théry, 61–73. Paris: Éditions de l'École des Hautes Études en Sciences Sociales.

———. 2016. *Mariage et filiation pour tous. Une métamorphose inachevée*. Paris: Seuil.
———. 2022. *Moi aussi. La nouvelle civilité sexuelle*. Paris: Seuil.
Verlegh, Désirée, Henc van Maarseveen, and Sandra Korthuis. 1984. "Het huwelijk de rechtsorde uit." *Nederlands Juristenblad* 18 August.
Weber, Max. (1917) 2004. "Science as a Vocation." In idem, *The Vocation Lectures*, translated by Rodney Livingstone, 1–31. Indianapolis; Cambridge: Hackett.
Wibaut-Van Berlekom, M., and F. Wibaut. 1932. *Wordend huwelijk*. Haarlem: H. D. Tjeenk Willink & Zoon N. V.
Wikipedia. "Recognition of same-sex unions in Europe." *Wikipedia*. Accessed August 28, 2023. https://en.wikipedia.org/wiki/Recognition_of_same-sex_unions_in_Europe.
Wollstonecraft, Mary. (1792) 2004. *A Vindication of the Rights of Woman*. London: Penguin.

II

Legal responses to non-state marriages and proposals for reforms

5 Addressing non-state marriages in state law

Responses from the Netherlands

Susan Rutten

5.1 Introduction

Marriage is an age-old concept. For a long time, marriage belonged to the private domain. Marriages were concluded according to traditions within one's own community. This has changed in many parts of the world, and many states have taken the arrangement of marriage to themselves. Marriage registers have been created. This has allowed states to have a view on existing marriages, and as a result, citizens can also enjoy the legal protection to be derived from marriage. States themselves decide which marriages are given legal status and legal effect. In this chapter, the focus will be on states that see marriage in its civil relations, in which the state has usurped the monopoly over marriages, and in which marriage is not left to religious, cultural or ethnic communities. However, even if a state recognises only civil marriages, people continue to marry according to the traditions of their own community, whether or not in addition to a civil marriage.

The Netherlands is such a state. Dutch law considers marriage only in its civil relations (Dutch Civil Code 1992, Art. 30, s. 2). Nevertheless, non-state marriages, i.e. marriages that are not concluded in accordance with state law, also called informal marriages, have been established in the Netherlands for decades. These marriages have long escaped the attention of the legislature and politics. After all, they were marriages that had no legal meaning and therefore belonged in the private domain. Many problems did not come to light. That changed when practices around certain non-state marriages became known that were harmful to those directly involved or to society. Non-state marriages became portrayed in a negative light. The Dutch government wanted to gain more insight into what was going on outside the official state law in the field of non-state marriages: why were they concluded, how often and what were the consequences of these marriages? The calmness in communities in which customary or religious marriages were the standard was ended, done with the (relative) freedom to decide oneself on marriage; state law required people to enter civil marriages, and communities had to obey that rule. Customary marriages became non-state marriages. They continued to exist but were subordinated to civil marriage. Authorities and communities became alert to

DOI: 10.4324/9781003470786-8

the risks and dangers of traditional marriages that were not accompanied by a civil marriage. And so, policymakers and legislators had to respond to these developments.

In this chapter I describe how Dutch state law contributed in dealing with the de facto normative pluralism in marriages: state law that required civil marriages whereas informally, people adhered to customary and religious marriages as described by customary or religious law. I explain how the Dutch legislator and judiciary have dealt with this struggle over the years. Based on these developments and considering suggestions that have been described in literature, I consider several tools and mechanisms that could be useful in settling the dilemma of leaving sufficient room and freedom for non-state marriages (thus granting freedoms to people in their private domain) and at the same time protecting victims and society against the possible negative and harmful practices that can accompany non-state marriages (see also Akhtar, Probert, and Moors 2018, 367–75).

5.2 Current Dutch law

5.2.1 Non-state marriages in the Netherlands

Non-state marriages occur in all kinds of variants in the Netherlands. How often these marriages take place turns out to be difficult to determine (Rutten a.o. 2015, 166). Non-state marriages can be religious marriages (i.e. marriages that are concluded in a manner that conforms to religious standards, Rutten a.o. 2015, 50), customary marriages and marriages in which partners commit themselves to each other through a spiritual ceremony. Although the categories are not always easy to distinguish from each other, the qualification may be important because religious marriages legally have a different position from other non-state marriages. Examples of religious marriages that are established in the Netherlands are Christian or ecclesiastical marriages, Jewish marriages, Muslim marriages, Hindu marriages and marriages according to any other religion. Customary marriages are still very common within Roma communities. Examples of the third and last category are humanistic relationship celebrations and informal marriages within Wicca (Leun and Leupen 2009, 15).

In many situations, non-state marriages take place after a civil marriage has been concluded. However, it also occurs that non-state marriages are concluded without a civil marriage taking place at all or are concluded prior to a civil marriage (Rutten a.o. 2015, 67–72). Significantly, spouses often declare that their non-state marriage is regarded as and is experienced to be their real marriage (Rutten a.o. 2015, 81–83, 105–6). The civil marriage or consular marriage is often referred to as an administrative act, a necessary 'registration'.

Motives for entering a non-state marriage without or prior to a civil marriage can be of various kinds. A lack of required documents could be the reason, or the legitimation of having an intimate relationship, overcoming a deficit that would be an impediment to enter a civil marriage, maintaining financial or social benefits, having no interest in a civil marriage or whatever other reason (Moors 2014; Rutten a.o. 2015, 106–12; Uddin 2018, 401–26).

5.2.2 *Legal status of non-state marriages under Dutch law*

5.2.2.1 *Legal status under civil law*

Dutch family law is governed in the first Book of Dutch Civil Code. Only civil marriages are recognised under Dutch law (Dutch Civil Code 1992, Art. 1:30 s. 2). According to Dutch rules on private international law, to be found in Book 10 DCC, all marriages that are entered into in the Netherlands are subjected to Dutch marriage law (Dutch Civil Code 1992, Art. 10:29). The only exception concerns marriages that are established at foreign consulates in the Netherlands. Those marriages are valid as long as neither of the spouses possesses Dutch nationality (Dutch Civil Code 1992, Art. 10:30). As far as religious marriages, or, more specifically, marriages with a religious ceremony and in the presence of a religious authority are concerned, they are allowed only if they are preceded by a civil marriage (Dutch Civil Code 1992, Art. 1:68).

As a result, regarding marriages concluded in the Netherlands, only civil marriages and consular marriages have legal effect. All other marriages are non-state marriages that do not have legal effect and are legally considered not to exist. Foreign marriages can be recognised only if the marriage is validly concluded according to the law where the marriage took place (Dutch Civil Code 1992, Art. 10:31). As a result, foreign non-state marriages will not be recognised in the Netherlands.

5.2.2.2 *Legal status under criminal law*

Since state marriages under Dutch law are restricted to civil marriages, only spouses of a civil marriage are legally qualified as spouses. Non-state marriages as such are not criminalised. They are only punishable if they meet the requirements of another criminal act, e.g. if it is a forced marriage, which would be punishable as an act of coercion (Dutch Criminal Code 1881, Art. 284). Only religious authorities who violate the order set under civil law, and thus cooperate in a religious marriage without a prior civil marriage, are punishable (Dutch Criminal Code 1881, Art. 449).

The question has arisen whether qualifications awarded to a non-state marriage under civil law should also be followed under criminal law. At first glance, that might seem logical. However, the legitimate question that can be asked is whether, from the point of view of criminality and criminalisation, a civil marriage should be approached differently from a non-state marriage. Two decisions of the Dutch Supreme Court have shone a light on this (Dutch SC 3 July 2018 and Dutch SC 1 December 2009). In the case decided in 2018, the court had to decide whether the spouse of an Islamic marriage concluded in Iraq, who was maltreated by her husband, could considered a spouse as meant by Dutch Criminal Code (1881, Art. 304, s. 1). It follows from this article that if the guilty party committed the crime against his or her spouse, this would result in an aggravating circumstance and may lead to an increase in the maximum prison sentence by one third.[1] The Supreme Court determined that, when interpreting the term spouse, criminal law should follow the system of personal and family law as laid down in the Civil Code as much as possible. Since the Iraqi marriage could be recognised as a valid marriage in the Netherlands despite being an Islamic marriage, spouses were also referred to as such in the application of criminal law. The man was therefore rightfully convicted of assault under the aggravating circumstance that the crime had been committed against his wife.

In the second case of 2009, the Supreme Court had to determine whether a non-state marriage could lead to a situation of bigamy, which is punishable under Dutch law (Dutch Criminal Code 1881, Art. 237). The case concerned a Moroccan man who had entered an Islamic non-state marriage in Morocco in 1988 and entered a civil marriage with another woman in the Netherlands 10 years later in 1998. The second marriage was dissolved by divorce a few years after that, in 2002. In 2005 the man had his first Moroccan marriage judicially confirmed in Morocco, so that this marriage could also be considered a legally valid marriage with retroactive effect, i.e. since 1988. The man requested to register the (first) 1988 marriage, presumably to allow his first wife to come over to the Netherlands, which initially was refused. According to Dutch Civil Code (1992, Art. 10:31), Dutch authorities do recognise such marriages retroactively unless they infringe upon Dutch public policy. What then followed was that the man was accused of bigamy since after the divorce of his second wife it appeared that in 1998, when he entered his second marriage, he was supposedly already married to another wife. However, to be punishable, Dutch criminal law requires that he *intended* to enter a double marriage. The man took the position that there was no such intent because at that time there was no question of a legally valid first marriage. The Court of Appeal and the Supreme Court did not go along with this. The Court of Appeal considered that the man was legally married under Moroccan law (because of the retroactive effect of the marriage confirmation in 2005) and that the man knew in 1998 that he had previously been married in Morocco. The Supreme Court expressly considered that being ‘lawfully’ married was not part of the offence and agreed with the Court of Appeal’s judgement that the defendant was married under Moroccan law at the time he was charged. It follows from this decision that if partners are married in a non-state marriage

1 According to Art. 90octies of Dutch Criminal Code (1881) this article also applies to registered partnerships.

and want to validate this marriage, they should think carefully about the possible consequences.

5.2.2.3 Legal status of family life

It often occurs that people who enter a non-state marriage live together as a couple. If spouses start a family life, with or without children, they are entitled to the protection that is offered to family life by human rights conventions and by national state law. The most often invoked human right provision in this respect is Article 8 of the European Convention on Human Rights (ECHR). This article can be invoked by itself or in conjunction with the right to equality, protected by Art. 14 ECHR. Thus, where a non-state marriage can be equated with another relationship, its family life should be protected in the same way as the other relationship. This means that rights that follow from family life, and are attributed to that other relationship, should in the same way be granted to members of a non-state marriage family.

Under Dutch law, only two kinds of relationships are legally recognised in law (Dutch Civil Code 1992, Book 1) marriage and registered partnership. Both are based on the principle of monogamy. Both institutions are open to both same sex-couples and couples between persons of a different gender. The legal effects of marriage and registered partnership are almost similar. Other relationships, like cohabitation without registration, are not regulated. Specific legislation (e.g. in the context of taxation, social security provisions, migration and asylum law) or case law may decide to attribute certain consequences to such cohabitation relationships. An example that shows how this can turn out is the following asylum case that was decided on 26 September 2017 by the District Court of The Hague. A Syrian man and Ethiopian woman met in Lebanon and entered an Islamic marriage there. Owing to the man's unlawful residence in Lebanon, this marriage could not be taken up in the Lebanese register. Because of the war in Syria, the partners could not travel to Syria to have the marriage registered in the family book in Syria either. The man obtained an asylum residence permit in the Netherlands. The wife wished to stay with her husband in the Netherlands. Under Dutch law, she could claim this by proving that she was either the spouse of the man or was so dependent on him that she belonged to his family (Dutch Alien Law: Art. 29, sect. 2). In the present case, there was no legally valid marriage under Lebanese law and the marriage could therefore not be recognised in the Netherlands. Informal marriages concluded outside the Netherlands are considered as partnership relationships by the Dutch immigration service (IND), if there is a durable, exclusive relationship. The woman therefore had to prove that there was a lasting family relationship with the man. The court considered that in this case, although the woman had not submitted any official documents, she did submit an Islamic marriage certificate that formed a connecting factor for at least the alleged partnership. In view of additional circumstances and statements, the Dutch authorities could not simply refuse the requested residence.

5.3 Developments in Dutch law

5.3.1 Changing policies

5.3.1.1 From multiculturalism to rejection[2]

If one looks at the Dutch policies towards minorities over time, it was only at the end of the 1970s that an ad hoc policy was pursued based on the idea that the stay of most newcomers in the Netherlands was temporary (WRR Report 1979). The aims were the integration of foreign migrant workers into society and remigration, in both cases preserving their own identity WRR Report 1979). In the 1980s, when it became clear that the presence of migrants would be permanent, the policy aimed at the full participation of minorities in society, with equal opportunities, rights and obligations and without discrimination. The minority and the majority should be open to each other's perspectives and values and adaptation was required on both sides (WRR Report 1979). During those decades, there was open discussion about whether to accept cultural diversity. Implicitly this was about the question of legal pluralism: never in its strong form (the acceptance of officially coexisting legal systems in which communities can each autonomously determine and have control over the law applicable to them), but in its weak variant (the acceptance of normative pluralism but with the state always having the last say). The atmosphere and political climate changed in the 1990s and at the start of the new century, political discussions were influenced by right-wing politicians who pointed at incompatibilities between Western and Islamic values, especially regarding the oppression of women. Although this view did not receive general support, policy shifted from a minority policy to an integration policy (Memorandum Integration Policy 1994; Report Integration Policy 1999; Report Integration Policy 2002). Similarities rather than differences between people were accentuated. In reality, this resulted in tensions between existing values and views in society and pressure on minorities to conform to the positions of the majority. The Scientific Council for Government Policy and the Government itself emphasised in various reports the need to reduce the distance between native and foreign citizens. 'Shared citizenship' and 'participation' became key concepts. A more obligatory integration policy was considered necessary (Memorandum Integration Policy 2011). The coexistence of normative systems was not something that should be striven after; on the contrary, a fear for parallel societies arose. In the second decade of the 21st century, the government switched from a minority- or integration-approach to a policy based

2 Or, as Donders calls it, from pluralism to populism (Donders 2020).

on themes. Issues affecting minorities or migrants were separated and placed under various specific themes. During all those developments, human rights have always played an important role. On the one hand were human rights that 'favoured' religious and cultural diversity (Memorandum Fundamental Rights 2004), on the other hand, and increasingly, human rights were invoked that were considered at risk when allowing religious and cultural values and practices. This atmosphere, which emphasised the discriminatory and harmful aspects of some cultural and religious practices, led to the development of policies in which women were protected against oppressive normative regimes and systems. The negative aspects of non-state marriages were emphasised by civil society groups that advocated for the victims of those marital practices and by organisations that monitored state security. Politicians followed. As far as non-state marriages have become part of a government policy at all, they were sheltered by action programmes that combat harmful traditional practices.

5.3.1.2 Action agendas

Various action agendas from ministers and notes from members of parliament have been launched with the aim of combating harmful traditional practices (Future Family and Child Protection 2021; Action Agenda Harmful Practices 2020; Note Self Determination 2020; Note Marriage without Discrimination 2019; Programme Against Violence 2018–2021; Action Plan Self Determination 2015–2017). Many measures were taken, and new policies were developed as a result of those plans. Female genital mutilation, forced marriages, polygamous marriages and honour-related violence are consistently mentioned as harmful practices. The ambition of the Dutch government is to prevent and to tackle harmful practices and to help victims of harmful practices at an early stage (Action Agenda Harmful Practices 2020). Notes from specific members of parliament, mostly from right-wing parties, were focused on more specified targets and aimed for example against the oppression of people by a religion or culture, and at promoting agency (Note Self Determination 2020), or even at combating non-state marriages (Note Marriage without Discrimination 2019). Based on the government's Action Agenda Harmful Practices 2020, various measures saw the light: a programme had been developed in which municipalities, police, stakeholders and other partners in the social field and the government cooperated to combat (domestic) violence (Programme Against Violence 2018–2021), agencies where violence could be reported and where one could go for help were set up, programmes to arrive at changes from within the migrant communities were established, information campaigns were launched, increased expertise was promoted, research projects were initiated, legal instruments were or were intended to be developed, etc. Owing to a disproportionate focus on non-state marriages in which fundamental values of Dutch society were not respected or were considered to threaten Dutch security, *all* non-state marriages received a negative connotation; non-state marriages were lumped together and were suspiciously faced with distrust.

5.3.2 Responses by law

In the past, academics in the Netherlands focused mainly on sociological and anthropological research into marriages within minority groups (Dessing 2001; Peeters, de Koning, and Bartels 2005; Sterckx and Bouw 2005; Storms and Bartels 2008; Szepietowska, Dekker, and Özgümüs 2011; Moors 2014; Sportel 2014). More recently, the Dutch government also wanted to initiate its own research in order to gain more insight into non-state marriages in Dutch society. This would make it possible to arrive at better and more effective policies. While scientific research was conducted as objectively as possible, many of those government-commissioned studies originated primarily from a negative view on non-state marriages (Hooghiemstra 2003; NCTb 2006; Cornelissens, Kuppens, and Ferwerda 2009; Leun and Leupen 2009; Nanhoe, Lünnemann, and Pels 2013; Smits van Waesberghe a.o. 2014; Sterckx a.o. 2014; Rutten a.o. 2019; Esser, Ten Voorde, and van Nieuwenhuizen 2020).

The picture that all this research shows is at least twofold. On the one hand, it has become clear that the conclusion of non-state marriages is common, even without being accompanied by a civil marriage. These marriages occur within various communities and can be linked to religion, tradition, culture or (other) philosophy of life. Many of these marriages are not problematic, either at the time of their formation, during the marriage or at its termination. If spouses in a non-state marriage believe it is important to be considered legally married, they can yet enter in a civil ceremony. However, if partners do not solve their issues, a second finding is that in such situations those who are involved in non-state marriages may lack legal protection.

In that respect the research has also uncovered several bottlenecks that can come to the surface in non-state marriages. The first is that human rights and other (fundamental) interests can be compromised, precisely because the marriages are established and exist outside the eye of the state authorities. Examples include marriages that spouses (or one of them) are forced to enter, the risk of a wife being oppressed by her spouse during the marriage or obstacles encountered in the termination of a non-state marriage. A second bottleneck that has been identified is that non-state marriages are concluded where state law prohibits those marriages. In this way, non-state marriages are used to circumvent state law (Rutten a.o. 2015, 109–10; Rutten a.o. 2019).

The next two paragraphs will discuss the response of the Dutch state law to these findings. A distinction will be made between remedies that offer a certain protection to existing non-state marriages (legal measures, Section 5.3.2.1), and remedies intended precisely to protect against non-state marriages, either because those marriages violate human rights or fundamental interests or because they are abused for the purpose of circumventing state law (Section 5.3.2.2).

5.3.2.1 *Legal measures that protect non-state marriages*

Non-state marriages are not regulated. The only rule that regulates non-state marriages, and is restricted to religious marriage ceremonies only, is the rule that requires a previous civil marriage (Dutch Civil Code 1992, Art. 1:68). Because non-state marriages take place outside the official legal order, the legislature leaves them untouched as much as possible. Nevertheless, sometimes in concrete issues, when legal questions arising from non-state marriages are referred to the court, it can offer a certain protection to the relationship, thereby accepting the actual existence of non-state marriage. For example, women who claim payment of the dower (bridal gift) from the Dutch court often see their claim granted, although the dower is agreed for an Islamic marriage that itself may have no legal status in the Netherlands.

Women who ask the Dutch court to order their husbands to cooperate in a religious divorce are also usually granted their claim. Here, too, the existence of a religious marriage ceremony is recognised by the court as a fact. The wife wants a divorce, but the man refuses to cooperate in a dissolution of the religious marriage. As a result, the wife may be forced to remain in her non-state marriage and is still considered the wife by the husband and by her community, and as a result she is prevented from taking up a new life of her own (van Eijk 2017, 2019; Kruiniger 2018). Because of the separation between church and state, but also because religious marriages have no legal status, Dutch judges cannot terminate a religious marriage. The legal basis on which courts condemn men to cooperate in a religious divorce is the tort. Non-cooperation is then regarded as an unlawful act towards the woman. The Supreme Court had accepted this construction by 1982 (Dutch Supreme Court 22 January 1982). In the Netherlands, this phenomenon of so-called 'marital captivity' occurs mainly within certain (orthodox) Jewish and Muslim communities (van Eijk 2017).

This legal basis approved by the Supreme Court has been included in a new bill that came into force on 1 July 2023 (Official Gazette [*Staatsblad*] 2023, 118). The law introduces two concrete new articles. Firstly in the Dutch Civil Code (1992), in Art. 1:68 a second section is added obliging a party to a religious relationship to cooperate in the termination of that relationship if the other party so requests, unless this cannot reasonably be required in view of important interests. Secondly in the Code of Civil Procedure, in the provision regulating what spouses can apply for in the context of divorce proceedings as ancillary provisions, a section is added (Dutch Code of Civil Procedure 1828, Art. 827 sect. 1), stating that as an ancillary provision, it may also be requested based on Dutch Civil Code (1992, Art. 6:162) (the general tort act provision), an order to cooperate in the termination of a religious relationship that exists beside a (civil) marriage.

The bill to this effect was introduced after extensive research had shed more light on often distressing situations of women who are in so-called marital captivity (van Eijk 2017; Kruiniger 2018) and after civil society organisations had set up large lobbies to improve the position of these women. With its 1982 ruling, the Supreme Court had already paved the way to give women in marital captivity access to civil courts in order to bring their religious marriage to an end. Since then, this route has been successfully followed many times. This shows that there was a need for a provision, that there existed a mechanism that turned out to be legally feasible and that there seemed to be sufficient support for such a provision. With this new law, the legislature does not aim to recognise non-state practices. The legislature aims primarily to protect the interests of the spouse who is in marital captivity, including her human rights.

5.3.2.2 *Legal measures that offer protection against non-state marriages*

As described earlier, as a result of various developments and new gained insights, the legislature has taken initiatives to come up with laws or proposals for laws to combat non-state marriages or at least the harmful practices that may be accompanied by non-state marriages. Intervention by the legislature may be required where human rights or harmful practices are at stake. Various mechanisms have been used by the Dutch legislature.

First, legal provisions have been made specifically against certain marriages or to the harmful practices that can go along with those marriages. One example is the already discussed Article 1:68 of the Dutch Civil Code (1992) that obliges a religious marriage ceremony to be preceded by a civil marriage. This rule, which determines the order between a civil and religious marriage, has been debated several times (Memorandum Civil and Religious Marriages 2001, 2). To date, however, the rule has always managed to hold up. The legislature has put forward several reasons to justify that order. For example, the Dutch government wants to have insight into existing marriages, if only because all kinds of rights, obligations and provisions are linked to being married. In addition, it is considered (essential) that state authorities will have control over the conclusion of marriages, particularly to protect one or both spouses-to-be. Finally, legislators considered that, if informal marriages without prior civil marriage were to be permitted, there would be people who did not realise that they were not legally married or what legal protection they lacked (Rutten 2016-1, 789–92). The criminalisation of clergy who participate in the conclusion of a religious marriage without a previous civil marriage can be explained in the same light.

In Dutch society, several incidents occurred in which a non-state marriage was established between spouses who had not chosen each other freely themselves, only in order to prevent the situation from escalating and serious honour-related violence from taking place. Non-state marriages were thus used as a solution in situations of coercion. There was some societal resistance to this. At that time, the insight also began to arise that non-state marriages could also bring other problems, such as marital captivity. Several civil society organisations asked with great fanfare for attention to be paid to this problem, not least in Dutch politics. This has led an amendment to be submitted by a Member of Parliament to criminalise marriage parties who participate in a religious marriage ceremony without a prior civil marriage (Amended Bill Proposal 2020). Meanwhile, research had also shown that in the Netherlands there were many situations of religious marital captivity that could have particularly harmful implications, especially for women (van Eijk 2017; Kruiniger 2018). Incidentally, harmful consequences from non-state marriages were reported, but one of the biggest problems turned out to be the fact that those marriages took place out of sight of official authorities (Rutten a.o. 2019, 12, 176). The authors of the amendment were concerned about the possible negative consequences of religious marriages, the fact that civil marriages were not accepted by everyone; and that this sometimes resulted in forced marriage and in a lack of freedom for and violence against women. They also warned against the emergence of a parallel society in which illegal marriages would be established in religious places of worship. Various bodies (e.g. Council for the Judiciary and the Public Prosecution Service) were asked to advice on the proposal. They all expressed a negative opinion (Response Memorandum 2021). The proposal would affect many marriages and harm many spouses in situations where the non-state marital situation was not at all problematic. Therefore criminalising all those situations would be over-inclusive and could deter women in religious marriages from seeking the protection of secular authorities, for example against marital captivity (Explanatory Memorandum 2021). Consequently, the proposed amendment was ultimately not passed. The criminalisation of non-state marriages now is (fortunately) off the table.

5.4 Mechanisms to address non-state marriages

This section will discuss the mechanisms that were used by the Dutch legislature in regulating aspects of non-state marriages. In the findings of an EU project conducted between 2010 and 2013 into religious diversity and secular models in Europe (RELIGARE), it was identified that in family law cases, marriage was one of the issues most frequently submitted to the courts (Summary Report 2013, 18). As soon as non-state marriages give rise to legal issues, or the parties ask for legal protection or governmental intervention because human rights are at risk of being violated, states must respond.

This can be done in law via different mechanisms. Many states in Europe allow religious marriages, even if they do not attach any legal force to them. Completely banning these marriages is therefore not seen as a fruitful solution. On the other hand, full recognition of non-state marriages, in the sense that they can validly coexist with civil state marriages and parallel institutions, is not on the table in the Netherlands either.

Mechanisms that will be further elaborated are those that address to a certain extent marital pluralism and allow certain religious standards and practices that are compatible with state law. Those are human rights, the inclusion of specified standards in state law, and the use of open standards and general concepts in state law.

5.4.1 The use of human rights

The first mechanism that will be discussed is the use of human rights as a means of accommodating non-state marriages and the interests of spouses in such marriages, and its limits. Human rights traditionally play an important role in discussions about diversity and law, especially when Islam and Islamic family law are discussed (Rohe 2012, 67–93; Jänterä-Jareborg 2013, 155–70). Human rights may serve either to protect religious practices and values or, on the contrary, to protect against those practices.

Human rights that aim to protect religious practices and values can be both freedom-rights (like the freedom of religion or right to marry and found a family) as well as social rights (like the right to have your family life be protected). These rights can be invoked on their own but also in combination with the right to equality. In the Netherlands, we have seen some equalisation of non-state marriages and other relationships in areas such as family reunification and tax law (see Section 5.2.2.3 of this chapter; Cf. Akhtar, Nash, and Probert 2020). From the right to protection of family life, combined with respecting the right to equality, even more could be expected – for example when it comes to the attribution of other possible rights deriving from family law, like parentage or custody rights (Rutten 2016-2, 45–57).

From the right to freedom of religion, it follows that people have a right to marry in accordance with the standards of their own religion. This right is not absolute and may be restricted under certain circumstances. The Dutch legislature has restricted this right by requiring that a civil marriage be concluded first before a religious marriage ceremony takes place. One may wonder whether the motives that Dutch legislators advanced (see Section 5.3.2.2 of this chapter) may justify this restriction (Rutten 2016-1, 789–92). Can the protection of future spouses be guaranteed just by regulating the order of the marriage ceremonies knowing that non-state marriages de facto nevertheless can and will take place? It follows from research that the marriage order as required by Dutch civil law is not known to everyone. The legally prescribed order does not seem to be a suitable or at least sufficient solution. Policymakers have chosen to also use additional instruments: several information campaigns have been initiated to inform communities with less access to information about Dutch state marital law (Action Agenda Harmful Practices 2020; Programme Against Violence 2018–2021). And finally, why restrict the prescribed marriage order only for religious marriage ceremonies, leaving unaffected other non-state (customary) marriages and non-marital relationships? So far, Dutch Civil Code 1992, Art. 1:68 did not succeed in banning religious marriages without prior civil marriage. After all, citizens keep prioritising social, religious and cultural norms imposed on them by their community or traditions, rather than following state civil law. It would be recommendable to only focus on abusive non-state marriages and offer protection against them, leaving as much room as possible for religious non-state marriages that are not problematic.

While human rights can, on the one hand, provide scope for religious marriages and their interests involved, on the other hand they can also impose restrictions on these marriages, especially where those practices would lead to a violation of other people's human rights. Some human rights treaties refer explicitly to certain harmful and cultural practices and call upon state parties to take measures to counter these practices (esp. Art. 5 of the Convention on the Elimination of All Forms of Discrimination against Women and the Istanbul Convention combating domestic violence and violence against women). Traditional or religious practices that do not respect this minimum norm must then be addressed, particularly to protect victims from these human rights violations. By placing religious, cultural or traditional practices explicitly in the light of human rights and framing them as human rights, a moral and political statement is made, and responsibility for the state to act becomes clear. Human rights are seen as democratic achievements. They represent fundamental values that should apply to everyone and protect everyone. They are laid down in treaties and have a direct effect in many states. Human rights can also be a direct reason for taking measures by a state, including legislative measures. In the Netherlands, it was human rights that gave rise to the legislation aiming to combat marital captivity (Deogratias 2019).

5.4.2 *Including specified standards in state law*

Legislators can make an important contribution to the multicultural debate by setting clear standards. Certain cultural or religious practices may be explicitly forbidden or explicitly accommodated. Explicit prohibition seems to be taking place increasingly in recent years. Explicit facilitation of cultural and religious diversity was especially propagated by proponents in the 1980s and 1990s, when diversity was not yet seen as a threat to society. Now that the globalisation of Western societies has progressed much further than a few decades ago, there is even more reason to think about how state legislation can respond sustainably to the changing society. The actual and enduring diversity of society might demand to go back to old theories, such as Rawls' concept of political liberalism, and to give it a new look. Or, as Fadel describes it, with reference to John Rawls' theory: '[Political liberalism] regulates the family from the perspective of what is required "to reproduce political society over time" in a manner consistent with its ideal of treating all citizens as "free and equal"' (Fadel 2012, 168). If that idea were translated into legislation, I would argue that religious marital pluralism should be incorporated into legislation.

By including specific provisions in state legislation, the law will gain clarity and give certainty about whether certain religious and cultural practices are permitted or not, in what circumstances and under what conditions. In doing so, a legislator can respond to the desirability and necessity of regulating the issue; he can offer a solution for problems and situations that have manifested themselves in practice; he can involve and weigh up all the interests at stake, and he can determine the limits in the religion–state relationship. A legislator can thus arrive at an appropriate regulation that fits in with the system of the law.

The Dutch legislature used this technique selectively to regulate aspects of non-state or religious marriages. The first example is Dutch Civil Code (1992, Art. 1:68 para. 1), prescribing that a religious marriage must be preceded by a civil marriage. Connected to this provision is the provision criminalising the religious authority that does not respect this rule (Dutch Criminal Code 1881, Art. 449). Non-state marriages as such are not punishable; however if they at the same time are polygamous marriages or forced marriages, they are not allowed under civil law and punishable under criminal law (Dutch Criminal Code 1881, Art. 237, 284). Finally, the legislature created specific provisions for spouses who are held in their marriages against their will, by offering them tools to have the termination of their non-state and religious marriages realised (Dutch Civil Code 1992, Art. 1:68 para. 2; Dutch Code of Civil Procedure 1828, Art. 827) and by classifying the keeping of a spouse in her marriage as criminal coercion, punishable under the general criminal act of coercion (Dutch Criminal Code 1881, Art. 284).

What is important for those provisions to become successful and accepted and supported in society is that they must be tailored to the specific issue that needs to be addressed. Non-state marriages were not forbidden completely; they were 'only' subjected to an order requirement. Another example of tailor-made thinking is that not *all* non-state marriages have been made punishable, but only non-state marriages that are problematic and unacceptable. An attempt to criminalise all parties involved in religious marriage ceremonies was not accepted since it would unnecessarily affect unproblematic religious marriages. And the obligation to cooperate in a religious divorce exists only where the other spouse submits a request to this effect. Spouses that do not care about the continuation of their religious marriage will not be confronted with this obligation. Furthermore, before granting such a claim, the court must assess the interests at stake. The introduction of this new provision in the law met remarkably little resistance.

5.4.3 *The use of open standards and general concepts in state law*

From the perspective that the law is shaped by the state, not only can legislators choose to include specific provisions on cultural and religious practices, but they can also choose to use open norms and to use regulatory law, leaving plenty of room for party autonomy and freedom of contract.

5.4.3.1 *Open standards*

Where the legislature uses open standards, it is judges who will give further substance to the rule in concrete situations. In doing so, the court has the option of considering all the circumstances of the case, including the religious or cultural context, and thus including non-state values and practices. In family law, open concepts are the best interests of the child as well as the family life concept. Those are neutral and generally accepted terms. When assessing the best interests of the child, the culture or religion in which a child is raised may be taken into consideration. When assessing persons belonging to a family, the family concept as it is perceived in the culture of the person(s) involved may be considered. Open standards thus offer a flexibility that enables courts to do as much justice as possible to the concrete circumstances of a case.

Several examples from Dutch law illustrate what can be achieved by using open standards. Perhaps the most remarkable one is where the legislature, following up on established case law, has chosen the tort act as a legal basis for claiming cooperation in a religious divorce. Thus, it is not religious marriage that is directly protected, but the wrongful act, or at least tortious neglect, that manifests itself as the corollary of religious marriage. The reason for introducing these new provisions is not the idea of accommodating non-state marriages. Rather, the reason is that the legislature wants to protect 'captivated' spouses. Tortious behaviour and human rights violations justify interference from the legislature; a safe solution that can be achieved without blaming religion. A second example of an open norm is criminal acts that can be used to also combat harmful traditional practices. Coercion, which is punishable under Dutch Criminal Code (1881, Art. 284), was given as an example. It made sense that the Dutch legislature in its explanatory memorandum had stated explicitly that both forced marriages and being kept in a marriage against one's will fall under the scope of the criminal act provision of coercion. Finally, as a third example, it has been shown that by using the generally accepted concept of family life, non-state marriages can be offered a certain protection.

5.4.3.2 *Party autonomy*

Another possibility, which also offers a real opportunity to facilitate religious diversity, is freedom of contract (party autonomy) (e.g. Summary Report 2013, 19; Jänterä-Jareborg 2014-1, 79–101; Jänterä-Jareborg 2014-2, 14–15; Rutten 2017, 14–15). In this technique people do have the option to organise themselves via contractual agreements. Party autonomy is even seen as the basic principle for regulating family relations, including those of ethnic and religious minorities under state law (Foblets 2014, xiv–xv). There are those who speak about a theory of cultural voluntarism (Eekelaar 2010, 344–55). In this approach, it is left as much as possible to the people themselves how and by what standards they want their family law relationships to be governed. Parties themselves are best suited to assess their own situation and to meet their own needs. Marriage law offers much scope for this (Estin 2012, 111; Rohe 2014, 69). Not the government, but the spouses themselves determine, through a prenuptial or nuptial agreement, whether and to what extent they wish to be held to religious norms and values before, during and at the end of the marriage. They may agree on requirements that are derived from non-state law, for example on a bridal gift; they may include marital conditions that they are allowed to agree upon under religious law, for example that the husband will not marry a second wife or that, if there is a divorce, the parties will cooperate in the realisation of a religious divorce. If a valid contract has been concluded, whatever parties have agreed with each other shall be regarded as law. If one of the parties does not fulfil his or her contractual obligation, a claim based on non-performance can be instituted.

5.5 Concluding observations

What emerges from these Dutch developments, is that when the government of a secular state has an eye for non-state marriages, even if this arises initially from a negative attitude towards such marriages, it can lead to some results. It has led to the legal regulation of several issues in the Netherlands. It has stimulated both the government and religious communities to think more thoroughly about the compatibility of religious and cultural values and practices on the one hand with entrenched values and standards on the other. It has even led to the first initiatives to establish cooperation and dialogue between the government and religious communities.

Three mechanisms that a secular government could deploy in its law have been considered further: the use of human rights, the inclusion of specified standards or provisions in state law and the use of open standards and general concepts in state law.

Human rights seem to be an appropriate mechanism, because of their fundamental character and their direct effect. They can be used both to offer protection for non-state marriages, as well as offering protection against harmful practices that may in concrete situations accompany those marriages. The right to equality enables non-state marriages to receive equal protection with other forms of (not legally recognised) relationships.

For specific provisions in state law to be successful, it seems desirable or even necessary that they are tailor-made and aim at real needs, be motivated by convincing interests and count on sufficient support. Finally, the use of open standards and party autonomy seems to be an interesting mechanism because it is a neutral and secular concept that can allow all circumstances of a case to be considered, including religious and cultural ones.

References

Action Agenda Harmful Practices. 2020. "Action Agenda Harmful Practices. Actieagenda Schadelijke Praktijken." https://www.rijksoverheid.nl/documenten/beleidsnotas/2020/02/18/actieagenda-schadelijke-praktijken#:~:text=In%20deze%20actieagenda%20staat%20een,huwelijken%20en%20vrouwelijke%20genitale%20verminking.

Action Plan Self Determination. 2015–2017. "Self-Determination Action Plan. Actieplan Zelfbeschikking 2015–2017." https://open.overheid.nl/documenten/ronl-archief-129aa883-f0e0-47f8-bc35-62bfdb851314/pdf.

Akhtar, Rajnaara C., Patrick Nash, and Rebecca Probert. 2020. *Cohabitation and Religious Marriage: Status, Similarities and Solutions.* Bristol: Bristol University Press.

Akhtar, Rajnaara C., Rebecca Probert, and Annelies Moors. 2018. "Informal Muslim Marriages: Regulations and Contestations." *Oxford Journal of Law and Religion* 7 (3): 367–75.

Amended Bill Proposal: TK 36123, no. 2. See also: TK 2020/21, 35348, no. A. Background Note: TK 2019/20, 34565, no. 3.

Cornelissens, Agnes, Jos Kuppens, and Henk Ferwerda. 2009. *Huwelijksdwang: Een verbintenis voor het leven?* Den Haag: WODC.

Deogratias, Benedicta. 2019. *Trapped in a Religious Marriage: A Human Rights Perspective on the Phenomenon of Marital Captivity.* Cambridge: Intersentia.

Dessing, Nathal M. 2001. *Rituals of Birth, Circumcision, Marriage and Death among Muslims in the Netherlands.* Leuven: Peeters.

Donders, Yvonne. 2020. "Diversity in Europe: From Pluralism to Populism?" In *European Populism and Human Rights*, edited by Jure Vidmar, 52–71. Leiden: Brill.

Dutch Civil Code. 1992.

Dutch Code of Civil Procedure. 1828.

Dutch Criminal Code. 1881.

Dutch SC 1 December 2009. ECLI:NL:HR:2009:BJ2779.

Dutch SC 3 July 2018. ECLI:NL:HR:2018:1053.

Dutch Supreme Court 22 January 1982. *Nederlandse Jurisprudentie* 1982, 489.

Eekelaar, John. 2010. "From Multicultural to Cultural Voluntarism: A Family-Based Approach." *The Political Quarterly* 81 (3): 344–55.

Eijk, Esther van. 2017. *Wel gescheiden, niet gescheiden? Een empirisch onderzoek naar huwelijkse gevangenschap in Nederland.* Maastricht: Maastricht University.

———. 2019. "Khul' Divorce in the Netherlands: Dutch Muslim Women Seeking Religious Divorce." *Islamic Law and Society* 26 (1–2): 1–28.

Esser, L. B., J. Ten Voorde, and N. van Nieuwenhuizen. 2020. *De aanpak van schadelijke praktijken: een juridisch perspectief.* Den Haag: WODC.

Estin, Ann Laquer. 2012. "Unofficial Family Law." In *Marriage and Divorce in a Multicultural Context: Multi-Tiered Marriage and the Boundaries of Civil Law and Religion*, edited by Joel A. Nichols, 147–66. Cambridge: Cambridge University Press.

Explanatory Memorandum. 2021. Explanatory Memorandum to an amended bill, TK 2021/22, 36123, 3.

Fadel, Mohammad H. 2012. "Political Liberalism, Islamic Family Law, and Family Law Pluralism." In *Marriage and Divorce in a Multicultural Context: Multi-Tiered Marriage and the Boundaries of Civil Law and Religion*, edited by Joel A. Nichols, 164–99. Cambridge: Cambridge University Press.

Foblets, Marie-Claire. 2014. "Preface: Family, Religion and Law in Europe: Embracing Diversity from the Perspective of Cultural Encounters." In *Family, Religion and Law: Cultural Encounters in Europe*, edited by Prakash Shah, Marie-Claire Foblets, and Mathias Rohe, xiii–xv. Farnham: Ashgate.

Future Family and Child Protection. 2021. "Future Scenario of Family and Child Protection. Toekomstscenario kind- en gezinsbescherming." https://open.overheid.nl/documenten/ronl-79dad0a9-c043-4a8b-8d15-f65d288242d2/pdf.

Hooghiemstra, Erna. 2003. *Trouwen over de grens: Achtergronden van partnerkeuze van Turken en Marokkanen in Nederland.* Amsterdam: Meulenhoff.

Jänterä-Jareborg, Maarit. 2013. "Religious Personal Laws, Freedom of Religion, Human Rights and Public Policy in Private International Law." In *The 90th Birthday of Boutros Boutros-Ghali: Tribute of the Curatorium to its President*, 101–18. Leiden: Martinus Nijhoff Publishers.

———. 2014-1. "On the Cooperation between Religious and State Institutions in Family Matters: Nordic Experiences." In *Family, Religion and Law: Cultural*

Encounters in Europe, edited by Prakash Shah, Marie-Claire Foblets, and Mathias Rohe, 79–101. Farnham: Ashgate.

———. 2014-2. "Cross-border Family Cases and Religious Diversity: What can Judges Do?" In *Family, Religion and Law: Cultural Encounters in Europe*, edited by Prakash Shah, Marie-Claire Foblets, and Mathias Rohe, 143–63. Farnham: Ashgate.

Kruiniger, Pauline. 2018. *Niet langer geketend aan het huwelijk*. Maastricht: Maastricht University.

Leun, Joanne P. van der, and Avalon J. Leupen. 2009. *Informele huwelijken in Nederland: Een exploratieve studie*. Leiden: Universiteit Leiden. Accessed November 19, 2023. https://scholarlypublications.universiteitleiden.nl/access/item%3A2885691/view.

Memorandum Civil and Religious Marriages. 2001. *Memorandum on Civil Marriage and Religious Marriage*. State Secretary for Justice, November 5, 2001. Parliamentary Papers II 2001/02, 28078, 1.

Memorandum Fundamental Rights. 2004. *Memorandum on Fundamental Rights in a Pluralistic Society. Nota Grondrechten in een pluriforme samenleving*, 2004, TK 2003–2004, 29614, nr. 2. https://www.parlementairemonitor.nl/9353000/1/j9vvij5epmj1ey0/vi3amazxtxyh.

Memorandum Integration Policy. 1994. *Outline memorandum on Integration Policy for Ethnic Minorities. Contourennota Integratiebeleid Etnische Minderheden*, 1994, TK 1993–1994, 23684, nrs. 1–2. https://repository.overheid.nl/frbr/sgd/19931994/0000009618/1/pdf/SGD_19931994_0006851.pdf.

———. 2011. *Memorandum Integration, Bonding, Citizenship. Nota Integratie, binding, burgerschap*, 2011, TK 2010–2011, 32824, nr. 1. https://zoek.officielebekendmakingen.nl/kst-32824-1.pdf.

Moors, Annelies. 2014. *Motieven om islamitische huwelijken aan te gaan*. Utrecht: FORUM.

Nanhoe, Anita, Katinka Lünnemann, and Trees Pels. 2013. *Eer en partnergeweld onder Hindostanen: Een verkennende studie naar de rol van eer en huwelijksdwang bij partnergeweld onder Hindostanen en de mogelijkheid van preventie*. Gemeente Rotterdam.

NCTb. 2006. *Informele islamitische huwelijken*. The Hague: Ministry of Justice. *Het verschijnsel en de veiligheidsrisico's*. Nationaal Coördinator Terrorismebestrijding. https://www.nctv.nl/documenten/kamerstukken/2006/12/20/vijfde-voortgangsrapportage-samenvatting-dtn7.

Note Marriage without Discrimination. 2019. *Note 'Dutch Marriage Law Does not Discriminate: As a Woman or a Man in the Netherlands, Regardless of Your Origin and Religion, You are Free to Organize Your Love Life as You Wish'. Initiatiefnota van het lid Van Wijngaarden: Het Nederlands huwelijksrecht discrimineert niet: als vrouw of man ben je in Nederland, ongeacht je afkomst en religie, vrij om je liefdesleven zo in te richten als je wilt*, TK 2019–2020, 34565, nr. 4. https://www.tweedekamer.nl/kamerstukken/brieven_regering/detail?id=2020D21517&did=2020D21517.

Note Self Determination. 2020. *Note 'In the Netherlands You Decide about Your Own Life'. Initiatiefnota 'In Nederland beslis je over je eigen leven'*. https://www.rijksoverheid.nl/documenten/kamerstukken/2020/06/16/initiatiefnota-in-nederland-beslis-je-over-je-eigen-leven.

Official Gazette [*Staatsblad*] 2023, 118.

Peeters, M. de Koning, and E. Bartels. 2005. *Over het huwelijk gesproken; partnerkeuze en gedwongen huwelijken onder Marokkaanse, Turkse en Hindoestaanse Nederlanders*. Amsterdam: Vrije Universiteit Amsterdam.

Programme Against Violence. 2018–2021. *Programme 'Violence has no Place Anywhere'. Programma voor de aanpak van huiselijk geweld en kindermishandeling in de periode*, 2018–2021. https://www.rijksoverheid.nl/documenten/beleidsnota-s/

2018/04/25/geweld-hoort-nergens-thuis-aanpak-huiselijk-geweld-en-kindermishandeling.

Report Integration Policy. 1999. *Report Integration Policy Ethnic Minorities. Integratiebeleid Etnische Minderheden,* 1999, TK 1998–1999, 26426, nr. 2. https://www.rekenkamer.nl/archief/publicaties/rapporten/1999/03/04/integratiebeleid-etnische-minderheden.

———. 2002. *Report on Integration Policy for Ethnic Minorities. Rapportage Integratiebeleid etnische minderheden 2002,* TK 2002–2003, 28612, nr. 1. https://zoek.officielebekendmakingen.nl/kst-28612-1.pdf.

Response Memorandum. 2021. Response Memorandum of the Minister 13 December 2021, EK 35348, no. C, in response to report and memorandum of amendment to 'novelle' law proposal against marital captivity, October 5, 2022.

Rohe, Mathias. 2012. "On the Foundations of Human Rights: Religious and Secular Approaches in the West and in Islam." In *Tensions within and between Religions and Human Rights,* edited by Johannes A. van der Ven and Hans-Georg Ziebertz, 17–38. Leiden: Brill.

———. 2014. "Family and the Law in Europe: Bridging Together Secular Legal Orders and Religious Norms and Deeds." In *Family, Religion and Law: Cultural Encounters in Europe,* edited by Prakash Shah, Marie-Claire Foblets, and Mathias Rohe, 1–18. Farnham: Ashgate.

Rutten, Susan. 2016-1. "Hernieuwde bezinning op informele religieuze huwelijken." *Nederlands Juristenblad* 91 (12): 784–91.

———. 2016-2. "Ouderschap en ouderlijk gezag bij niet-erkende islamitische huwelijken." *Justitiële Verkenningen* 42 (4): 45–57.

———. 2017. *Gegeven de betekenis van islamitisch familierecht: Samenloop van Europese en islamitische familierechtsordes; Nederland als een voorbeeld.* Maastricht: Maastricht University.

Rutten, Susan, Esther van Eijk, Lisanne Drost, Khadija Kadrouch-Outmany, and Eliane Smits van Waesberghe. 2015. *Gewoon Getrouwd: Een onderzoek naar kindhuwelijken en religieuze huwelijken in Nederland.* Maastricht: Maastricht University.

Rutten, Susan, Eliane Smits van Waesberghe, Richard Blauwhoff, Esther van Eijk, Pauline Kruiniger, Leyla Reches, Elles Ramakers, and Inge Rook. 2019. *Verboden huwelijken: Onderzoek naar de werking van de Wet tegengaan huwelijksdwang in de praktijk.* Den Haag: WODC.

Smits van Waesberghe, Eliane, Iris Sportel, Lisanne Drost, Esther van Eijk, and Elja Diepenbrock. 2014. *Zo zijn we niet getrouwd: Een onderzoek naar omvang en aard van huwelijksdwang, achterlating en huwelijkse gevangenschap.* Maastricht: Maastricht University.

Sportel, Iris. 2014. *Maybe I'm Still His Wife: Transnational Divorce in Dutch-Moroccan and Dutch-Egyptian Families.* Oisterwijk: Wolf Legal Publishers.

Sterckx, Leen, and Carolien Bouw. 2005. *Liefde op maat: Partnerkeuze van Turkse en Marokkaanse jongeren.* Amsterdam: Het Spinhuis.

Sterckx, Leen, Jaco Dagevos, Willem Huijnk, and Jantine van Lisdonk. 2014. *Huwelijksmigratie in Nederland: Achtergronden en leefsituatie van huwelijksmigranten.* Den Haag: Sociaal Cultureel Planbureau.

Storms, Oka, and Edien Bartels. 2008. *De keuze van een huwelijkspartner: Een studie naar partnerkeuze onder groepen Amsterdammers.* Amsterdam: Vrije Universiteit.

Summary Report. 2013. Accessed November 24, 2023. https://cordis.europa.eu/docs/results/244635/final1-religare-final-publishable-report-nov-2013-word-version.pdf.

Szepietowska, Ewa K., Anne-Floor Dekker, and Fatma Özgümüs. 2011. *De doos van Pandora: Huwelijksmigratie onder vluchtelingengroepen in Nederland.* Amsterdam: Vluchtelingen Organisaties Nederland.

Uddin, Islam. 2018. “Nikah-Only Marriages: Causes, Motivations, and Their Impact on Dispute Resolution and Islamic Divorce Proceedings in England and Wales.” *Oxford Journal of Law and Religion* 7 (3): 401–26.
WRR Report. 1979. *Report of the Scientific Council for Government Policy, WRR, on Ethnic Minorities. WRR-Rapport Etnische minderheden*, 1979. https://www.wrr.nl/publicaties/rapporten/1979/05/09/etnische-minderheden.

6 A study of Muslim marriage (and divorce) practices in England and Wales

Making a case for reform

Rehana Parveen

6.1 Introduction to the religious make-up of England and Wales

According to the 2021 Census the population of England and Wales was 59,597,300, nearing 60 million; the largest it has been (ONS 2022). The Census included a question on religion that asked 'What is your religion?', with a drop box of options to choose from. Although taking part in the Census is a legal requirement, responding to the religion question is voluntary. The religion question itself has been subject to criticism, as it is argued that it assumes participants to be religious and should have been framed more neutrally in order to ensure that those of no religion answered the question (Humanists UK 2021).

Notwithstanding the criticisms in the lack of nuance around the religion question, it should still be noted that 94% of the overall population in England and Wales did in fact answer this question and that this figure is higher than previous years. The responses reveal the most common religious group in England and Wales remains 'Christian' at 46.2% of the overall population, though, for the first time this group has decreased to less than half of the population. The second most common response was 'no religion' at 37.2% of the population, an increase of 12% from 2011. Islam remains the largest religious group after Christianity, and Muslims have continued to increase as a proportion of the population from 4.9% in 2011, to 6.5% in 2021. This translates to a current figure of around 3.9 million people who identify as Muslims within England and Wales. For other larger faith groups such as Buddhism, Hinduism, Judaism and Sikhism there were some small differences from the 2011 Census but not as significant as the decrease of Christianity or the increase in Islam and in those of no religion (ONS 2022).

Much of what the 2021 Census tells us about Muslims living in England and Wales follows established historical patterns; that Muslims are often highly concentrated in certain regions and that those who described themselves as Muslim had the youngest average age at 27. The next youngest average age is for those who report as having no religion. Muslims as a religious group are therefore increasing in numbers and, in comparison to the overall population,

DOI: 10.4324/9781003470786-9

are younger though the Census cannot tell us how 'practising' or 'observant' individuals within this group may consider themselves. It is a crude marker for the purposes of identity without revealing much about the lived experiences of Muslims other than to indicate that Muslims as an identifiable group clearly form a significant religious minority within England and Wales. The complexities concerning Muslim communities, the different strands of Islam that they follow, the different ideological positions that they take, the transnational ties that they maintain and the development of Muslim communities within the United Kingdom have been the subject of detailed and nuanced academic research (Lewis 2011; Gilliat-Ray 2012; Bowen 2014; Bowen 2015; Mustafa 2015; Lewis and Hamid 2018).

Interestingly, there are some similar patterns emerging between those identifying as Muslims and those who report as having no religion. Both groups have continued to increase in significant numbers. Both groups have younger average ages than the overall population. This would indicate, perhaps, that the religious make-up of England and Wales is heading in more diverse directions, arguably, on some matters in more polarised directions. However, there are some shared points of contention between Muslims and those of no religion when it comes to the regulation of family life and the role of the state in regulating formalised relationships, particularly when it comes to entry into marriage. Both may argue that a legal framework which prioritises Christian norms marginalises their lived experiences and in effect excludes them from accessing law (see, later in this chapter). Attempting to capture the diversity of the population will impact how English law seeks to frame some of the challenges that it faces in regulating family life. Family law is increasingly expected to accommodate and regulate the multiple and diverse ways in which parties enter and manage their intimate and familial relationships as well as the consequences of the breakdown of those relationships. Minorities, such as Muslims, can find themselves having to challenge what are accepted as the perceived norms around family life in order for their family practices to be included within law and its legal framework. Muslims as minority communities within England and Wales are neither homogenous nor insignificant. It is important therefore that the norms of Muslim family life are part and parcel of the conversations concerning their regulation. Muslim behaviours should not be perceived as needing to fit in or be accommodated within the law as an afterthought; rather they should form part of the complex discussions about the changing landscape of family life for Britons. Some of the recent debates around marriage laws have highlighted the overlapping concerns between Muslims and non-religious groups, such as Humanists, in the state's failure to recognise their particular types of marriage ceremonies (Humanists UK 2020, 2022).

In this chapter I argue that, despite claims to 'neutrality', English family law relies on Christian and Eurocentric norms that are embedded into its legal framework. Notwithstanding the increasingly diverse ways in which adult relationships are formed, English family law remains highly exclusionary as to the types of relationships that are recognised and protected by the state. Exploring the practices of British Muslims in their marriages and divorces highlights the ways in which some of these exclusions manifest themselves. The first two sections of this chapter address the significant body of literature that examine Muslim marriage and divorce practices. I engage with some of the complexities that have arisen when Muslims enter into marriage ceremonies that are not recognised by the state. In terms of Muslim divorce practices, the media and academic debates have largely centred around the existence of sharia councils and their role in providing Muslim women with a religiously sanctioned divorce. For both marriage and divorces practices I argue, in many respects, Muslims are behaving in a manner not dissimilar from their contemporary non-Muslim counterparts but that Muslims regulate their behaviour from within an Islamic framework. Muslim marriage and divorce practices need to be understood from both within this framework and modern family life more generally. In the third section I draw together my criticisms of English law's claim to neutrality, highlighting the ways in which Christian and Eurocentric norms are incorporated into English law as the assumed 'normal' ways in which all adults are expected to enter and exit from relationships. I draw out some of the colonial aspects of these norms and in the final section I consider how English family laws can begin to disentangle itself from those legacies. Such disentangling will be to the benefit of British society more generally, not just Muslims.

6.2 Muslims and English family law

We now have a significant and rich body of literature that has explored certain and specific aspects of Muslim marriage within English law (R. C. Akhtar 2015, 2018a, 2018b; Parveen 2018, 2020) and divorce practices (Shah-Kazemi 2001; Bano 2012; Bowen 2015). This topic has also been explored across a wide range of settings outside of England and Wales most recently by Moors and McBrien (2023). In England and Wales we also have case law that has highlighted some of the contradictions and confusion in the law, particularly concerning recognition of Muslim nikah-only (Islamic religious) marriage ceremonies (Probert 2002; Vora 2016; Jackson and O'Sullivan 2017).[1]

The most recent debates concerning Muslim marriage practices have centred on the lack of legal recognition afforded to nikah-only marriages and the impact of the lack of recognition (Jackson and O'Sullivan 2017; Uddin 2018; Probert 2020).

1 Although both historically and in contemporary society there are a number of cases which have addressed the issue of a 'non-marriage', there are a number of recent decisions that have specifically concerned the nikah-only marriage. See, for example, the following cases: *Dukali v. Lamrani* (2012) EWHC 1748 (Fam), *MA v. JA & the AG* (2012) EWHC 2219 (Fam), *Sharbatly v. Shagroon* (2012) EWCA Civ 1507, *K v. K* (2016) EWCH 3380 (Fam), *Akhter v. Khan* (2020) EWCA Civ 122.

In England and Wales, for a marriage to be recognised as valid it must comply with the requirements of the Marriage Act 1949 and its subsequent amendments. The recognition and validity of marriages have largely been dependant on ensuring that the formalities around the marriage ceremony are fully complied with. This includes the steps for notice prior to the ceremony, the conduct of the ceremony itself including the recognition of the officiant conducting it, the requirement of an authorised venue and compliance with registration requirements post the ceremony. In policing the ceremony and its related elements, English law has had to rely on what are seen as normative practices around marriage ceremonies as the benchmark against which to judge compliance (*Hudson v. Leigh* 2009). Perhaps understandably, these have historically reflected Christian and/or European marriage ceremonial norms. In the case of *Hudson*, when discussing the types of rituals and ceremonies that may fail to effect a legal marriage, Bodey J questions whether a 'full dress-rehearsal' would amount to a legally valid marriage. His dress-rehearsal depicts a marriage scene with a vicar who has used the full wording of the marriage service, wedding-outfits, bridesmaids, flowers, music, an Order of Ceremony – all of which point to the 'normal' or expected rites of a marriage ceremony. Bodey J struggles to think of other examples of 'questionable' ceremonies which in his words, 'do not appear fanciful'.

Failures to meet the legal requirements for a valid marriage ceremony have resulted in confusing and at times contradictory outcomes when marriages have been declared valid, void or non-qualifying (in earlier case law this is referred to as a non-marriage) (Probert 2002; Gaffney-Rhys 2010). In the event of a non-qualifying marriage, couples are unable to access important rights and privileges that hang on the existence of a state-recognised marriage. Probert argues that the 'restrictive, inconsistent and complex' set of laws around marriage in England and Wales can be traced as far back as to the Marriage Act 1836 (Probert 2021). Probert demonstrates how the development of marriage laws and their amendments have addressed matters of diversity in a piecemeal manner and often reforms have been framed as alternatives to the requirements of the rites of the Church of England (Probert 2021). This is an important observation as it highlights how deeply embedded and legally normalised Christian ceremonial marriage practices are within English family law. Christian marriage norms are the default, not only in terms of a cultural practice, but within the legal framework, as the established markers of what a valid marriage ceremony should consist of. Sandberg points out that the ad hoc reforms that have taken place have been bolted on to a legal framework that itself is no longer fit for purpose (Sandberg 2021).

Reforms can lead to greater misunderstandings and confusion when they are being framed as alternatives to a particular regime rather than permitting practices legitimacy in their own right. Take, for example, the requirement that a marriage ceremony must take place in an authorised venue. Probert states that the historical system of licensing premises for the purposes of marriage has its roots in suspicion of those who did not conform to the established

Church and a desire to know where they were meeting (Probert 2021). There is therefore an element of religious control that is historically associated with approval of premises. In any event, English law not only accommodates marriages taking place in a church as an authorised venue, but it also assumes venue in a place of worship carries the same significance for all marriage ceremonies. In an effort to accommodate Muslim practices, the law permits registration of mosques as places of worship, thereby allowing Muslims the same opportunities for marriage recognition. This assumes that the venue has the same significance and consequences for Muslim marriages as it does for Christian marriage ceremonies. However, for Muslims, the venue is irrelevant to the validity of their religious marriages. Many Muslims do not marry in a mosque; indeed, for many, their marriage ceremonies take place at home, in a wedding or other hall, at a restaurant, in a marquee or any suitable venue (Edge 2013; Grillo 2015). Having a nice venue for the marriage ceremony may be important to many Muslims, but it will not be critical to the validity of the nikah as a religious marriage.

Incorporating alternative provisions into English law that in effect allow Muslims to mirror the norms of Christian marriage practices may provide some limited opportunities for legal recognition, but this fails to explore Muslim marriage practices on their own terms. As has been documented very few mosques are registered for the purposes of marriage (Grillo 2015), and there is little indication for any such demand from Muslims. In their recent study, although Ali et al. found some support for Muslim marriages taking place in mosques, it was also noted that that Muslims do not instinctively consider mosques a natural location for their marriages (Ali, Jones, and Shahid 2020). Possibly, in future, younger generations of Muslims, accustomed to the norms of British society, may prefer their marriage ceremonies to take place in a mosque, as implied by Ali et al., but this is by no means conclusive. There is only limited research on unmarried Muslim men and women and their approaches to marriage, making it difficult to identify trends accurately (Mohee 2012). For legal frameworks to assume that legal recognition can or even should be achieved by enabling Muslims to mirror Christian/Eurocentric marriage practices is at best simplistic. More likely it will result in exclusionary practices. It places the responsibility on Muslims and other minority communities (including those in the non-religious category) to comply with English law requirements that are falsely presented as neutral and secular, when in actuality they are a reflection of a Christian historical context, that has developed into a Eurocentric context.

The issue of unregistered marriages and their legal status within English law has attracted the widespread attention of academics, judges, politicians, the media and social commentators. It has been recognised that this issue disproportionately impacts on women generally and more recently on Muslims. Although exact figures are unknown, estimates indicate that a significant proportion of Muslims do not marry in accordance with the formalities of English law whether intentionally or otherwise. The figures that are suggested have included 80% in press releases and from two-thirds to four-fifths of Muslim marriages in various research including a Channel 4 (2017) commissioned documentary. Attempting to get a clear picture of how widespread this is has produced these highly contradictory figures. For example, Ali et al. found only 18 respondents from a total of their 88 participants were in nikah-only marriages, indicating a much smaller minority (Ali, Jones, and Shahid 2020). However, if we were to remove from that figure of 88 all those who married abroad then the 18 respondents in nikah-only marriages would form almost a third of the participants in their study. Whichever figure is accepted, it is clear that a significant proportion of Muslims getting married in the United Kingdom enter nikah-only marriages. Probert points out that religious-only marriages are not a new phenomenon even if this issue currently disproportionately impacts Muslims (Probert 2023) and that there is nothing new or uniquely challenging about them given the history of English marriage laws.

In the body of academic literature that has explored nikah-only marriages, it has been recognised that English law is confusing and contradictory in determining the boundaries between valid, void and non-marriages (Parveen 2018; Probert 2020). The legal consequence for couples in nikah-only marriages is that, despite the confusion, they are usually treated by the law as cohabitants. As is the case for cohabitants more generally, a lack of legal recognition has gendered implications for women. The most significant implication of which is the financial vulnerability of the weaker partner. This vulnerability is most acute at the point of any separation or at the death of the financially stronger partner, particularly if the vulnerable partner must rely on intestacy laws to establish financial claims. In the event of divorce or death most financial legal protections are contingent on a legally recognised marriage.

Nikah-only marriages occupy an important social and religious space for Muslims but no real legal space. Socially, parties to them are bound by a relationship that is recognised by their religion and by the communities in which they participate. Indeed, such couples will refer to themselves as 'married' and as 'husband' and 'wife'. In the event of dissolution, they will require a religiously sanctioned process in order to terminate that relationship. At the same time, in the legal space the nikah-only marriage does not exist, and the law will treat such couples as cohabitants; a term highly unlikely to be used by Muslim couples themselves in describing their relationships, and the term does not meaningfully articulate the lived experiences of those couples. A nikah-only marriage is simultaneously both a marriage and a non-marriage depending on the context in which it is being addressed.

Some of the academic literature has sought to explore the motivations behind why a couple may enter a nikah-only marriage. (Akhtar 2018b; Uddin 2018; Ali, Jones, and Shahid 2020). As noted (Parveen 2020) this issue is at least as complex as asking why non-Muslims choose to cohabit rather that obtaining state protection through recognised marriages. From the research to date, for some Muslims it is a choice not to be bound by state regulation, for others it is a lack of knowledge or misguided assumptions as to the availability of legal protections and for many it is a lack of importance ascribed to the civil requirements. In its Nuffield funded study of marriage ceremonies conducted outside of the legal framework ('the Nuffield study'), Probert et al. (2021) engaged with 170 participants who had conducted or entered into a non-legally binding wedding ceremony. Although most participants were Muslim, a significant proportion were not, including Humanists.

All of the research to date identifies that the nikah is more crucial for most Muslims in legitimising their relationships than compliance with the formalities of English law. The continuing high rates of cohabitation for the British population more generally indicate that establishing relationships outside the formalities of marriage legislation will increasingly be the norm. As I have argued, if a Christian-based marriage ceremony is unimportant for a significant proportion of the non-Muslim British population why would it be any more important for Muslims (Parveen 2020)? Clearly, the piecemeal way in which the current law has developed, allowing Muslims the option either to undergo a separate civil ceremony or to combine legal formalities with their nikah ceremonies, has not had the desired impact. The Nuffield study built on earlier academic literature in attempting to explore some of the motivations for non-legally binding marriage ceremonies. Unlike most of the previous literature, the Nuffield study investigated the experiences of Muslims within the broader context of other faith, non-faith and inter-faith communities. It highlighted the barriers faced by all of these different groups. The participants of the Nuffield study, at times, seemed baffled by the perceived arbitrariness, undue complexity, inefficiency and unfairness of the restrictions on non-Christian ceremonies.

The Nuffield study also countered the oft-cited claim that parties to non-legally binding ceremonies are completely unaware of their lack of legal status. Whilst they may not be cognisant of all the complexities, it was evident that most were aware of their lack of legal status. The narrative around Muslim marriage practices has been to present them as uniquely challenging in this context without attempting to situate them within broader developments around cohabitation and alternative types of marriage ceremonies (Parveen 2020). The Nuffield study addresses some areas of commonality amongst these different groups and helped to inform the Law Commission in its consultation on weddings (Commission 2022). The Law Commission's recommendations will be addressed later in this chapter, but for now I argue that English law has normalised and embedded Christian and Eurocentric marriage ceremonial practices, thereby creating an exclusionary framework. In its attempt to address diversity it has sought to provide alternatives to its *own existing framework* that may have helped some Muslims some of the time in recognising their relationships, but its rigidity and inflexibility continues to marginalise those who stray too far from the 'normal' marriage ceremony envisioned by the law. 'Accommodation' of Muslim marriage practices has been based on 'assimilation' of Muslim marriage practices into Christian or Eurocentric paradigms, with little meaningful impact on Muslims. At the same time those same

Christian practices are less relevant to an increasingly non-religious proportion of the rest of British society.

6.3 Muslim divorce practices

The earlier research into Muslim family practices was dedicated primarily to Muslim divorce practices and the existence of sharia councils as religious bodies (Shah-Kazemi 2001; Bano 2012). Concerns were raised regarding the creation and operation of a 'parallel legal system' that would enable Muslims to be governed by 'sharia law'. Much of the current work on Muslim marriage practices has been founded on the earlier literature, which explored sharia councils as religious bodies. In investigating their processes for making religious determinations on the validity and dissolution of Islamic marriages, academics documented the high proportion of female users of sharia council services and noted the high proportion of nikah-only marriages that were coming for adjudication before sharia councils. Conversely, it is the prospect of a divorce that often brings to light the lack of status of the nikah and the lack of protection for the financially vulnerable partner. It is therefore academic research on sharia councils and divorce practices that first identified nikah-only marriages as sites of enquiry. While this chapter is not dedicated primarily to matters of divorce, if the law makes financial protection contingent upon a recognised marriage and a state-sanctioned divorce, then the interrelationship between civil marriage, civil divorce and financial protection is established by the state. It is the state that that chooses to protect the institution of marriage rather than emphasising socially valuable relationships (Bonthuys 2016). The state's resistance to providing a comprehensive framework of protection for cohabitees has resulted in an unnecessarily acute distinction being drawn between a recognised and a non-recognised marriage ceremony. There have been widespread calls for reform of the regulation of cohabitee rights, and clearly any reforms will provide protection for those in nikah-only marriages. Most recently this topic has been addressed by the Women and Equalities Committee (2022) of the UK Parliament in its Report on the Rights of Cohabiting Partners.

Aside from the issues of legal recognition and financial vulnerability, there is one other significant issue that having a civil marriage or civil divorce does not necessarily assist with: religious marital captivity for women. Even where there is a civil divorce, Muslim women may feel that in the eyes of their religion and their communities they are not divorced until a religious determination has been made. The need for a religious divorce and what a sharia council can offer in such circumstances has been subjected to considerable academic and media critique (Parveen 2017). The existence and role of sharia councils has produced a rich body of academic literature, supported by a significant amount of field work, including inter alia (Shah-Kazemi 2001; Douglas et al. 2011; Bano 2012; Bowen 2015; Parveen 2017; Azzouz 2021). This is despite claims that 'not much is known about how they actually operate across the country' (Casey 2016).

The media criticism of sharia councils often produces sensationalised claims drawing on colonial and racists stereotypes that perpetuate perceptions of brown Muslim women as victims without agency and in need of saving from savage brown Muslim men by civilised white saviours (Razack 2008). The academic critique does, however, demonstrate both the barriers faced by Muslim women in obtaining a religious divorce via sharia councils and the positive outcomes that can be achieved by them (Norton and Ahmed 2012). It remains the case that much of the critique concentrates on Muslim women's experiences through markers of gender equality such as the differential access to religious divorce. The women's practice of Islam and the spiritual benefits in accessing religiously sanctioned divorce processes are insufficiently prioritised. The impact on spirituality as a means through which Muslim women and indeed Muslim men navigate their personal relationships has begun to receive more detailed attention. Recently, both Mohee (2012) and Kalra (2025) in Chapter 9 have addressed the significance of Muslim women's 'Muslimness' and spirituality in negotiating their identities. Further attention must be paid to the ways in which Muslim women's spiritual equality is enhanced by the provision of services that allow them a religious determination and what the impact would be to their spirituality by the loss of such services. The significance of spiritual equality for Muslim women has not been fully explored.

Like Muslim marriage practices, I argue that the role of sharia councils also needs to be contextualised within broader discussions of contemporary family life. When sharia councils are discussed as an anomaly sitting outside of all 'norms' of family law, this contributes to the othering of Muslims and promotes a hierarchy of acceptable ways in which to enter and exit from relationships. The work that sharia councils do should be understood within the broader conversations concerning alternative dispute resolution ('ADR'), the lack of legal aid, the state's role in the governance of adult relationships and the gendered implications of these (Diduck 2016; Heenan 2021). Most recently introduced, the no-fault divorce process has been welcomed by many stakeholders. It supports a type of 'hands-off' approach to divorce whereby judicial oversight is largely limited to the process of divorce and compliments the current policy approach to family law. Bano's (2012) extensive body of work on sharia councils has attempted to draw together the complexities of the relationship between the state and sharia councils and some of the ongoing debates within British Muslim communities on the role of sharia councils. More recently, in examining the relationship of the state with Muslim communities, Bano has highlighted how fixed notions of democracy serve to ascribe meanings and values in problematic ways for minority Muslim communities. Bano (2023) points out the orientalist tropes of Muslims lacking credentials of freedom and democracy when attempts are made to complicate the democratic notions that seek to govern the exercise of communal and private spaces. One the one hand the state is putting in place policies and measures that encourage adults to manage the outcomes of breakdowns in relationships for themselves. Despite the gendered consequences, this is framed as supporting the autonomy of adults. On the other, the state remains highly suspicious of Muslims adopting an Islamic framework to this end, framing use of sharia councils as a failure to integrate and indicative of a lack of agency on the part of Muslim women.

It should be noted there is no consensus among Muslim communities themselves on the significance or role that sharia councils should play. With the focus on Muslim divorces secured through sharia councils, very little attention has been paid to those Muslims who obtain their religious divorces through alternative means, such as the husband pronouncing a Ṭalāq, parties agreeing to separate or via access to online resources. We know very little from those women who remain trapped in religious marriages (irrespective of whether they have a civil marriage or civil divorce), and there seems to be little state responsibility in assisting their release from those religious bonds in a manner that accords with the women's religious beliefs. Although there has been state intervention where the marriage is perceived as a 'forced marriage', this has been critiqued for 'othering' minority women (Mitra-Kahn and Gill 2012) and demanding their exit from their culture as a prerequisite to state protection (Enright 2009). A sharia council, at the very least, provides Muslim women who require for their own personal religious, spiritual or community reasons a religious divorce, the opportunity to obtain one. The banning of sharia councils would not remove Muslim women's need for a religious divorce. Forcing Muslim women to remain trapped in a religious marriage or obtain a divorce in a manner that does not align with their own agencies, religious practices or desires is neither empowering for them nor a promotion of gender-equal status.

Deogratias (2019) explored the issue of marital captivity using a human rights legal framework to critique the role of the state and argued for a greater burden to be placed on the state to ensure that it complies with its positive human rights obligations. State accountability, it was argued, produces better outcomes for those trapped in religious marriages rather than leaving the burden on religious or faith communities to create solutions. As argued by Deogratias, a human rights lens might allow for the development of a right to divorce (as a corollary to the right to marry) or the inclusion of marital captivity as a form of violence against women. However, Deogratias' framing of the state, human rights and secular laws as 'neutral' without fully exploring how family laws are embedded with particular Christian or Eurocentric assumptions remains extremely problematic. Aftab states neutrality is a fallacy as it ignores the influence of religion, particularly Christianity, in shaping family laws (Aftab 2019). Further there are colonial legacies embedded within these frameworks making the claim to neutrality particularly duplicitous. Christianity in Europe is inextricably linked to whiteness. As Stratton (2016) states, Christianity is 'understood as an expression of whiteness' and that 'colonialism included the giving of Christianity to the lower races as a way of elevating them'.

Muslims wishing to order their lives using an Islamic framework should not come as a surprise and that this may be permitted, encouraged, supported or even promoted by the state is often met with panicked responses indicating deep fears and mistrust of Muslims and Muslim communities (Bano 2008). The liberal language of 'integration' is often used to deny Muslims opportunities to establish and develop in their own right with the emphasis and onus placed on them to conform to the agreed perceived norms of the majority. Those norms that maintain Christian and Eurocentric practices are reproduced in 'secular' laws and presented as neutral. Policy suggestions are often predicated on a desire for a particular type of 'integration', where the focus is on the promotion of nebulous 'British Values' as a method for achieving 'community cohesion' (Casey 2016). Muslims entering and exiting from relationships without conforming to the formalities of English law are framed as behaving in a manner that is incompatible with 'UK law', a threat to 'Britishness' and an indication that they are responsible for their own failure to access their rights. When British non-Muslim cohabitees enter relationships without any legal status and very few rights, this is rarely framed as an issue of 'incompatibility with UK law'. Rather it is addressed as a development of society and understandable changing social conditions.

6.4 The law's claims to neutrality and the Eurocentric approaches to family law

In the Nuffield study an interesting observation about marriage law is made by some of the participants and summarised in the quote from one of them: 'white people are the norm . . . and Christians are the norm, or not just the norm but the desirable or the best'. This quote addresses some of the embedded notions within Eurocentric legal frameworks that decolonial, postcolonial and critical race academics and theorists have sought to unpack more generally.

The exploration of Muslim marriage and divorce practices through a lens of 'integration' results in policies that would, on the face of it, support Muslim 'integration'. This framing carries with it all the loaded assumptions as to European superiority to which Muslims must conform. Many Muslims within Europe have come from many different parts of the world, each with different historical interactions with their previous European colonisers (Shehada 2011). Indeed An-Naim argues that 'Islamic Family Law' is a colonial fabrication; European colonisers displaced sharia in every other aspect of the legal systems of colonised Muslims but permitted a discrete field of so-called 'Islamic Family Law'. As a result, colonial administrators created isolated and archaic family law norms (An-Na'im 2019). Bano states that the emergence of Muslim family law in the United Kingdom must be understood as part of specific historical, social and political conditions under which postcolonial emerges (Bano 2023).

Increasingly, law and legal actors tell themselves that law is moving or ought to move in the direction of a framework that is 'secular', 'neutral' and 'objective'. In a keynote address Sir James Munby (the then President of the Family Division) stated that although historically this country is part of the

Christian west with an established Christian church 'we sit as secular judges serving a multi-cultural community' and that the starting point of the common law is to hold an 'essentially neutral view of religious beliefs' and further that 'all [tenets, doctrines or rules of any section of society] are entitled to equal respect, so long as they are "legally and socially" acceptable' (Munby 2013). Thus, legal decision-making is presented as an objective application of legal frameworks that are race, religion and gender neutral and assume law can be universally applied in the same way to all groups and all members of society. Roy identifies a common theme that runs throughout critical perspectives of law which include a rejection of liberal legalism, legal objectivity and neutrality and an ideological commitment to a contextual analysis of the law (Roy 2008). Universalism is a key component of the claim to a neutral, secular state and its laws, and this framing has been specifically unpacked in the discourse around human rights (Mutua 2001) and international law (Anghie 2006). Claims to universalism and neutrality often mask value-laden behaviours and practices that are privileged as 'normal'. Shehada (2011) states the 'individual European citizen is abstracted, homogenised, "degendered", and universalized'. In contrast, Muslims are portrayed as 'non-universal, particular and different'. This framing is evident in the ways in which both civil marriage and divorce laws are universalised whilst Muslim marriage practices are particularised and uniquely problematised. Decolonial and postcolonial scholars have highlighted a fear or moral panic over 'sharia' rooted in colonial fears that Islam is a religion of savages that will supersede Christianity and needs to be controlled by superior civilised Europeans (Mutua 2001). Muslim women are identified as the beneficiaries of the saving missions of Europeans (Razack 2004; Abu-Lughod 2013). This has permeated its way into legal frameworks and policy discussions and in the ways in which the relationship between Muslim women and secular states is framed. We can see this in European case law where Muslim women's choice of dress is scrutinised without recognising their subjectivity, their freedom of choice or their individual spirituality (Alghrani, Ali, and Marshall 2019). The secular space makes value judgements about behaviours but cloaks them in the language of the abstract and universalised and thereby places the onus on Muslims to conform in order to attain these 'objective' standards.

6.5 Proposals for reform

Two key proposals for reform affecting Muslim marriage and divorce practices in England and Wales are briefly compared and explored in this section. First, the independent review into the application of sharia law in England and Wales ('the Review') (Siddiqui 2018), which primarily addressed religious tribunals but included recommendations on marriage law as a way of attempting to restrict religious tribunals. Secondly, a set of proposals comes from the Law Commission (2022) in its consultation on weddings. In its final report on 19 July 2022 the Law Commission recommended comprehensive reform in the form of an entirely new scheme to govern weddings. The Law Commission specifically included Muslim marriage practices in its analysis. It assessed the disparate ways in which the current law creates an exclusionary framework and how the law contributes to a higher proportion of ceremonies declared as non-qualifying ceremonies. In comparing the proposals of the Law Commission and the Review we can see the significant difference in the recommendations when Muslim family practices are understood and given legitimacy in their own right.

In October 2015 the government commissioned the Review to 'understand whether, and the extent to which, sharia law is being misused or applied in a way that is incompatible with the law within sharia councils'. This is a very vague and odd framing, and the imprecise language makes it difficult to understand exactly which 'law' was being investigated. The subsequent bullet-pointed terms of reference attempted to expand on this overarching aim, but it remains problematic for several reasons. It uses the language of 'compatibility' not unlike the language of 'integration' with the onus on Muslims to become 'compatible'. The expanded terms of reference attempt to draw out this framing more explicitly with the enquiry panel directed to seek out examples of best practice to assure compliance and compatibility with UK law. Leaving aside the misnomer that is 'UK law', this aspiration is embedded with colonial and Eurocentric assumptions; namely, that only those aspects of Muslim behaviour that are 'compliant' or 'compatible' with English law are indicators of best practice. Further, that state law (and by implication Western state law) sets the standard for best practice and that 'best practice' cannot be achieved from the practices of minority diasporas themselves. This aim internalises a colonial notion of the ways in which minority religious and cultural norms ought to be accommodated, with the supremacy of state law unquestioned. It emphasises 'Western' and European hegemony and supports my earlier arguments about the ways in which 'accommodation' of Muslim family practices is viewed as the provision of alternatives that fit within the current legal framework.

The Review reluctantly conceded the impracticality of any attempts to ban sharia councils and its three main recommendations lack innovation or creativity. It recommended that the Marriage Act should be amended to require a civil marriage ceremony to be conducted before or at the same time as a religious ceremony and sought to criminalise a celebrant or officiant to an Islamic marriage for any failure in this regard. This completely ignores the myriad of reasons why Muslims enter religious-only marriages (Sandberg 2019). Secondly, it recommended awareness and education campaigns to educate and inform Muslim women. Again, ignoring research that tells us many Muslim women are aware of their lack of legal status. In addition, the notion that Muslim women particularly need to be educated and informed as to their rights and responsibilities is patronising. Similar language or tone is not used when addressing the persistent misunderstandings around the 'common law marriage' myth, which despite numerous public campaigns is alive and well

(Barlow 2020). Thirdly, some regulation of sharia councils was seen as desirable and necessary.

The Review's recommendations retreat to the safe space of placing the onus on Muslims to conform to a legal framework of marriage laws that is becoming progressively unsuitable for Britons more generally and fails to pay attention to wider family law developments (Thompson and Sandberg 2016). The language of 'compatibility' and 'integration' continues to frame Muslim communities as homogenised guests who must be encouraged or even forced to follow 'our laws and customs' in order to fully participate in 'our societies', even where those laws and customs are unfit for increasing numbers of non-Muslim members of British society. The need to educate Muslim women presumes, without centring their voices or their religious, spiritual and social needs, that their lack of education is a core factor in this debate and that with the right education their practices will become compatible. The need for 'accommodation' of Muslim practices is perceived throughout as demanding special problematic attention of the law. The Review did not attempt to situate Muslim family practices within broader social changes nor did it attempt to draw any comparisons with cohabitation (Thompson and Sandberg 2016).

The approach of the Law Commission (2022) in its consultation and final report was significantly better than the Review. The Law Commission recognised the complexity of marriage laws, the changing landscape of families and the ways in which the law itself does not work for many couples. Muslims were included as couples for whom the law created unnecessary barriers. In acknowledging and problematising *the law*, it was able to recommend comprehensive reform that would enable more Muslim marriages to be recognised without necessarily exceptionalising Muslim family practices as uniquely difficult. Instead, the reforms suggested would make the legal framework of marriage recognition simpler and easier for couples to achieve legally recognised marriage status. The reform is to be welcomed, though in my view it does not go far enough in providing a minimalist framework that the state should adopt in recognising marriages (Parveen 2020).

6.6 Conclusion: Future directions

Muslims marriage (and divorce) practices demonstrate the importance of marriage (and divorce) to Muslims. They establish how British Muslims are, in many respects, behaving like their British non-Muslim counterparts by entering adult relationships that do not conform with the formalities of the Marriage Act 1949 and its amendments but that they regulate their behaviour within an Islamic framework. Their motivations are complex, and the lack of legal financial protections can produce gendered outcomes. Although many may be aware that their relationships lack legal status, they may not be fully cognisant of the extent to which the financially vulnerable partner may be exposing themselves. Many of these same arguments could be made for British non-Muslims who assume their cohabitation status provides them with greater financial protection than is currently available to them.

It is entirely possible to understand the nuances and complexities of communities and their social norms without resorting to orientalist and racist tropes. Once we begin to unpack the colonial, Eurocentric and Christian values and norms embedded within our legal systems the exclusionary nature of the current framework becomes apparent. Legal frameworks do not become value neutral simply by being promoted as 'secular', 'objective' or 'neutral'. A legal framework of marriage that polices the details of a marriage ceremony is inevitably dependant on identifying ceremonial norms against which compliance is judged. In an increasingly diverse society the law must develop in a manner that will truly recognise that diversity rather than exclude it. Elsewhere I (Parveen 2020) explore a minimalist approach to the legal framework of marriage that would allow parties greater freedom to enter into a marriage ceremony of their choice, with a post ceremony registration process. I argue that there are many significant events which the law addresses through 'after the event' registration processes, and marriage is no more or less significant in acquiring state recognition. If Muslim marriage practices are revealing the limitations of our current laws, then we need to explore the ways in which couples wish to marry including religious and non-religious ceremonies. There needs to be a shift in the focus of the law away from the policing of ceremonies to recognising the different ways in which couples enter into marital relationships. Ultimately, this will be to the benefit of any couple wishing to undertake a marriage ceremony in a manner that is currently not recognised.

References

Abu-Lughod, Lila. 2013. *Do Muslim women need saving*. Cambridge, MA: Harvard University Press.

Aftab, Amira. 2019. "Religious Accommodation in the Secular State: The Sharia Debate in Australia, Canada and United Kingdom." In *Studies in Law Politics and Society*, edited by Austin Sarat, 85–108. Bingley: Emerald Publishing Limited.

Akhtar, Rajnaara C. 2015. "Unregistered Muslim Marriage: An Emerging Culture of Celebrating Rites and Compromising Rights." In *Marriage Rites and Rights*, edited by P. Mody, R. Probert, and J. Miles, 167–92. London: Bloomsbury Publishing.

———. 2018a. "Modern Traditions in Muslim Marriage Practices, Exploring English Narratives." *Oxford Journal of Law and Religion* 7 (3): 427–54.

———. 2018b. "Unregistered Muslim Marriages in the UK: Examinig Normative Influences Shaping Choice of Legal Protection." In *Personal Autonomy in Plural Societies, A Principle and Its Pradoxes*, edited by M. Graziadei, A. D. Runteln, and M. C. Foblets, 140–55. London: Routledge.

Alghrani, Amel, Amal Ali, and Jill Marshall. 2019. "Leyla Sahin v Turkey." In *Feminist Judgments in International Law*, edited by Loveday Hodson and Troy Lavers, 203–30. Oxford: Hart Publishing.

Ali, Shaheen Sardar, Justin Jones, and Ayesha Shahid. 2020. "To Register or not to Register? Reflections on Muslim Marriage Practices in Britain." *Nordic Journal of Law and Social Research* 41–66.

Anghie, Antony. 2006. "The Evolution of International Law: Colonial and Postcolonial Realities." *Third World Quarterly* 27 (5): 739–53.

An-Na'im, Abdullahi Ahmed. 2019. "The Postcolonial Fallace of 'Islamic Family Law'." In *The Cambridge Companion to Comparative Family Law*, edited by Shazia Choudhry and Jonathan Herring, 254–79. Cambridge: Cambridge University Press.

Azzouz, Fouzia. 2021. *Muslim Marriage and Divorce Practices.* Bristol: University of Bristol.

Bano, Samia. 2008. "In Pursuit of Religious and Legal Diversity: A Response to the Archbishop of Canterbury and the "Shari'a Debate" in Britain." *Ecclisiastical Law Journal* 283–309.

———. 2012. *Muslim Women and Shariah Councils: Transcending the Boundaries of Community and Law*. Basingstoke: Palgrave Macmillan.

———. 2023. "Sharia Councils and Muslim Family Law: Analysing the Parity Governance Model, the Sharia Inquiry and the Role of the State/Law Relations." In *The Sharia Inquiry, Religious Practice and Muslim Family Law in Britain*, edited by Samia Bano, 95–127. London: Routledge.

Barlow, Anne. 2020. "Modern Marriage Myths: The Dichotomy between Expectations of Legal Rationality and Lived Law." In *Cohabitation and Religious Marriage: Status, Similarities and Solutions*, edited by Patrick Nash and Rebecca Probert Rajnaara Akhtar, 39–51. Bristol: Bristol University Press.

Bonthuys, Elsje. 2016. "A Patchwork of Marriages: The Legal Relevance of Marriage in a Plural Legal System." *Onati Socio-Legal Series* 1303–23.

Bowen, Innes. 2014. *Medina in Birmingham, Najaf in Brent: Inside British Islam.* London: Hurst.

Bowen, John R. 2015. *On British Islam: Religion, Law and Everyday Practice in Shariah Councils.* Princeton: Princeton University Press.

Casey, Louise. 2016. *The Casey Review: A Review into Opportunity and Integration.* London: Department for Communities and Local Government.

Channel 4. 2017. "The Truth About Muslim Marriage (Documentary)." True Vision Aire Channel 4.

Deogratias, Benedicta. 2019. *Trapped in a Religious Marriage: A Human Rights Perspective on the Phenomena of Marital Captivity.* Cambridge: Intersentia.

Diduck, Alison. 2016. "Autonomy and Family Justice." *Child & Family Law Quarterly* 28 (2): 133–50.

Douglas, Gillian, Norman Doe, Sophie Gilliat-Ray, Russell Sandberg, and Asma Khan. 2011. *Social Cohersion and Religious Law: Marriage. Divorce and Religious Courts.* Cardiff: Cardiff Law School.

Edge, Ian. 2013. "Islamic Finance, Alternative Dispute Resolution and Family Law: Developments Towards Legal Pluralism?" In *Islam and English Law: Rights Responsibilities and the Place of Shari'a*, edited by Robin Griffith-Jones, 116–43. Cambridge: Cambridge University Press.

Enright, Máiréad. 2009. "Choice, Culture and the Politics of Belonging: The Emerging Law of Forced and Arranged Marriage." *The Modern Law Review* 72 (3): 331–59.

Gaffney-Rhys, Ruth. 2010. "Hudson v Leigh – the Concept of the Non-Marriage." *Child and Family Law Quarterly* 22 (3): 351–65.

Gilliat-Ray, Sophie. 2012. *Muslims in Britain: An Introduction.* Cambridge: Cambridge University Press.

Grillo, Ralph. 2015. *Muslim Families, Politics and the Law: A Legal Industry in Multicultural Britain.* Farnham: Ashgate.

Heenan, Anna. 2021. "Haley v Haley: Family Arbitration and the New Frontier of Private Ordering." *The Modern Law Review* 84 (6): 1385–98.

Hudson v. Leigh. 2009. EWHC 1305 (Fam).

Humanists UK. 2020. "High Court Rules Humanist Marriage Recognition Failure is 'Discriminatory', but Stops Short of Formal Breach Due to Ongoing Review."

Accessed June 12, 2023. https://humanists.uk/2020/07/31/humanist-marriage-case-outcome/.

———. 2021. "Why Bother Answering the Religion Question on the Census at All?" March 9. https://humanists.uk/2021/03/09/why-bother-answering-the-religion-question-on-the-census-at-all/.

———. 2022. "Humanist Marriages: No Justification for Delay Following Law Commission Report." Accessed June 12, 2023. https://humanists.uk/2022/07/19/humanist-marriages-no-justification-for-delay-following-law-commission-report/.

Jackson, Leyla, and Kathryn O'Sullivan. 2017. "Muslim Marraige (Non) Recognition: Implications and Possible Solutions." *Journal of Social Welfare and Family* 39 (1): 22–42.

Kalra, Simran. 2025. "Religious Knowledge and Legal Rights: A Study of Nikah and Secular Marriage among South Asian Muslim Women in England." In *Relationships Rights and Legal Pluralism: The Inadequacy of Marriage Laws in Europe*, edited by Mateusz Stępień and Anna Juzaszek. London: Routledge.

Law Commission. 2022. *Celebrating Marriage: A New Weddings Law*. London: Crown.

Lewis, Philip. 2011. *Young, British and Muslim*. New York: Continuum International Publishing Group.

Lewis, Philip, and Sadek Hamid. 2018. *British Muslims: New Directions in Islamic Thought, Creativity and Activism*. Edinburgh: Edinburgh University Press.

Mitra-Kahn, Trishima, and Aisha Gill. 2012. "Modernising the Other: Assessming the Idealogical Underpinnings of the Policy Discourse on Forced Marriage in the UK." *Policy and Politics* 40 (1): 107–22.

Mohee, Samia. 2012. *Young British South Asian Muslim Women: Identities and Marriage*. London: University College London.

Moors, Annelies, and Julie McBrien. 2023. *Muslim Marriage and Non-Marriage: Where Religion and Politics Meet Intimate Life*. Leuven: Leuven University Press.

Munby, James. 2013. "The Sacred and the Secular: Religion, Culture and the Family Courts." *Law Society's Annual Family Law Conference in the UK*, October 29, 2013.

Mustafa, Asma. 2015. *Identity and Politcal Participation among Young British Muslims: Believing and Belonging*. Basingstoke: Palgrave Macmillan.

Mutua, Makau. 2001. "Savages, Victims, and Saviours: The Metaphor of Human Rights." *Harvard International Law Journal* 42 (1): 201–46.

Norton, Jane Calderwood, and Farrah Ahmed. 2012. "Religious Tribunals, Religious Freedom, and Concern for Vulnerable Women." *Child and Family Law Quarterly* 363–88.

ONS. 2022. *Census 2021 Guidance Note on Religion Questions and Religion Outputs*. London: ONS.

Parveen, Rehana. 2017. "Do Sharia Councils Meet the Needs of Muslim Women?" In *Gender Justice in Family Law Disputes: Women, Mediation, and Religious Arbtiration*, edited by Samia Bano, 142–65. Waltham: Brandeis University Press.

———. 2018. "Religious-Only Marriages in the UK: Legal Positionings and Muslim Women's Experiences." *Sociology of Islam* 6 (3): 1–24.

———. 2020. "From Regulating Marriage Ceremonies to Recognizing Marriage Ceremonies." In *Cohabitation and Religious Marriage: Status, Similarities*, edited by Patrick Nash, Rebecca Probert, and Rajnaara C. Akhtar, 85–101. Bristol: Bristol University Press.

Probert, Rebecca. 2002. "When are We Married? Void, Non-Existent and Presumed Marriages." *Legal Studies* 22 (3): 398–419.

———. 2020. "Determining the Boundaries Between Valid, Void and 'Non-Qualifying' Marriages: Past, Present and Future?" In *Cohabitation and Religious Marriage: Status, Similarities and Solutions*, edited by Patrick Nash, Rebecca Probert, and Rajnaara C. Akhtar, 15–27. Bristol: Bristol University Press.

———. 2021. “Getting Married: The Origins of the Current Law and Its Problems.” *Ecclesiastical Law Journal* 255–66.

———. 2023. “Religious-Only Marriages in England and Wales.” In *The Sharia Inquiry, Religious Practice and Muslim Family Law in Britain*, edited by Samia Bano, 11–26. London: Routledge Focus.

Probert, Rebecca, Rajnaara Akhtar, Sharon Blake, Tania Barton, and Vishal Vora. 2021. *When is a Wedding not a Marriage? Exploring Non-Legally Binding Ceremonies.* London: The Nuffield Foundation.

Razack, Sherene H. 2004. “Imperilled Muslim Women, Dangerous Muslim Men and Civilised Europeans: Legal and Social Responses to Forced Marriages.” *Feminist Legal Studies* 12 (2): 129–74.

———. 2008. *Casting Out: The Eviction of Muslims from Western Law and Politics.* Toronto: University of Toronto Press.

Roy, Alpana. 2008. “Postcolonial Theory and Law: A Critical Introduction.” *Adelaide Law Review* 29 (1–2).

Sandberg, Russell. 2019. “Criminalising Imams Will Not Solve the Problem of Unregistered Marriages.” Accessed June 20, 2023. www.familylaw.co.uk/news_and_comment/criminalising-imams-will-not-solve-the-problem-of-unregistered-marriages.

———. 2021. *Religion and Marriage Law: The Need for Reform.* Bristol: Bristol University Press.

Shah-Kazemi, Sonia Nurin. 2001. *Untying the Knot: Muslim Women, Divorce and the Shariah.* London: The Nuffield Foundation.

Shehada, Nahda. 2011. “The Portrayal of Islamic Family Law in Europe.” In *Critical Research in the Social Sciences: A Transdiciplinary East-West Handbook*, edited by Roger Heacock and Edouard Conte, 241–57. Ramallah: Ibrahim Abu-Lughod Institute of International Studies.

Siddiqui, Mona. 2018. *The Independent Review into the Application of Sharia Law in England and Wales.* Government Report – Secretary of State for the Home Department, London: Crown.

Stratton, Jon. 2016. “With God on Our Side: Christianity, Whiteness, Islam and Otherness in the Australian Experience.” *Journal of Media & Cultural Studies* 30 (16): 613–26.

Thompson, Sharon, and Russell Sandberg. 2016. “The Sharia Law Debate: The Missing Family Law Context.” *Law and Justice* 177: 181–92.

Uddin, Islam. 2018. “Nikah-Only Marriages: Causes, Motivations and Their Impact on Dispute Resolution and Islamic Divorce Proceedings in England and Wales.” *Oxford Journal of Law and Religion* 7 (3): 401–26.

Vora, Vishal. 2016. “Unregistered Muslim Marriages in England and Wales: The Issue of Discrimination through ‘Non-Marriage’ Declarations.” In *Muslims in the UK and Europe II*, edited by Yasir Suleiman, 129–41. Cambridge: Centre of Islamic Studies, University of Cambridge.

Women and Equalities Committee. 2022. *Rights of Cohabiting Partners.* London: House of Commons.

7 Legal pluralism's perspectives and human rights challenges in marriage and divorce norms

The case of Muslims in Europe

Amal Alqawasmi

7.1 Introduction

Empirical data research has clearly shown that Muslim family law is unofficially applied across Europe (Mustasaari and Al-Sharmani 2018; Bone 2020; Khalfaoui 2020). This is more likely to involve marriage and divorce norms rather than other family matters and with different levels of coordination within national borders among the several Muslim communities in a given country (Akhtar, Probert, and Moors 2018; Alqawasmi 2021). The role of the state is limited; these norms usually regulate marriage and divorce cases without noticeable intervention or regulation by a state official authority. It depends a great deal on the level of legal recognition and cooperation between the authority and the Muslim communities, not only when it comes to religious rights, but also on the practical and procedural side of marriage and divorce cases. The result is instability and a lack of formality before the state with unprotected family rights (Uddin 2018; Jaraba 2020, 30).

However, there are individual Muslims who are aware of this and try to officially fulfil their family status, for example, by taking part in an officially recognised civil marriage, either before or after the religious marriage in an Islamic centre, in order to combine their religious marriage with a civil ceremony, which is the official and legal form in front of the state. Even though this is recommended among many Muslims, it is still not generally the norm in Europe (Probert, Rebecca, and Shabana Saleem 2018, 383–84; Bone 2020, 166). This situation brings new legal and social challenges in Europe since the lack of officiality has led to unprotected family rights and legal uncertainty. Moreover, there is a deep concern about creating segregated communities within European societies that regulate their family issues outside the control of the state (Alqawasmi 2021, 983–84). All this brings important responsibilities and challenging issues for the European legal system.

This chapter discusses the case of these marriage and divorce norms in relation to legal pluralism perspectives and human rights challenges as follows. First, there are different orientations in defining and dealing with the concept of legal pluralism; it can be defined by the presence of more than one legal order in a social field, including both state and non-state sources of law. And

DOI: 10.4324/9781003470786-10

it is also defined by the coexistence of a multiplicity of legal systems whenever they are legitimate and recognised by the state. So what is the correlation between the different definitions and the consequences when perceiving the term of empirical legal pluralism in regard to family and religious norms? Second, taking into consideration the case of empirical legal pluralism, what are the main confrontation issues raised in regard to social cohesion, concerned rights, and the nature of Muslim family law? Third, how can different interpretations and understanding of the concepts of justice and equality influence the question of human rights raised when discussing Muslim marriage and divorce provisions?

7.2 Different approaches in defining legal pluralism

The concept of legal pluralism has a particular importance when it comes to the presence of multiple legal orders with different sources of law within a pluralistic society, and how their functionality is being evaluated and how they are interacting with each other (Büchler 2016, 73). So what are the points of interests raised for discussion in relation to Muslim family norms?

Starting from the wide variety of literature on legal pluralism and given the complexity that surrounds the concept within interdisciplinary interests,[1] the first and simplest definition is to describe legal pluralism as the presence of more than one legal order in a social field (Griffiths 1986, 1). The attention here is placed on how these legal orders interact, which is also analytically defined as the coexistence of multiple sources of law within the same society (Chiba 1998; Benda-Beckmann 2002, 65–68). This includes both state and non-state sources of law and confirms the view that a law is not just the one that is created and applied by the state, but also includes other different legal orders, where there is a choice of socio-legal standards other than the state-centred law. This choice can be made by individuals and communities as well, and it can be created by the state itself or be the result of the personal interests of the parties concerned (Chiba 1998, 242). Thus, according to this first definition, legal pluralism is the coexistence of different legal orders in one place, whether they are officially recognised by the state or not.

Defining legal pluralism is closely related to defining the various perspectives of law, therefore leading to different definitions of legal pluralism (Benda-Beckmann 2002, 48–51; Tamanaha 2008, 390–96). When the only legal system is that of a state, especially in the modern nation state where there is one dominating jurisprudence, the concept of legal pluralism is, to a certain extent, contrary to legal centralism. Therefore, wherever the law is the one created and applied by the state only, a narrow and strict concept of legal pluralism is presented. This leads to a second definition of legal pluralism which

1 Vanderlinden (2013, 234–36) discussed more the complexity of the concept of legal pluralism especially when it comes to understanding the relationship between law and society.

is the possibility of the coexistence of a multiplicity of legal systems whenever they are legitimate because they are recognised by the state. This second definition of legal pluralism is clearly based on the idea of a single unified legal order that should be cohesive and homogeneous under the sovereignty of the state.[2]

On the other hand, the previously mentioned first definition of legal pluralism – as the coexistence of a multiplicity of legal systems from a plurality of sources that are not limited to the state – is contrary to the idea of a central dominating legal system since these other legal orders are not necessarily officially recognised (Shah 2020). This concept of legal pluralism is more evident in a pluralistic society when it comes to family law because it is related to one's private life which is most likely to be influenced by cultural and religious identity. Therefore, this approach refers to the space where people from multiple backgrounds regulate their family issues in accordance with their own culture or religion, which is not necessarily the legal order of the state. One should keep in mind that this kind of coexistence does not mean that all these multiple legal systems within the same geographic area interact in harmony since there can also be conflicting situations (Griffiths 1986, 7; Tamanaha 2008, 400–1).

Thus, the empirical data related to the case of marriage and divorce norms in Europe can be called 'empirical legal pluralism', and consequently this term can be defined by the existence of pluralistic legal norms in family issues within European societies that are applied unofficially without the recognition of the state. And that is exactly where the current Muslim family norms are taking place and where they can be properly studied and analysed (Benda-Beckmann 2002, 74).

In summary, an overall analysis of the different approaches in defining the term of legal pluralism will describe the coexistence of different legal orders in one place, with different levels of influence of the state's authority over the legitimacy and officiality of non-state systems. However, the functionality of these different legal orders will not be limited by this, and an interaction between them will be seen in the real life of the pluralistic society concerned whether all these legal orders are classified as official or not (Chiba 1998).

When it comes to religious norms and provisions, one should bear in mind that they are not just to be judicially determined and then isolated. A process of interactive analysis, productive dialogue, and realistic confrontation should take place for a better legal understanding and solutions as well. In pluralistic societies, law is a vital instrument in legally accommodating the diverse normative orders, as is an in-depth understanding of how they were produced and how they should regulate behaviour within religious communities. The

2 Worth mentioning that this will lead to the discussion about the difference between strong and weak legal pluralism as outlined by Griffiths (1986); see Bunn-Livingstone (2002, 49–54); Shah (2005, 2).

law plays a fundamental role in developing technical and procedural frameworks to produce effective methods for regulating religious diversity. All this is marginally accepted by the idea of the exclusive dominating law of the nation state. There is a real need not to treat religious communities as different units within a society. It is crucial to understand that religious norms and provisions influence the members of a religious community in the same way that state law does (Riles 2008, 294–96).

Muslim marriage and divorce norms represent a case of empirical legal pluralism that will continue to exist and be applied in Europe, having an effect on society even if not officially recognised. This situation leads to uncertainty and unprotected family rights (Alqawasmi 2021, 983–84). This, in turn, highlights the related research questions of how these operating norms should be appropriately categorised in any discourse of legal recognition, and what policy of legal pluralism will be adopted by the state concerned as a positive approach to diversity within the legal order, especially while considering religious sensitivity and lack of officiality.

7.3 A confrontation when accommodating legal pluralism

Discussing Muslim marriage and divorce norms in Europe brings a number of challenges that should be analysed and evaluated from different perspectives. In the following sections, I will discuss the challenges that are mostly influencing the lives of individuals and communities, as well as whole societies.

7.3.1 The question of social cohesion

Literature on legal pluralism highlights a clear concern about adopting pluralistic legal structures, especially family laws, because this would have a negative effect on the social cohesion of society. This cohesion is undoubtedly of particular importance for the welfare of all societies, including pluralistic ones. This point of view is based on the fact that accommodating legal pluralism in family issues would weaken the common values of modern, secular, and democratic societies, which are based on sharing an awareness and understanding of legal unity. Moreover, it would create more segregated communities within a national society, which is not compatible with a modern nation state (Poulter 1999, 39; Macdonald 2003, 133–52; Menski 2020, 21).

Noteworthy here is the fact that legal unity is based on the idea that all people are subject to the law created by the state, which has the sole competence of legal legislations. This is evident in the state private laws, including family laws, which its people are supposed to be subject to. Thus, assigning this authority in family laws to a religious community would be in contradiction with legal unity. This idea actually represents one of the main objections towards legal pluralism (Griffiths 1986, 4–5; Tamanaha 2008, 402–7). This case of legal pluralism where different legal structures coexist in family law codes places the duty of the state at stake when it comes to guaranteeing clarity, justice, and equality before the law for all its people. In other words, it would challenge legal certainty since it most probably would create doubts in people as to which legal order they are supposed to follow (Zumbansen 2017, 193).

However, empirical data shows that there is a parallel of Muslim family provisions that are locally governed by Muslim communities and not controlled by the state. The core issue here is how to apply the law in these cases of empirical legal pluralism, using an approach that preserves legal certainty in a modern secular state in order to avoid creating segregated communities. On the other hand, the state also has a responsibility to accommodate and respect religious and cultural diversity. This challenging issue therefore needs a balanced socio-legal evaluation in order to achieve the desired social cohesion. Therefore, the question here is basically directly connected to how the state evaluates the different concepts of legal pluralism, and what possibilities of accommodating different legal structures the legal system can accept. All this regardless of the other legal order, whether it is the Muslim family one or another, since it is a primary discussion that concerns the concept of legal pluralism.

The functionality of the procedures and norms adopted by the different social groups or communities within a society is a main concern in legal pluralism research since this plays a vital role in understanding this sensitive interaction between individuals and their community and all of society as well. This is particularly connected to strengthening social cohesion within pluralistic societies. But it is still a question confronting different points of interests as well (Bhamra 2007; Locchi 2016, 139–48; Büchler 2016, 86–88).

7.3.2 The concerned rights

Freedom of religion and family life aims to guarantee freedom of choice and action for individuals and has a legal effect as well (United Nations 1948, Art. 2 and Art. 18; Council of Europe 1950, Art. 2, Art. 8 [1] and Art. 9). So how will this officially be accommodated for individual Muslims when considering their religious marriage and divorce norms?

There is a concern that giving officiality to these norms within Muslim communities will have an impact on individual rights within these communities, especially vulnerable individuals, mostly women. Religious communities in general are questioned whether they treat men and women equally and offer both the same freedom of choice and do not discriminate if either the husband or wife refuses to comply with what the community considers to be a religious norm that should be followed. Therefore, will this continue if Muslim communities are officially granted permission to keep applying religious family norms among their members who also have their own rights as individuals too (Bader 2003, 277–79; Shachar 2005, 65–69)?

It is argued that giving legal authority in family issues to Muslim communities will strengthen their authority to place internal restrictions and more limitations on their members in the name of religious values and norms.[3]

Consequently, the right of the community as a group to apply Muslim family provisions contradicts the rights of the members of this community to follow their own choices as individuals. This has an impact on vulnerable members in the community. Therefore, the concern is primarily the rights of these individuals within their community, which could be weakened or even lost because of the collective right and the authority given to this community in family issues. Conservative interpretations and traditional legal opinions may add restrictions and limitations of individual rights, especially when it comes to women.[4] This raises more challenges since the state has the duty to protect individual human rights under international law too.

But these challenges would arise if these communities have official authority over their members and there is no control by the state. Instead, the state must ensure that individual human rights are protected and that all the members of these communities have full access to law and justice. The role of the state is essential in keeping a balance between the right of the Muslim community as a group to apply religious family provisions and the human rights of the individuals as well. Any given officiality in this case should reinforce the role of the law, ensure equal access to the law, and guarantee the freedom of individuals because it will be under the control of the state and not an authority that is given exclusively to a religious community (Estin 2011, 822).

The challenge is that the state should not ignore the existence of empirical legal pluralism or simply act as an observer. Family provisions should be subject to state control, and state officials and judges should be well informed of the circumstances, especially when it comes to vulnerable members. Standing against Muslim family provisions will not eliminate the challenge, nor protect the individual's rights. It is actually solving the problem by denying it (Bader 2003, 278).

It would be more effective to open potential channels and promote public debates with these communities in order to identify all the practices within the community, including those that limit individual rights, and to raise awareness about the need to also strike a balance between individual and group rights (Bader 2009).

Muslim women who consider themselves religious and belong to religious communities come from various backgrounds and also have different levels of education and awareness. Many are able to participate in complex family law negotiations and face challenging issues with more or less desired outcomes.[5]

3 Shachar (2001, 17–18) discussed the so-called perils of multicultural accommodation.

4 Shachar (2001, 45–62) and Büchler (2016, 88–90) have discussed in particular the case of family law and the construction of collective identity.

5 See, for example, the reflection on personal narratives from Muslim women using a Šarīʿah council to obtain an Islamic divorce in the United Kingdom as Bano and Pierce (2013, 229–30) discussed.

As such, one should not generalise that they are always the vulnerable members in their religious communities since there is an individual effort towards achieving more effective rights, which can be institutionally supported.

7.3.3 The plurality inside Muslim family law

Muslims in Europe, whether they are residents or citizens, are pluralistic. They are of different origins, whether they were born in Europe or immigrants. In addition, their religious values and norms differ. Therefore, there are different Muslim communities all over Europe, as well as in every single European state. This affects, in turn, how they follow their religious marriage and divorce norms as well as their socio-legal choices.

Islamic law is known to be pluralistic, and there are different juridical schools and a variety of schools of thought even though they share the general framework of Islamic jurisprudence. As such, it is normal to find different interpretations of texts on the topic from the Qur'ān and the Sunnah, which leads to various possible applications as well (Kamali 1991, 191; Hallaq 2005, 150–77). In another words, no specific Muslim family provisions are being followed by the pluralistic Muslim communities in Europe. Some choose to follow the model of their country of origin to a certain extent if they are immigrants. However, the majority try to benefit from the different schools of legal thought and traditions within the framework of Islamic jurisprudence. In any case, the result is that multiple forms of marriage and divorce norms are being applied unofficially in Europe (O'Sullivan and Jackson 2017, 22–23; Akhtar, Probert, and Moors 2018, 367–75; Jaraba 2020, 29; Menski 2020, 13–28). Given the situation, the challenge lies in determining to what extent it is effectively possible to systemically codify one Muslim family law, not only when it comes to Muslim communities, but also for the European national authority concerned.

This process of identifying the appropriate form of Muslim family provisions in Europe must then be elaborated and codified by highly qualified specialists in this field. The real situation of Muslim communities and the influence of the surrounding social and cultural values should be taken into consideration, as long as the needed developments best fit the European societies where this law is supposed to be officially recognised. All this underlines an important issue, that those involved in such a process should have the approval of Muslim communities and the national authority too. This calls for a trusted and qualified committee that can take on such a responsibility transparently and represent the parties involved (Poulter 1999, 211).[6]

6 The Šarī'ah council in the UK, for example, has important experience in this field. There are critical analyses and reflections on this experience and its functionality, especially when it comes to gender issues, and conservative selections from the framework of Islamic law (Bano and Pierce 2017; Bone 2020; Marotta 2021).

On the other hand, even though Muslims in Europe are pluralistic, they can be classified as Europeans too. They can be unified under every national European state they live in, whether they live there as residents or citizens. Living in Europe, they all share the same circumstances that influence their family lives. This common and shared identity is important when discussing which model of Muslim family provisions they should follow since laws should always respond to the needs of a society in a balanced interaction.

The plurality of opinion in Islamic jurisprudence can be useful in this regard because it leads to adaptation and flexibility in the application of laws as well (Hallaq 2009, 118). Therefore, researchers, scholars, and socio-legal experts can benefit from the various schools of legal thought by adapting a model for most Muslims in Europe. This flexibility should be used when it comes to elaborating this legal structure. A case described by Ferrari (2006, 61) in a comparison of the traditions of canon law, Jewish law, and Islamic law shows that the authority of the religious legislator in the tradition of canon law is linked to the centralised, pyramidal structure of the Church authority, where there is uniformity and only one legally correct answer. However, the 'interpretation' of law in Jewish and Islamic traditions is linked to a socio-religious structure that is a network where there can be different solutions to the same problem, all of which are equally correct from the legal point of view.

7.4 Challenges facing human rights

One of the core challenges when discussing Muslim marriage and divorce provisions is the discussion of its incompatibility with the constitutional and human rights that are legally approved in Europe. The main objection is not towards Islam as a religion but towards traditional interpretations and legal opinions in several issues involving Muslim family provisions. This mostly targets the difference between men and women in several family legislations such as their different rights and duties in marriage, divorce, child custody, and polygamy (Krivenko 2009, 56–57).

When it comes to European countries, the international conventions on human rights are an essential element in public policy with the different European societies sharing many common values and norms, including family law (see Council of Europe 1950, 1961; United Nations 1962, 1966, 1979a, 1989). Therefore, any family provisions or norms that are not compatible with those supporters of human rights will not be applied or recognised in any form, even if justified for cultural or religious reasons.

One of the main conventions in this regard is the United Nations Convention on the Elimination of All Forms of Discrimination against Women (CEDAW) of 18 December 1979. The convention is known for its rigidity in concentrating on the absolute equality of rights between men and women in all aspects. This is evident in the concept of gender equality adopted by CEDAW as explained in Art. 1 by stating that

> the term 'discrimination against women' shall mean any distinction, exclusion or restriction made on the basis of sex which has the effect or purpose of impairing or nullifying the recognition, enjoyment or exercise by women, irrespective of their marital status, on a basis of equality of men and women, of human rights and fundamental freedoms in the political, economic, social, cultural, civil or any other field.
>
> (United Nations 1979a, Art. 1)

In family matters, Article 16 of this convention, for example, requires all the state parties to take all appropriate measures to eliminate discrimination against women in all marriage and family matters and in particular shall ensure that men and women have equal access to family law institutions like marriage, divorce, and custody (United Nations 1979a, Art. 1). Moreover, in the 'Women and Religion in Europe' resolution, the Parliamentary Assembly calls on the member states of the Council of Europe to take several actions to protect the rights of women from all violations related to religion. And among these actions the member states are called to 'refuse to recognise foreign family codes and personal status laws based on religious principles which violate women's rights, and ceasing to apply them on their own soil' (Parliamentary Assembly, Council of Europe 2005). The European states therefore have a legal obligation to take appropriate action to achieve this equality of rights and responsibilities between women and men who start a marriage, during their marriage, its dissolution, and in all other related family issues.

When it comes to Muslim family law, traditional interpretations usually consider the different roles that are given to men and women within a marital relationship and inside family life as well, where they are supposed to complement each other in the appropriate manner (Syed 2004b, 49–57). Muslim family law, when officially applied, indicates that absolute equality as firmly stated in CEDAW is not compatible with Muslim family principles (Krivenko 2009, 115). This view is actually confirmed by the reservations expressed by the Arab and Islamic countries that are signatories to the CEDAW regarding Art. 16, which calls for equality between men and women in all marriage and family matters. There are also other countries that did not accept the principle of gender equality in the family set out in Art. 16. For example, France, Switzerland, and Korea expressed their reservations regarding the right to choose the family name. Ireland expressed another reservation that concerns the rights of guardianship, adoption, and custody of children born out of wedlock, while Thailand had reservations on all the contents of Art. 16 (United Nations 1979b).

Therefore, even though the concept of gender equality is accepted in Europe in general, it continues to be considered differently.

Moreover, it is important to underline that the concept of gender equality in family law in Europe ensures equal position and status for men and women but allows men and women to take different positions in their family life and in their marriage. Whether these different positions are influenced by culture or religion, freedom of choice in their roles in their private family life is respected. Therefore, if they choose to take complementary but different positions and have equally important roles in their family, no one can say that gender equality has been violated. This is not very different from the general idea of the different but complementary roles assigned to husband and wife under Muslim family law. Thus, considering Muslim family principles as a challenge to human rights and gender equality is more likely to be a matter of the different ways that the concept of equality is applied rather than a case of being in contradiction with the principle of the equal value and dignity of both men and women.

On the other hand, even if several Arab and Muslim majority countries have expressed their reservations about specific articles in the CEDAW, there is a general tendency towards a reform of Muslim family law known as personal status code. Several amendments have been approved in response to the developments and changes affecting the family, especially the increased participation of women in their societies.[7]

Moreover, major efforts are being made by non-governmental organisations and women's activist groups to promote the importance of accommodating justice and equality in countries where Muslim family law is officially applied.[8] This is based on the idea that all parties fully agree that the concept of justice is of particular importance as an ethical value, and Islam as a religion prioritises the values of justice, fairness, and the dignity of men, women, and children, regardless of their family status, And the philosophy of law in Islam is based on the idea of the need to achieve justice as a main objective.[9] At the same time, justice is influenced by the backgrounds and real circumstance of people in society. As such, what can be seen as justice in a given period of time, or in a certain place, may be considered injustice in completely different circumstances. This is one of the main reasons why there are various opinions in Islamic jurisprudence on a specific issue in different times or places.

Within the framework of Islamic jurisprudence, it is normal to have various interpretations and opinions on many issues by Muslim scholars and expert

7 Keeping in mind that any modification in family law codes is affected directly by the country's political situation, such as upcoming elections, political conflicts, or an unstable political situation which is seen in Arab and Islamic countries (Welchman 2007, 151–55).

8 See, for example: Musawah (n.d.) ('equality' in Arabic) the global movement for equality and justice in the Muslim family.

9 See, for example, the verses from the Qur'ān:

(Indeed, Allah commands you to render trust to whom it is due and when you judge between people to judge with justice. Excellent is that which Allah instructs you. Indeed, Allah is ever Hearing and Seeing) Qur'ān 4:58.

(Indeed, Allah orders justice and good conduct and giving to relatives and forbids immorality and bad conduct and oppression. He admonishes you that perhaps you will be reminded) Qur'ān 16:90 (The Qur'ānic Arabic Corpus 2013).

jurists in Islamic law since Islamic jurisprudence is basically a human effort, where multiple schools of thought and different views are recognised and respected. It is a process where scholars and jurists derive solid legal rules from the primary sources of Islam, the Qur'ān and the Sunnah, which encompass the principles, values, and ethics of Islam, and not a body of laws. The various experiences and new problems that emerge in different societies are always taken into consideration, and their impact is acknowledged within this ongoing human effort to develop the appropriate legal opinion on different issues. Therefore, Muslim family law, wherever it is officially accommodated, is not divine, and it is completely incorrect to say that it cannot be changed. On the contrary, it must be revised by experts and scholars to reflect the changes that influence every society, taking into consideration that achieving justice should always be the priority as one of the main objectives and challenges of any law, whether in legislation or in its applicability.

Countries that have Muslim family law in their official legal system do not ignore the need to constantly update and revise their codes. However, there is still a need for a greater concerted effort by women's rights activists, sociologists, counsellors, and constitutional experts to work with Islamic law experts in order to find concrete solutions to equality for both men and women in all aspects of Muslim family law. The new challenges, interests, and needs of different societies should be taken into consideration to achieve justice as the main objective in this regard. It is important to underline here that this process of finding solutions to present-day challenges within the framework of Islamic jurisprudence will differ from one society to another based on the influence exerted by local factors and cultures. And this plurality resulting from the different interactions is important in searching for the best way to achieve full protection of rights.

Any discussion on the incompatibility of certain aspects in Muslim family provisions should be based on Šarīʿah law and its legal effects and applicability in society, not on the individual or selective practices influenced by a specific tradition or custom. In fact, many cases of women's rights, in Muslim countries also, are the result of the traditional and patriarchal, male-dominant behaviour that Islam as a religion stands against (Mashhour 2005, 564).

It is also useful to understand the philosophy with which the concepts of justice and equality have been accommodated within the main principles of Muslim family law. The reservations made by several countries in applying Muslim family law using equality as stated in CEDAW were justified by considering this equality as sometimes contrary to the equal distribution of different rights and duties within family life and not a discrimination against women. For example, a husband has the duty to give a dowry – mahr – to his wife upon their marriage and also has the duty to provide for his wife and children. A wife, instead, has no obligation to provide for her husband even if she is able to and strongly recommended to do so, especially if her husband is in need. As a consequence, and in specific situations, men are given twice the inheritance because of their greater financial responsibilities. This is considered to be a kind of equal distribution of rights and duties between men and women inside marriage. However, men do not always take twice the share of an inheritance. In fact, there are several cases where men and women take the same shares and others where women take more than men. It all depends on the familial relationship (Syed 2004b, 85–96). It is therefore incorrect to say that the rule regarding inheritance in Islamic law is to give men more than women since there are different situations with various distributions of the shares.

When it comes to Ṭalāq, the objection is that the husband has direct access to this while the wife does not, which is contrary to the principle of gender equality. This objection would be correct if Ṭalāq was the only way to dissolve a marriage in Muslim family law, which is not the case. The dissolution of a marriage under Muslim family law can be carried out in specific ways. First, it can be by the will of the individual, which is unilateral divorce, and is known as Ṭalāq. This is basically the husband's right but can also be the wife's right if it was registered as a condition in their marriage, and it is known as Ṭalāq-i-tafwīḍ. Second, it can be by mutual consent of both husband and wife: Ṭalāq mubāra'ah, or Khulʿ. Third, it can be with the judgement of an authorised Šarīʿah judge, which can vary, depending on the case that comes before the judge. This can be the annulment of the marriage, known as Faskh, or can be another form of Ṭalāq, called Tafrīq, or it can be judicial, called Khulʿ (Assartawi 1997; Syed 2004a; Mashhour 2005, 571–77; Al-Ashqar 2009, 368–72).

Therefore, both husband and wife may dissolve their marriage. However, when it comes to Ṭalāq, the man has direct access since he is legally bound to pay all the related financial rights to the woman including the mahr. This considers the duties of the husband and does not discriminate against the woman. When the dissolution is a unilateral Ṭalāq divorce, the wife has a right to the mahr and all financial rights regardless of who initiated the proceedings.

Polygamy is also considered an institution in Muslim family law that most challenges the principle of equal rights for men and women. This is not only because it can be classified as a man's prerogative in marriage, but also because of its effects on a woman's financial rights in marriage and its negative consequences on her psychological health and emotional stability as well. This has been clearly stated by the UN Committee on the Elimination of Discrimination against Women, which concluded that 'polygamous marriage contravenes a woman's right to equality with men, and can have such serious emotional and financial consequences for her and her dependents that such marriages ought to be discouraged and prohibited' (UN Committee on the Elimination of Discrimination against Women 1994, para. 14). In addition, the CCPR[10] clearly notes in its General Comment No. 28 that

> Equality of treatment with regard to the right to marry implies that polygamy is incompatible with this principle. Polygamy violates the dignity

10 The Centre for Civil and Political Rights (CCPR Centre) is an independent, non-governmental organisation seeking to realise its vision through universal ratification and implementation of the International Covenant on Civil and Political Rights (ICCPR).

> of women. It is an inadmissible discrimination against women. Consequently, it should be definitely abolished wherever it continues to exist.
> (United Nations Human Rights Committee 2000, 68th Session)

These UN bodies therefore clearly consider polygamy to be a violation of the equal treatment and human dignity of women (Kreuzer 2009, 688).

Discussing polygamy within the framework of Islamic jurisprudence clarifies that mentioning it in the Qur'ān was basically a limitation, and not a permission, to the existing polygamy practiced without any restrictions by many peoples, including Arabs before Islam.

This restriction in the Qur'ān sets the condition that all wives are to be treated equally, and if a man fears that he will be unable to do so then he should marry only one wife (Syed 2004b, 41–44; Mashhour 2005, 568).

This fundamental condition is currently interpreted differently in official Muslim laws on personal status. Tunisia, for example, has forbidden polygamy because it is considered impossible nowadays for a man to provide for more than one wife (Code of Personal Status in Tunisia 1956, Art. 18). The literature on Islamic jurisprudence also states that any wife has the right to put a condition in her marriage contract according to the Hanbali school that her husband will not marry another wife during their marriage. Even without this condition, the wife may ask for a divorce if negatively affected by her husband's polygamy (Assartawi 1997). This can already be found in various states that officially apply Muslim family law (see Moroccan Family Code 2004, Art. 40; Jordanian Personal Status Code 2010, Art. 37; Egyptian Personal Status Code 1985, Art. 11). In addition, polygamy is legislated differently according to what is considered appropriate in every society. In Morocco, no case involving polygamy can proceed without the court's permission (Moroccan Family Code 2004, Art. 41), whereas in Jordan, the court is required to officially inform the first wife whose permission, however, is not required (Jordanian Personal Status Code 2010, Art. 13). Polygamy is therefore restricted by more or less strict conditions or procedures in many Muslim countries since it is by default a legislation that is subject to restrictions and limitations. This should clearly be taken into consideration, especially when it comes to the changes that influence every society.

Thus, the flexibility of Islamic jurisprudence is vital in adapting to different circumstances and is a real possibility when accommodating the new aspects of equality between men and women in Muslim family provisions where Muslim women should not feel obliged to choose between following their religion in their private family life and their equal rights with men in family life too.

Whenever human rights concerns are highlighted, the goal is not simply to guarantee equality between women and men under the law but to also defend this in everyday life, which is still a challenge in European societies (Büchler 2016, 101).

What has been achieved at the level of human rights legislation is obviously the result of human experience made up of barriers and challenges until they become an essential component of modern democratic states. This is based on the principle of the full acknowledgement and protection of the dignity and freedom of every individual regardless of any categorisation that might result in discrimination or a lack of acknowledgement of rights. Consequently, respecting diversity is a cornerstone of human rights legislation. And this, in turn, confirms the need for continuous consolidation and argumentation of this point in accordance with the demand of every society, especially when it is a pluralistic one.

This will bring further discussions about the influence of different values and norms on the current concept of human rights, whether or not it will be more cohesive for universal human rights to be considered as a normative general framework rather than a detailed one, and the related impact on the application of the concerned laws.

7.5 Conclusion

Disregarding the fact that empirical legal pluralism exists will not improve the rights of more vulnerable people and women. And underestimating its effect will not prevent members of Muslim communities from being subject to informal religious provisions in their family life. There is no guarantee that human rights within family law can be protected outside the control of the state. Therefore, the role of state law is important when reconsidering the different aspects involved in dealing with Muslim family norms within a liberal democratic legal system.

Family laws in Europe have gone through different stages to obtain these modern models, which are still subject to modifications in order to adapt to ever-changing circumstances. Considering this, two points of discussion are raised. First, to what extent can it be focused on the core values of human rights standards as connecting factors, and not limited to a singular vision, to improve its universal dimension and its vital applicability in pluralistic societies? Second, to what extent can the flexibility of Muslim family norms effectively guarantee human rights and justice within European societies? Any possible official accommodation of Muslim family norms needs to take these into account. These are major challenges in this regard and can be part of the solutions as well.

References

Akhtar, Rajnaara C., Rebecca Probert, and Annelies Moors. 2018. "Informal Muslim Marriages: Regulations and Contestations." *Oxford Journal of Law and Religion* 7 (3): 367–75.

Al-Ashqar, U'mar. 2009. *Towards an Authentic Islamic Culture*. Translated by K. Nusibah. Amman: Dar Al-Nafaes.

Alqawasmi, Amal. 2021. "Marriage and Divorce Practices in Islamic Centers in Italy." *Oñati Socio-Legal Series* 11 (4): 959–89.

Assartawi, Mohammad. 1997. *The Explanation of the Personal Status Law. The Dissolution of Marriage*. Amman: Dar-Alfiker.

Bader, Veit. 2003. "Religious Diversity and Democratic Institutional Pluralism." *Political Theory* 31 (2): 265–94.

———. 2009. "Legal Pluralism and Differentiated Morality: Shari'a in Ontario?" In *Legal Practice and Cultural Diversity*, edited by Ralph Grillo, Rojer Ballard, Alessandro Ferrari, André J. Hoekema, Marcel Maussen, and Prakash Shah, 48–72. Farnham: Ashgate Publishing Ltd.

Bano, Samia, and Jennifer L. Pierce 2013. "Personal Narratives, Social Justice, and the Law." *Feminist Legal Studies* 21 (3): 225–39.

———, eds. 2017. *Gender and Justice in Family Law Disputes: Women, Mediation, and Religious Arbitration*, 46–73. Waltham: Brandeis University Press.

Benda-Beckmann, Franz von. 2002. "Who's Afraid of Legal Pluralism?" *Journal of Legal Pluralism* 47: 37–82.

Bhamra, Meena. 2007. "On Cultural Diversity: The Importance of Normative Foundations for Legal Responses." In *Law and Ethnic Plurality: Socio-Legal Perspectives. Immigration and Asylum Law and Policy in Europe*. Vol. 13, edited by Shah Prakash, 9–30. Leiden: Martinus Nijhoff Publishers.

Bone, Amra. 2020. "Islamic Marriage and Divorce in the United Kingdom: The Case for a New Paradigm." *Journal of Muslim Minority Affairs* 40 (1): 163–78.

Büchler, Andrea. 2016. *Islamic Law in Europe, Legal Pluralism and Its Limits in European Family Laws*. New York: Routledge.

Bunn-Livingstone, Sandra L. 2002. "Juricultural Pluralism vis-à-vis Treaty Law: State Practice and Attitudes." In *Juricultural Pluralism vis-à-vis Treaty Law*. Leiden: Brill Nijhoff.

Chiba, Masaji. 1998. "Other Phases of Legal Pluralism in the Contemporary World." *Ratio Juris* 11 (3): 228–45.

Code of Personal Status in Tunisia. 1956.

Council of Europe. 1950. "Convention for the Protection of Human Rights and Fundamental Freedoms." https://www.coe.int/en/web/human-rights-convention/the-convention-in-1950#.

———. 1961. "European Social Charter." https://www.coe.int/en/web/european-social-charter/home.

Egyptian Personal Status Code. 1985.

Estin, Ann. 2011. "Family Law, Pluralism, and Human Rights." *Emory International Law Review* 25 (2): 811–28.

Ferrari, Silvio. 2006. "Adapting Divine Law to Change: The Experience of the Roman Catholic Church, with Some Reference to Jewish and Islamic Law." *Cardozo Law Review* 28 (1): 53–66.

Griffiths, John. 1986. "What is Legal Pluralism?" *The Journal of Legal Pluralism and Unofficial Law* 18 (24): 1–56.

Hallaq, Wael B. 2005. *The Origins and Evolution of Islamic Law*. Cambridge: Cambridge University Press.

———. 2009. *An Introduction to Islamic Law*. New York; Cambridge: Cambridge University Press.

Jaraba, Mahmoud. 2020. "Khulʿ in Action: How Do Local Muslim Communities in Germany Dissolve an Islamic Religious-Only Marriage?" *Journal of Muslim Minority Affairs* 40 (1): 26–47.

Jordanian Personal Status Code. 2010.

Kamali, Mohammad Hashim. 1991. *Principles of Islamic Jurisprudence*. Revised ed. Cambridge: Islamic Text Society.

Khalfaoui, Mouez. 2020. "Current Muslim Understandings of Classical Family Law in a Modern Secular Context: Germany as a Case Study." *Journal of Muslim Minority Affairs* 40 (1): 117–27.

Kreuzer, Karl. 2009. "Clash of Civilizations and Conflict of Laws." *Revue Hellenique de Droit International* 62 (2): 629–94.

Krivenko, Ekaterina Yahyaoui. 2009. *Women, Islam and International Law: Within the Context of the Convention on the Elimination of all Forms of Discrimination Against Women*. Vol. 8. Leiden: Brill.

Locchi, Maria Chiara. 2016. "Legal Pluralism in Multicultural Societies: New Perspectives for Comparative Constitutional Law." In *Le droit compare et./Comparative Law and*. Actes de la conference annuelle de Juris diversitas, 139–48. Aix-en-Provence Marseille: Universitaires d' Aix – Marseille Presses.

Macdonald, Roderick A. 2003. "L'hypothèse du pluralisme juridique dans les sociétés démocratiques avancées." *Revue De Droit* 33 (1–2): 133–52. Université De Sherbrooke.

Marotta, Anna. 2021. *A Geo-Legal Approach to the English Sharia Courts, Cases and Conflicts*. Comparative Law in Global Perspective Series. Vol. 1. Leiden: Brill.

Mashhour, Amira. 2005. "Islamic Law and Gender Equality Could There Be Common Ground: Study of Divorce and Polygamy in Sharia Law and Contemporary Legislation in Tunisia and Egypt." *Human Rights Quarterly* 27 (2): 562–96.

Menski, Werner F. 2020. "Rethinking Legal Theory in the Light of South – North Migration." In *Migration, Diasporas and Legal Systems in Europe*, edited by Shah Prakash and Menski Werner, 13–28. Abingdon; New York: Routledge Cavendish.

Moroccan Family Code (Moudawana). 2004.

Musawah, N. D. "A Global Movement for Equality and Justice in the Muslim Family." Accessed November 18, 2023. www.musawah.org/. Musawah ("equality" in Arabic) the global movement for equality and justice in the Muslim family. www.musawah.org/.

Mustasaari, Sanna, and Mulki Al-Sharmani. 2018. "Between 'Official' and 'Unofficial': Discourses and Practices of Muslim Marriage Conclusion in Finland." *Oxford Journal of Law and Religion* 7 (3): 455–78.

O'Sullivan, Kathryn, and Leyla Jackson. 2017. "Muslim Marriage (Non) Recognition: Implications and Possible Solutions." *Journal of Social Welfare and Family Law* 39 (1): 22–41.

Parliamentary Assembly, Council of Europe. 2005. "Resolution 1464: Women and Religion in Europe." https://pace.coe.int/en/files/17372#trace-3.

Poulter, Sebastian. 1999. *Ethnicity, Law and Human Rights: The English Experience*. Oxford: Oxford University Press.

Probert, Rebecca, and Shabana Saleem. 2018. "The Legal Treatment of Islamic Marriage Ceremonies." *Oxford Journal of Law and Religion* 7 (3): 376–400.

The Qur'ānic Arabic Corpus. 2013. *Language Research Group*. University of Leeds. Accessed December 1, 2023. https://corpus.quran.com/translation.jsp.

Riles, Annelise. 2008. "Cultural Conflicts." *Law and Contemporary Problems* 71 (273).

Shachar, Ayelet. 2001. *Multicultural Jurisdictions: Cultural Differences and Women's Rights*. Ser. Contemporary Political Theory. Cambridge: Cambridge University Press.

———. 2005. "Religion, State, and the Problem of Gender: New Modes of Citizenship and Governance in Diverse Societies" *Mcgill Law Journal* 50 (1): 49–88.

Shah, Prakash. 2005. *Legal Pluralism in Conflict: Coping with Cultural Diversity in Law*. London: Glass House Press.

———. 2020. "Are There Asian Diasporic Laws in Britain? Reconsidering the Presuppositions of Legal Pluralism." *Quaderni di diritto e politica ecclesiastica*, no. 1: 201–20.

Syed, Mohammad Ali. 2004a. *Rules of Dissolution of Marriage in Islamic Law*. Albany: State University of New York Press.

———. 2004b. *The Position of Women in Islam: A Progressive View*. Albany: State University of New York Press.

Tamanaha, Brian Z. 2008. "Understanding Legal Pluralism: Past to Present, Local to Global." *Sydney: Sydney Law Review* 30 (3): 375–411.

Uddin, I. 2018. "Nikah-Only Marriages: Causes, Motivations, and Their Impact on Dispute Resolution and Islamic Divorce Proceedings in England and Wales." *Oxford Journal of Law and Religion* 7 (3): 401–26.

United Nations. 1948. "Universal Declaration of Human Rights." In *Universal Declaration of Human Rights*. https://www.un.org/en/about-us/universal-declaration-of-human-rights

———. 1962. "Convention on Consent to Marriage, Minimum Age for Marriage and Registration of Marriages." https://www.ohchr.org/en/instruments-mechanisms/instruments/convention-consent-marriage-minimum-age-marriage-and#.

——— 1966. "International Covenant on Economic, Social and Cultural Rights." https://www.ohchr.org/en/instruments-mechanisms/instruments/international-covenant-economic-social-and-cultural-rights.

———. 1979a. "Convention on the Elimination of All Forms of Discrimination Against Women." https://www.ohchr.org/en/instruments-mechanisms/instruments/convention-elimination-all-forms-discrimination-against-women.

———. 1979b. "Reservations to the Convention on the Elimination of All Forms of Discrimination against Women." https://treaties.un.org/pages/ViewDetails.aspx?src=TREATY&mtdsg_no=IV-8&chapter=4&clang=_en.

———. 1989. "Convention on the Rights of the Child." https://www.ohchr.org/en/instruments-mechanisms/instruments/convention-rights-child.

United Nations Committee on the Elimination of Discrimination against Women. 1994. "General Recommendation No. 21." https://www.un.org/womenwatch/daw/cedaw/recommendations/index.html.

United Nations Human Rights Committee. 2000. *CCPR General Comment No. 28: Article 3 (The Equality of Rights Between Men and Women)*. UN Doc. CCPR/C/21/Rev.1/Add.10. https://sjd.gov.jo/EchoBusV3.0/SystemAssets/PDFs/AR/AppliedLegislations/a7walsha5seye.pdf.

Vanderlinden, Jacques. 2013. *Les Pluralismes juridiques*. Brussels: Primento.

Welchman, Lynn. 2007. *Women and Muslim Family Laws in Arab States: A Comparative Overview of Textual Development and Advocacy*. Amsterdam: Amsterdam University Press.

Zumbansen, Peer C. 2017. "The Rule of Law, Legal Pluralism, and Challenges to a Western-Centric View: Some Very Preliminary Observations." *Osgoode Legal Studies Research Paper Series* 193.

III

Empirical research on the marital reality of individuals

8 Contestations about polygyny

Converts to Islam in the Netherlands

Vanessa Vroon-Najem and Annelies Moors

8.1 Introduction

On 6 October 2016, a Dutch TV programme, *Undercover in the Netherlands*, broadcasted an episode that showed how 'illegal Islamic marriages' are concluded in Dutch mosques. This episode of *Undercover*, a rather sensationalist commercial format with reporters going undercover to report on 'serious abuse', was one step in a sequence of events that would lead to major media hype, parliamentary questions and a law proposal.[1] References in this episode to polygyny certainly contributed to the hype.

The day before the airing of this episode, the largest right-wing liberal party (VVD) presented an initiative to further criminalise religious marriages that are concluded prior to a civil marriage.[2] This initiative started with the firm statement that 'the Dutch marriage law does not discriminate: in the Netherlands, as a woman or man you are free to arrange your love life the way you want, regardless of descent or religion'. It then continued with the phrase, 'in the Netherlands you decide yourself whom to fall in love with, whom to sleep with and whether or not to marry, and if so, with whom, and in which order you choose to do so'. Central to this initiative is the premise that 'undermining Dutch marriage law is not just a violation of the law', but also a 'rejection of the equality between men and women, the Dutch way of life and the history of emancipation that Dutch marriage law has gone through'.

According to the Dutch Civil Code, 'religious functionaries' are legally prohibited from concluding a religious marriage prior to a civil marriage (Dutch Civil Code 1992, Art. 68; Van der Leun and Leupen 2009, 8ff).[3] The initiative proposes and argues for an intensified enforcement of the existing rule, for example 'through undercover actions' on 'religious (often Islamic) dating

1 This chapter builds on Moors, de Koning, and Vroon-Najem 2018, where this TV episode is analysed extensively.

2 See Dutch Parliamentary Document (2019).

3 This regulation emerged in the early nineteenth-century Napoleonic period, when marriage became only a civil matter. In Belgium and France, concluding a religious marriage prior to a civil marriage is also prohibited.

DOI: 10.4324/9781003470786-12

sites', and to extend the law and make everyone who is directly and voluntarily involved in concluding an illegal (religious) marriage punishable by law.[4]

This initiative was written with the support of Shirin Musa, the director of Femmes for Freedom (FFF), an organisation that promotes marital freedom and the equality of men and women and fights against forced marriages, child marriages, forced abandonment, hidden women and marital captivity.[5] The text of the initiative includes two cases that Musa presented to substantiate the policy proposals. One of these cases concerns an illegal immigrant who finds a third wife through a dating site.[6] The *Undercover* episode presents precisely such a case: an actor impersonating a Muslim woman goes online to find a polygynous husband on a Muslim dating site. After meeting a man already married to two wives, the couple goes to the mosque to conclude the marriage. When they leave the mosque, the *Undercover* reporter confronts both the newlywed husband and the imam who concluded the marriage.

What is striking in the initiative, the cases Musa provided and the *Undercover* episode is that polygynous marriages are mobilised in order to make the case against religious-only marriages, the large majority of which are monogamous. Foregrounding polygynous marriages is a convenient way to support the notion that Islamic-only marriages are harmful for women. This, in turn, is then used as the main argument to further criminalise such religious-only marriages, although these marriages have no legal effect.

In this chapter, we first briefly discuss the problematisation of polygynous marriages in policy-making and the media and then shift the focus to the narratives of women who have entered such marriages. Our interlocutors are converts to Islam, to whom polygyny is an alien practice. Because of their thorough unfamiliarity with polygyny, they need to reflect seriously on how they entered such a marriage.[7] Through these women's reflexive narratives we can gain insight into how they signify and engage in a polygynous marital relationship.

Our interlocutors are not statistically representative for converts to Islam in the Netherlands. They all self-identify as observant Muslims, to whom living a

4 The initiative then presents five policy proposals, two of which directly concern entering a religious-only marriage. In the meantime the proposal has been amended; the criminalisation of witnesses has been removed (otherwise the state would need to define who is a witness, which goes against the separation of state and religion) as well as that of the parties entering such a marriage (avoiding the risk of further victimising the victim) (see Dutch Parliamentary Document (2020). Also, Femmes for Freedom has distanced itself from the criminalisation of spouses (2021).

5 See www.femmesforfreedom.com/.

6 The second case concerns the proposals on support for women who are left in their country of origin; a polygynous marriage is also at stake in this case.

7 Yet there are no firm lines of demarcation between these converts and Muslim-born women in the Netherlands, who are often the children of migrants. Also for the latter, 'polygyny' is often far removed from their life worlds. Some of these women may also have grown up with little Islamic education; they may go through a process that in some ways resembles the conversion of our interlocutors.

Muslim life matters a great deal. Whereas they do not commit to a particular school of Islamic thought, they have, to various extents, been inspired by the Islamic revival. This means that they follow a relatively literalist interpretation of the main sources of Islam, attempt to follow 'correct or pure Islam' and distance themselves from 'traditional cultural aspects'.[8]

This contribution is part of our long-term research with women converts to Islam in the Netherlands. Starting in 2014, Moors and Vroon-Najem worked together to explore how these women entered marriage (Moors, de Koning, and Vroon-Najem 2018; Moors and Vroon-Najem 2019).[9] For our project we conducted topical life story interviews, centring on how they found a spouse and entered marriage (Bertaux 1981), with 40 women converts (mostly between 2015 and 2019); we talked extensively with 10 women who had personal experience with polygyny and three women who would seriously consider such a marriage. As we purposely looked for women in a polygynous relationship, it is not possible to draw conclusions from these numbers about the prevalence of polygyny amongst converts, which remains very limited. Additionally, we asked dozens of other converts how they felt about polygyny and whether they would consider entering such a marriage themselves. Our fieldwork included participant observation at the conclusion of marriage contracts and weddings, attending lectures and courses on how to enter a Muslim marriage and many informal conversations with the various parties involved in these marriages. We also interviewed religious authority figures, both converts and born Muslims, to whom converts often turned for advice. Both authors have been involved in conceptualising the project, have done fieldwork that included joint interviews with our interlocutors and have worked together in analysing the material.

The introductory vignette already indicates that polygynous marriages are both legally prohibited and considered undesirable, if not reprehensible. In the following we first discuss how polygynous marriages have been turned into a problem in need of intervention (Bacchi 2015). As will be argued, the ways in which these marriages intersect with migrant/transnational marriages and with Islamic-only marriages has been an intricate part of this.

8.2 The problem with polygyny: State actors

In the Netherlands polygynous marriages are prohibited.[10] Historically, civil marriages, institutionalised in the early nineteenth century, have been

8 We have not included women who converted only for pragmatic reasons.

9 Research for this project is funded by the ERC advanced grant on 'Problematizing "Muslim Marriages": Ambiguities and Contestations' (Grant number: 2013-AdG-324180). Vroon-Najem started research on women's conversion to Islam in the Netherlands and the politics of belonging in 2006 (Vroon-Najem 2014, 2019), while Moors has a long history of research on Muslim marriage and particularly the dower (Moors 1995, 2008).

10 When a registered partnership became an option in 1998 the same rule applied; it is, however, possible to include more people in a cohabitation contract.

modelled after Christian marriages; that is, they were to be monogamous, heterosexual and concluded with the consent of the spouses without any possibility for divorce; women were obliged to obey their husbands. Whereas over time, the prohibition of divorce and the obedience rule were abolished, and same-sex marriages have been permitted since 2001, polygynous marriages have remained prohibited. Still, polygynous marriages that were concluded abroad (and were valid) could be recognised in the Netherlands, following the principles of International Private Law. This, however, did not apply to the effects of these marriages. For instance, men were allowed to bring only one spouse and her children to join them in the Netherlands.

In the 1990s the need for stricter rules became a topic of debate. By then, Islam had been labelled as standing in tense relation with Dutch culture and as the source of many societal problems.[11] From the 2000s on, there was a further growth of ethno-nationalism with public debate and policy becoming increasingly assimilationist as a result (Gingrich 2006; Geschiere 2009). With respect to polygyny, in 1993 the Dutch Supreme Court declared that the principle of monogamy is a principle of public order. This opened the door for refusing to recognise polygynous marriages in the Netherlands concluded abroad. In 2015, after years of debates about countering forced marriages, further restrictions were imposed. Polygynous marriages were mentioned in one breath with forced marriages; they were considered an indication of unfree partner choice (Bonjour and De Hart 2013, 70). Polygynous marriages concluded abroad were no longer recognised if one of the partners had the Dutch nationality or had the Netherlands as their main residence (Rutten 2016, 50). The main argument was that polygynous marriages are considered harmful for women.[12]

Besides the legal prohibition of polygyny, the women involved face two other ways in which these marriages are problematised. First, some of the marriages of women converts to Islam in the Netherlands are transnational as these women often marry a (post-)migrant from a Muslim majority country. Secondly, as observant Muslims, who do not want to enter a sexual relationship outside of a marriage, they often enter an Islamic marriage quite quickly. However, an Islamic-only marriage (without a prior civil marriage) is prohibited.

To start with migrant marriages, during colonial times the Dutch state was already concerned about 'native' men marrying Dutch women. Such marriages were often considered a shortcut to acquire Dutch nationality (Stoler 1992, 543).[13] Similar concerns about migrant marriages became salient again with the growing presence of labour migrants in the Netherlands in the 1970s;

11 Simultaneously, migrants from Muslim majority countries had become identified (and sometimes self-identified) as Muslims.

12 There is also a strong societal condemnation of those entering such marriages, which stands in contrast to the more nuanced way in which polyamory is evaluated (Roodsaz 2023).

13 More generally, until 1964, a woman who married a foreigner automatically lost her citizenship, while a foreign woman who married a Dutch man automatically became Dutch (De Hart 2006, 11).

such marriages were often deemed harmful for the women concerned. At first the focus was on the negative effects for Dutch women, but in the next decades such concerns were also extended to the daughters of migrants in the Netherlands who married a man from their parents' country of origin and to the women who were brought as so-called 'import brides' from Türkiye and Morocco to the Netherlands; in both cases the women were considered at risk of forced marriages (Bonjour and De Hart 2013, 67–68).

Undesirable migrant marriages were then regularly linked to 'Islam'. Polygynous marriages, cousin marriages and underage marriages were associated with Muslims and considered particularly negative for women. As an indication of unfree partner choice (forced marriage), policymakers developed a wide range of new regulations to counter them (Bonjour and Kraler 2014; Sterckx and Dagevos 2014; De Koning, Storms, and Bartels 2014).

Whereas these debates all centred on civil marriages, from the mid-2000s Islamic-only marriages also became a topic of debate (Moors 2013). The first hype emerged in 2005 when, in the context of the trial of the Hofstad network (an alleged terrorist organisation), it was reported that such Islamic marriages were concluded in these circles, often in a highly informal manner.[14] In 2008, Islamic marriages again became the focus of considerable public and parliamentary debate. This time, imams attached to Salafi-oriented mosques were accused of concluding such marriages, which might also be underage or polygynous marriages. They were seen as a way of developing a highly conservative 'parallel society' that self-segregated from Dutch society. In both cases – be they marriages in jihadi circles or those linked to Salafi-oriented mosques – the women entering these marriages were considered victims of the men involved.

8.3 Women converts and polygyny

Not only state actors but also scholars often argue that polygynous marriages are harmful for women. Liversage (2019), who did research on polygyny in transnational marriages, argues that in such marriages most of the advantages are for men and most of the hardship for women. While agreeing that in some cases women themselves may see advantages, they were not present in her study.[15] Also Joffe (2016) and Zeitzen (2008) focus in their work on equality and harm. Zeitzen acknowledges that whereas different marriage forms (both polyandry and polygyny) may exist in the same communities; in both cases they tend towards male domination. This then raises the question how the women who enter polygynous marriages signify these.

14 The Dutch security services considered such Islamic marriages as a threat to national security (NCTb 2006).

15 Liversage (2019) explains that this may be explained at least in part by the fact that the larger study from which she drew her cases focused on divorce.

For Muslims, marriage is important religiously; especially for converts, it is also important for social reasons. Quite often these women desire to enter marriage quickly: to keep sexual relations *halal*, to have companionship and to be able to start a Muslim family of their own. Since becoming Muslim is controversial among non-Muslims in the Netherlands and joining a local community of Muslims takes time, many women converts are between social circles for a while and may struggle with loneliness, particularly during Ramadan and Islamic holidays (Vroon-Najem 2014).

Lacking Muslim family and being unfamiliar with the stricter forms of Muslim dating, finding a husband is often a challenge. This makes women vulnerable to abuse, particularly since new converts tend to have an idealistic, rosy view of other Muslims (e.g. Roald 2012). This desire to find a spouse quickly without much knowledge or support can therefore have some serious downsides. In hindsight, our interlocutors often realised that they had been naïve and lacking knowledge about what an Islamic marriage entails (see also Moors and Vroon-Najem 2023). For single converts, being on their own makes it particularly difficult to assess and vet potential marriage partners. Online and offline, more experienced (convert) women warn each other about so-called 'marriage bandits':[16] men who present themselves as devout Muslims but who are in fact only pursuing quick sexual relationships. One of the red flags is when such a man proposes a convert to become his 'secret second wife'.[17]

Our interlocutors generally acknowledged that polygyny is allowed in Islam, but most did not consider it something they would choose for themselves. Many expressed ambivalence; they would not reject polygyny outright and mentioned some possible benefits, but the thought of sharing their husband remained quite unappealing or even a non-negotiable no-go. Nevertheless, many of them followed the opinion that a woman could not *prohibit* her husband outright from marrying more than one woman, but it was certainly named as a reason for divorce. Often, they underlined that whether polygyny is acceptable depends on whether a husband would be able to live a *righteous* polygynous life. They pointed out that such a man would need to be able to live up to his obligations: equal treatment of both wives in material and emotional terms. This is very difficult in the Netherlands, as marital life is legally and practically based on the model of one spouse only.

16 This term was coined by Zainab Bint Younes, a Canadian Muslim writer and blogger: see MuslimMatters.org, which publishes material about polygyny.

17 To avoid the 'marriage bandit', women are advised to find a trustworthy *wali*, a Muslim man who can act as a marriage guardian on their behalf; to educate themselves regarding the rights and duties entailed in a Muslim marriage; and to pursue a civil marriage as well since in the Netherlands a Muslim marriage is a private ritual without legal standing. However, in the case of polygyny, a civil marriage is unobtainable. This leaves women converts who choose this form of marriage with fewer options for legal protection than would be the case if a civil marriage with more than one person were allowed.

8.4 Age and positionality

A woman convert's assessment of polygyny varies depending on her age and positionality, which ties in with her options to find a marital partner. This becomes more difficult as women become older, have been married previously and already have children. Although a few of our interlocutors entered a polygynous marriage at a young age, it was mostly something to be considered by older women or women who had been married before.

Older women converts particularly mentioned that their perspective on the subject had changed over the years as they became more open to the possibility of being a second wife, or at least they could name some advantages. The difference in positionality between younger and older women was clearly visible in the life story of Aliya,[18] a divorced single woman in her forties at the time of our interview, whose assessment of polygyny had changed over the years. When she first married, she was in her twenties. At that time, she had demanded a stipulation in her Islamic marriage contract that her husband could not marry a second wife, something she considered 'the worst of the worst'.

The option to prohibit a husband from marrying a second wife through a stipulation in the Islamic marriage contract is subject of debate (in practice, the effect of such a stipulation is that a divorce is granted to the wife). Those advocating against such a stipulation argue that it is not possible to prohibit something that Allah has allowed. Aliya, however, considered it permissible:

> I know many scholars of Islam disagree but in Islam it is permitted to make a contract, and a marriage contract is a contract like any other. You are equal partners in that. So you can draw up rules, and if you both sign, that is valid. Many people say, 'Allah has allowed it so how can you ban it?' But then I think, Allah has allowed us to eat Brussels sprouts every day but that does not mean it is mandatory. If I put in my contract that I do not eat Brussels sprouts, that does not mean I do something forbidden, right? You cannot make something that Allah has allowed mandatory for everyone. Although I have to say, this is my own interpretation.[19]

When her future husband hesitated to agree with this condition, she almost cancelled the marriage.

In hindsight, she admits that at the time she had a very romantic image of marriage.

> Now, at age 46 [and single], my thinking is more like 'maybe it is not such a bad idea, polygyny'. Now I look at it from a different perspective. . . .

18 In order to protect the privacy of our interlocutors, we have used pseudonyms.

19 She also mentioned that some would argue that a man is not bound to abide by such a provision in the contract because within Islam polygyny is allowed, but she rejected this as well: 'that I would consider fraud; you have signed [a contract]!'.

> I can see wisdom in that it is allowed because there are many women who are left [without husbands] and especially good men who treat women well, those men remain married, you know. Rationally, now I have a different perspective, because when you are young, the only thing on your mind is 'he is mine, he is mine', but there is more to it [marriage] than that.

This sentiment was echoed by another interlocutor, Adinda. Like Aliya, she lectured occasionally for local (converted) Muslim women's groups. Adinda told us polygyny was not an issue in her own marriage; her husband did not desire to marry another woman. But she shared a moral story that circulated among the women in her social circle.

The story highlights the positive sides of polygyny and encourages women not to reject the thought out of hand. In this story, a husband tells his spouse that he desires to marry a second wife. He asks for her approval, but she answers that if he does so, she will leave him. He then abandons the idea as they have children together, and he decides it is not worth it. But then he suddenly dies, and the life of his widow is turned upside down. She is suddenly a single mother who needs to take care of her children by herself while depending financially on a business in peril. As the story goes, she becomes depressed and destitute. Then a friend tells her that she knows a brother [in Islam] who is interested in marrying a second wife: would she be interested to meet him? Now this woman is on the other side of the table and agrees to meet him. They like each other, and she asks to meet his first wife. At this meeting, his first wife admits she finds it very difficult and painful but nevertheless, she has hope that they can be like sisters. This act of sisterhood invokes in the woman at the centre of the story a positive form of jealousy as she realises 'she is the woman I could not be'.

Appreciating the shift in perspective in this story, Adinda explained why polygyny means letting go of your ego and being generous enough to accept sharing your husband, highlighting why polygyny is allowed in the first place: to save people (from loneliness and destitution). However, she added, we are now all very selfish, we are all like, 'he is *my* husband, he is mine!' In the life stories of our interlocutors who experienced being in a polygynous marriage, indeed, the ideal picture of Islamic sisterhood, wishing for the other woman what they wish for themselves, was challenging in regard to sharing their husband.

8.5 Second wives: openness or secrecy

Almost all the women we interviewed about polygyny highlighted the importance of openness and honesty. They highly valued the first wife being informed of a pending second marriage and the second wife being made aware that a potential husband is already married.

Several of our interlocutors experienced grief and heartbreak caused by secrecy. Initially feeling positive about polygyny, they found themselves caught up in considerable personal drama. Two of them started from a similar position of aiming for Islamic sisterhood as expressed in Adinda's moral story. One of them is Dagmar. Being her husband's first wife she felt that she could deal with her husband's wish to have a second wife and agreed to it being a possibility when they discussed it in general. However, when she found out, after the fact, that he had indeed gone ahead and married another woman, she felt terrible. It bothered her greatly that he had not consulted her beforehand. After two and a half years, she finally met his second wife herself. But despite her efforts to build an understanding, sending the second wife a 'welcome aboard' package, a relationship built on the concept of Islamic sisterhood never materialised. When this second marriage ended in a divorce, she made her husband promise that if he would ever consider marrying again, he would consult her beforehand and would make sure there were clear arrangements between both women to ensure equity.

Sakina experienced the precariousness of secrecy from the other end, being the secret second wife herself. She entered marriage as her husband's second wife with an idealistic vision of polygyny.

> I entered into that marriage thinking, 'nice, we will help and support each other with raising our children. If she is busy I will care for them and vice versa. We will learn from each other.' That is how I envisioned it.

In practice, her marriage remained a secret as her new husband failed to inform his first wife; he had convinced Sakina that it was for the best and that, in any event, the secrecy would only be temporary. However, before he took the step to tell his first wife, she found out on her own. As they were in a civil marriage, she threatened him with a costly divorce and the loss of custody of their children. He then radically distanced himself from Sakina and (Islamically) divorced her immediately. Although this caused her much anger and pain, after some time had passed, she nevertheless entered a polygynous marriage for a second time. This time, she made sure their marriage was out in the open from the beginning, and although she was on good terms with her husband's first wife, she no longer envisioned a shared life as 'sisters in Islam', as she had experienced the dilemmas and challenges of putting such ideals into practice.

In the stories of two much younger women who entered a polygynous marriage, secrecy again played a pivotal role in whether they evaluated their marital life positively or negatively. Both were in their early twenties when they were approached for marriage almost immediately after their conversion. In both cases, their suitors were already married. One of them was open about it, the other one kept it a secret. In the case of Selma, a few days after she said her *shahada*,[20] a fellow student proposed to marry her, telling her right away

20 On saying the *shahada* – 'I testify that there is no god but God and I testify that Mohammed is His messenger' – with the intention to convert, a person becomes Muslim.

that he was already married. Initially she rejected his offer. But as she liked him a lot, they stayed in touch, and she began to consider his proposal seriously. Eventually they agreed to marry. She asked him if he had informed his first wife, which he confirmed, and after 3 months the two women met each other.

Married for 7 years at the time of the interview, she told us that the fact that he was honest with his first wife was of great importance to her:

> Suppose my husband comes home and tells me 'a few days ago, I married a third woman', I would be devastated. If you have love and respect for each other, you need to inform one another. I cannot imagine doing something like that behind someone's back.

Reflecting on the general lack of acceptance of her choice, she admits that although the mother of her husband herself was a second wife, the practice was frowned upon by his female relatives, and she had not told her own family. The stigma of being a second wife amongst Muslims surprised her.

> Women who practise Islam in a serious manner but who go crazy when you tell them you are a second wife. I never understand that because it is in the Qur'an. So if you are indeed a practising Muslim, why are you so judgemental? Of course, you need to overcome some jealousy . . . but my husband is not my possession. Some people say, 'my husband is mine'. I think that is quite peculiar.

Sophie, on the other hand, who was also proposed to by a man she had met online within weeks of her conversion, was unaware that he was already married when she accepted his proposal. Soon after, she found out he had a child and confronted him with questions. He admitted he was still legally married but explained that he had married when he was very young, that the marriage was not working out and that a divorce was imminent. Trusting that this marriage was effectively over, she went ahead and married him Islamically. Soon, however, she found out that his first wife was pregnant with their second child, which he explained had happened when they had tried to save the marriage. Because of the pregnancy, he remained married to both.

By the time Sophie herself was pregnant with her second child, his first wife had had enough and wanted a divorce. Believing she was his only wife for a while, Sophie then found out her husband had secretly married again and fathered a child. She felt betrayed and deceived: 'Not so much because he had married again, but because he had hidden it from me'. After that, she decided it would be best if he left the house and lived on his own, but they remained married. The new second wife was informed as well. She had been married before and was divorced, with the care of four young children; she too decided to stay married. They both felt some empathy towards each other, and Sophie told her she could always contact her if she wanted to discuss something.

> Perhaps I can help her with things. After all, I was in her position once. I have ten years of experience [with polygyny], so I can handle it better. She struggles with it a lot, which is understandable. She is not ready to contact me yet but we are in it together. . . . My expectations [of marriage] have changed. Before, I had this dream image and now not so much. But that does not mean it cannot work out.

8.6 Polygyny as an option

Amongst our interlocutors, there was a consensus that men need to be able to handle multiple marriages correctly: promoting equality in both a material and an emotional (and sexual) sense. In practice, the second wife would often provide for herself. Whereas there was a profound dislike of the idea that a second wife would be on welfare, if she waived her right to be provided for, that was considered her right as well. Maria's marriage as a third wife was organised around such an agreement. Over 40, she had been married with children before she divorced, had a busy, well-paid job and was engaged in volunteer work in her spare time. She explained, 'In this life phase it is actually quite alright to have someone to share the good and bad times with, my passions and dreams, but who is not around all of the time. That is a real benefit!'

There were also others amongst our interlocutors who considered polygynous marriage an option, evaluating it more positively. Sometimes this was the case because they were used to living on their own and no longer desired to live with 'a full-time husband'. As a divorced convert in her late thirties explained, 'I would consider it an option to marry as a second wife. I have children, I do not necessarily want more children. Unless I meet Prince Charming, I would definitely be open to the idea'. Another convert considered polygyny an acceptable or perhaps even a desirable option, as she did not want to have children at all. Recognising the importance of marriage in Islam, she considered a part-time husband who had children with another woman a workable solution.

8.7 Conclusion

Both participants in public debate and policymakers consider polygyny undesirable; this is also the case for Muslims. Whereas marriage legislation has always prohibited polygyny, such marriages have become more strongly condemned because they are linked to two other forms of marriage that have become increasingly controversial since the 1990s: migrant marriages and Islamic marriages. Marriage with an 'imported' bride or groom from the country of origin was seen as a particular threat to integration and as harmful for the women, as these women were often considered the victims of forced marriages. Islamic marriages (conducted prior to a civil marriage) were also increasingly targeted as illegal, using the very same arguments to discredit this marriage format;

these marriages were seen as contributing to the development of parallel societies and as putting women at risk of forced marriage, enabling marriages of minors and polygynous marriages. As a result also polygynous marriages concluded abroad are no longer recognised if a Dutch national and someone having the Netherlands as their main residence were involved.

As our convert interlocutors were often married to a (post)-migrant, and for religious reasons rather quickly entered an Islamic marriage, they were already confronted with the problematisation of both forms of marriage. When they also then entered a polygynous marriage arrangement, they risked ostracisation not only by the majority population but also by Muslims. The ways in which they signified their engagement in these marriages was, not surprisingly, more complex and nuanced than the dominant perspectives presented in public debate. To them, as converts, discussions about integration did not make sense. Rather than self-segregating, they felt pushed out of the nation after conversion (see Vroon-Najem 2014). Most of our interlocutors did not consider polygyny an attractive option, yet those entering such a marriage did not consider themselves victims of a forced marriage.

The narratives of the women concerned point to a variety of positions. It is evident that age matters, in both their evaluation of these marriages and how they deal with them. Another major element, besides being the first or the second wife, was whether the husband can engage in polygyny in the correct way, which refers to equal treatment and honesty/openness.

Age matters in various ways. On the one hand, age tallies with experience. Young women who had entered a polygynous relationship often, in hindsight, considered themselves naïve, they had taken a risk and felt lucky if it worked out well. Older women, in contrast (or the same woman once she had grown older) would underline the problem that for them – often also divorced or widowed, and perhaps with children – it was very difficult to find a husband. They considered being married as a second wife a better option than remaining single, both because of the religious value of marriage and because they felt in need of someone who would support them. A few women explained that to them polygyny was a positive option, as they preferred a 'part-time' husband.

What mattered most in polygynous marriages was whether a husband could live up to the demands of such a marriage. He would need the financial means to maintain both wives and the emotional ability to treat them equally in time and attention. Another major aspect is whether he was open and trustworthy. Polygyny generally worked much better when both the first and the second wife had been informed (and sometimes consulted) in advance of the second marriage; polygynous marriages where one of the wives was held 'secret' did not last long.

More generally, the evaluation of polygynous marriages depends much on the positionality of those involved. Women entering such a marriage generally fare better if they themselves have access to material resources, a good network and legal and religious literacy. This is the case for all kinds of relationships, whether a civil marriage, an Islamic marriage or cohabitation. Polygynous marriages (not recognised as such in the Netherlands) are particularly condemned because it is Muslims who enter such marriages. Differences in the evaluation of polyamory in public debate speak for that. Yet the growing interest in polyamory may in some sense become helpful for women in polygynous arrangements. Whereas polygyny is prohibited because of its alleged harmfulness for women, the prohibition of such marriages and increased criminalisation – also because of the intersection with religious-only and migrant marriages – may cause harm. For our interlocutors, important considerations when evaluating polygyny included whether certain rules were followed, particularly equal treatment. However, also if a husband makes efforts to treat his wives equally, because of the criminalisation of polygyny, this is nearly impossible to arrange as there are no ways to provide both wives with an equal legal status. Whereas it is possible to make specific arrangements, this option is both costly and requires a high level of legal literacy. It is very unlikely that the state will make accommodations to Muslims, but discussions about whether there is a need and opportunity to provide better legal protection for all partners in a polyamorous relationship may benefit Muslim couples who opt for a polygynous life.

References

Bacchi, Carol. 2015. "The Turn to Problematization: Political Implications of Contrasting Interpretive and Poststructural Adaptations." *Open Journal of Political Science* 5 (1): 1–12.

Bertaux, Daniel. 1981. "From the Life-History Approach to the Transformation of Sociological Practice." In *Biography and Society. The Life History Approach in the Social Sciences*, edited by Daniel Bertaux, 29–45. Beverly Hills; London: Sage Publications.

Bonjour, Saskia, and Betty De Hart. 2013. "A Proper Wife, a Proper Marriage: Constructions of "Us" and "Them" in Dutch Family Migration Policy." *European Journal of Women's Studies* 20 (1): 61–76.

Bonjour, Saskia, and Albert Kraler. 2014. "Introduction: Family Migration as an Integration Issue? Policy Perspectives and Academic Insights." *Journal of Family Issues* 36 (11): 1407–32.

De Hart, Betty. 2006. "The Morality of Maria Toet: Gender, Citizenship and the Construction of the Nation-State." *Journal of Ethnic and Migration Studies* 32 (1): 49–68.

De Koning, Martijn, Oka Storms, and Edien Bartels. 2014. "Legal "Ban" on Transnational Cousin-Marriages; Citizen Debate in the Netherlands." *Transnational Social Review: A Social Work Journal* 4 (2–3): 226–41.

Dutch Civil Code. 1992.

Dutch Parliamentary Document. 2019. "34565 no. 3 (in Dutch)." Accessed November 26, 2023. https://zoek.officielebekendmakingen.nl/kst-34565-3.html.

———. 2020. "35348 no. 7 (in Dutch)." Accessed November 26, 2023. https://zoek.officielebekendmakingen.nl/kst-35348-7.html.

Femmes for Freedom. 2021. "Response to the Bill Combating Marital Captivity (in Dutch)." Accessed November 26, 2023. www.femmesforfreedom.com/files/publicaties/pdf/Internetconsultatie08082021.docx-1.pdf.

Geschiere, Peter. 2009. *The Perils of Belonging: Autochthony, Citizenship, and Exclusion in Africa and Europe*. Chicago: University of Chicago Press.

Gingrich, Andre. 2006. "Neo-Nationalism and the Reconfiguration of Europe." *Social Anthropology* 14 (2): 195–217.

Joffe, Lisa Fishbayn. 2016 "What's the Harm in Polygyny? Multicultural Toleration and Women's Experience of Plural Marriage." *Journal of Law and Religion* 31 (3): 336–53.

Liversage, Anika. 2019. "Polygyny, Wellbeing, and Ill-Being Amongst Ethnic Muslim Minorities." In *Wellbeing of Transnational Muslim Families*, 78–93. London and New York: Routledge.

Moors, Annelies. 1995. *Women, Property and Islam. Palestinian Experiences 1920–1990*. Cambridge: Cambridge University Press.

———. 2008. "Registering a Token Dower: The Multiple Meanings of a Legal Practice." In *Narratives of Truth in Islamic Law*, edited by Baudouin Dupret, Barbara Drieskens, and Annelies Moors, 85–104. London: I.B. Tauris.

———. 2013. "Unregistered Islamic Marriages: Anxieties about Sexuality and Islam." In *Applying Shari'a in the West: Facts, Fears and the Future of Islamic Rules on Family Relations in the West*, edited by Maurits Berger, 141–64. Amsterdam: Leiden University Press.

Moors, Annelies, Martijn de Koning, and Vanessa Vroon-Najem. 2018. "Secular Rule and Islamic Ethics. Engaging with Muslim-Only Marriages in the Netherlands." *Sociology of Islam* 6 (1): 274–96.

Moors, Annelies, and Vanessa Vroon-Najem. 2019. "Converts, Marriage, and the Dutch Nation-State: Contestations about Muslim Women's Well-Being." In *Wellbeing of Transnational Muslim Families. Marriage, Law and Gender, Studies in Migration and Diaspora*, edited by Marja Tiilikainen, Mulki Al-Sharmani, and Sanna Mustasaari, 22–38. Milton Park; New York: Routledge.

———. 2023. "When Islamic Marriage Travels to the Netherlands: Convert Muslim Women (Re)Signifying the Marriage Guardian and the Dower." In *Muslim Marriage and Non-Marriage: Where Religion and Politics Meet Intimate Life*, edited by Julie McBrien and Annelies Moors, 221–45. Leuven: Leuven University Press.

NCTb, Nationaal Coördinator Terrorismebestrijding. 2006. *Informele islamitische huwelijken. Het verschijnsel en de (veiligheids)risico's*. Den Haag: NCTb.

Roald, Anne Sofie. 2012. "The Conversion Process in Stages: New Muslims in the Twenty-First Century." *Islam and Christian-Muslim Relations* 23 (3): 347–62.

Roodsaz, Rahil. 2023. "(Un)Usual Suspects: Relational Capacities and Subjective Transformations in Polygynous and Polyamorous Practices in the Netherlands." *European Journal of Women's Studies* 30 (2): 181–97.

Rutten, Susanne. 2016. "Ouderschap en ouderlijk gezag bij niet-erkende islamitische huwelijken." *Justitiële Verkenningen* 16 (4): 45–57.

Sterckx, Leen, and Jaco Dagevos. 2014. *Huwelijksmigratie in Nederland. Achtergronden en leefsituatie van huwelijksmigranten*. Den Haag: SCP.

Stoler, Ann. 1992. "Sexual Affronts and Racial Frontiers: European Identities and the Cultural Politics of Exclusion in Colonial Southeast Asia." *Comparative Studies in Society and History* 34 (3): 514–51.

Van der Leun, Joanne, and Avalon Leupen. 2009. *Informele huwelijken in Nederland. Een exploratieve Studie*. Leiden: Universiteit Leiden.

Vroon-Najem, Vanessa. 2014. "Sisters in Islam. Women's Conversion and the Politics of Belonging: A Dutch Case Study." PhD diss., University of Amsterdam.

———. 2019. "Muslim Converts in the Netherlands and the Quest for a "Culture-Free" Islam." *Archives de sciences sociales des religions* 186: 33–51.

Zeitzen, Miriam Koktvedgaard. 2008. *Polygyny: A Cross Cultural Analysis*. New York: Berg Publishers.

9 Religious knowledge and legal rights

A study of nikah and secular marriage among South Asian Muslim women in England

Simran Kalra

9.1 Introduction

Within the Western context, family formation begins increasingly with cohabitation (Manning, Brown, and Payne 2021; Jónsson 2021). In countries such as England, social movements have successfully sought rights for opposite-sex couples to form legal unions that grant rights analogous to marriage, i.e., civil partnerships, thus avoiding the label of marriage, which has been condemned for its patriarchal baggage (Chan 2013, 49). This chapter explores the question of Islamic unions that are not recognised as marriage in English law but constitute religiously valid marital unions within the community. Some scholars have argued that these should be recognised by the state as a distinct category of union, with rights conferred by the nikah contract/nikah nama (Bone 2020) or alternatively be deemed void marriages (Fisher, Saleem, and Vora 2018, 557) that allow individuals to seek financial remedies under English laws. Contrasting with these legal liberalist interventions, I argue that the distinction between the two orders allows women to claim religiosity in seeking religious marriages and increases their access to Islamic rights and that women rely on the Islamic order to advance their access to secular justice and resist the patriarchal dynamics of the marriage market. Here, religiosity is seen to increase women's access to the state law and articulation of rights within the state legal framework, challenging accounts of law and religion as antithetical to each other.

I rely on Verter's theorisation of 'spiritual capital', which he developed by relying on Bourdieu's analysis of cultural capital (Verter 2003). Here, religious knowledge, practice and upbringing are seen to result in individuals' disposition, a habitus in which religion enables the reproduction of power dynamics and resistance thereto. Islam is thus not merely a means of religious salvation for women, but a means of self-identification and resistance to power dynamics within the intimate and the communal spheres and a means to change their circumstances using religious rules and artefacts.

Section 9.2 of this chapter provides an overview of the existing literature on women's rights in Islam in England and Western contexts where Islam is not

DOI: 10.4324/9781003470786-13

the state nor the majority religion. This is integrated with a critical analysis of the liberal legalism, feminism and multiculturalism that inform much of the policy reform agenda and scholarship on policy accommodation of religious practices by the state. Here, I highlight recent research that sheds light on the role of religion in protecting women's interests. Advancing that work, I urge scholars to undertake an analysis of the role of religion in advancing access to legal rights, not merely as a resource (such as access to religious leaders and religious tribunals), but as a source of spirituality that women can harness for rights invocation. This is followed by Section 9.3 on the policy debate to which the argument contributes. Here, I analyse the limitations of the literature on law reform by recognising nikah as marriage within the larger literature on multiculturalism. In Section 9.4, I provide a brief discussion on my methodology and sample, leading into a section on my research findings.

Section 9.5 explores the means and ends to which women in my sample relied upon their religion. I show that the women relied on the nikah to secure social acceptance of their relations, and to enhance their religious identity claims. Analysing this dependence on the nikah, I demonstrate that in fact, the nikah was a part of a larger religious-life project that enabled women's claims within their Islamic unions. In the second analytical sub-section, I argue that women sought to resist patriarchal power dynamics by relying on claims to religious knowledge and religious practice. Finally, I conclude the analysis by highlighting how gendered experiences of religious practice and education informed women's marital struggles.

I conclude by summarising my findings and identifying how policy interventions that focus solely on legal awareness and access to state legal apparatus are limited and need to be integrated with access to religious rights. The insights derived here are relevant for South Asian Muslim women in England, as well as Muslim-minority communities in Europe and North America, where nikah-only unions are on the rise.

9.2 Religion and women's rights

The literature on feminism and multiculturalism has debated the possibility of women's rights through religion. Okin notes that religious traditions inhibit the freedom of women and women's access to human rights and argues that in order to protect women, traditional religions should be eradicated (Okin 1999). This work has attracted criticism for its conceptualisation of non-Western religions as traditional and uncivilised and its limited understanding of these religions (Mahmood 2005; Phillips 2007; Abu-Lughod 2013). Aside from these failings, the work is also observed to be limited in its adoption of binary relations between religion and human rights. For instance, scholars such as Saba Mahmood have noted that religion has enabled women to live their lives in ways distinct from Western-secularised conceptualisations and to pursue goals that are not conceived and protected in Western liberal ordering (Mahmood 2005). Mahmood critiques Okin's work for failing to recognise that women's desires are varied and that the expectations of Western women (who are themselves not a homogeneous group) should not be universalised. This work contributes to scholarship on subjectivism and standpoint theory within feminist scholarship, which urges scholars to approach the question of women's rights from the perspective of the women in question, rather than that of the outsider researcher or the Western commentator.

Following suit from Mahmood's work and that of contemporaneous scholars such as Afshar (Afshar 1984), subsequent scholarship has observed that women's preferences and choices in pursuing religious lives and practices should be protected. Accordingly, scholars such as Akhtar have noted that women within the British Muslim community in England are increasingly turning toward their religion to organise their family life. Religiosity is perceived as a means to self-realisation (Akhtar 2018). As such, within the literature on Islamic unions in England, scholars have consistently noted the primacy attributed by women to religion for ordering family life (Shah-Kazmi 2001; Bano 2012; Parveen 2017; Akhtar 2018; Uddin 2018).

Explaining the relevance of religion to social life and life goals, Mohee notes that not only does religion offer an alternative life project, but it can also create a means of securing ends in both worlds (Mohee 2011). She argues that women within the British Muslim community resisted pressures for marriage within their family and community by arguing that Islam required them to be financially independent and capable of supporting their family alongside their husbands-to-be. They could accordingly pursue higher education instead of marrying early. Such work has challenged the assumption that religion and human rights are antithetical and that only Western cultural practices and liberal legalism can secure women's freedoms. Instead of a shift to local legal rights frameworks, individuals are seen to adopt hybrid identities (Bhabha 1994) that enable rights claims in both legal orders. In a similar vein, Uddin challenges the argument that religion acts to impede access to justice. He shows that religious leaders such as family or community imams enable women's access to the justice mechanism system, be it the Shari'a Councils or the state legal authorities (Uddin 2018). This also advances Bano's work on Shari'a Councils that noted the heterogeneity in their approaches and the possibility of justice through non-state religious tribunals when women seek to use these to their ends (Bano 2012).

Other work on religion and dispute resolution in family matters has noted the importance of religion as a source of succour. For instance, Parveen notes that faced with marital distress, women turn to their Islamic faith and seek religiously informed counselling (Parveen 2017, 230). Additionally, Shari'a Councils also adopt approaches that favour more progressive readings of Islamic texts and protect women's rights to refuse divorce-related mediation in cases of domestic abuse. Thus, here too, religion acts as a means of accessing women's rights. Qureshi's work shows us how women use their religious texts to 'speak to (their) life context(s)'(Qureshi 2016, 109). Her work notes how some women within her sample rely upon their faith to claim rights by prioritising religiosity (Qureshi 2016, 180). In addition, she notes the multifaceted identities that British Muslim women espouse: they are protective mothers before the social services, devout Muslims before the councils and use either legal order to advance their interests. Advancing this work, the chapter explores how women's religiosity and spiritual identity can advance their legal rights claims with respect to their adult-unions. To develop my claim, I now discuss the debate on recognition of Islamic unions as legal marriages.

9.3 Multiculturalism and the nikah union

In England, scholars have offered different ways of managing the regulatory diversity. Some scholars in countries such as England and the Netherlands have argued for the criminalisation of nikah-only unions (Nash 2017; Manea 2019). These arguments have found favour with a recent English parliamentary law review on the subject (Siddiqi 2018) and continue to place law and human rights as antithetical to religion. Here, multiculturalism is perceived as an ill that needs to be stamped out unless it is in line with the state legal order. Other solutions include subsuming nikah into the legal category of cohabitation, which in turn should be protected under law (Vora 2020); or classifying these as void marriages, which would enable parties to make financial claims as if they were married (Fisher, Saleem, and Vora 2018); or the statutory protection of cohabitees' rights, which in turn would protect nikah unions (Akhtar, Nash, and Probert 2020, 87). A final possible solution is treating the nikah as a new adult relationship status that is protected under the state law, which can be used to enforce the nikah contract (and to provide financial rights claims in case of dissolution) between the parties (Bone 2020).

All these solutions run contrary to radical feminist approaches that reject liberal legalism as a means of advancing women's rights. For instance, in 1984 Smart argued that women's interests are better protected outside the law, which has only reinforced women's subordinate position within the public arena and within the family (Smart 1984). In subsequent years she has suggested that feminists turn to non-law solutions and discouraged resorting to law for women's empowerment (Smart 1989). Similarly, with reference to marriage, Auchmuty has argued that a 'rejection of legal regulation has proved a better policy than appeals to its vaunted protection' (Auchmuty 2012). Instead of putting faith in the law, this scholarship argues that women must be made aware of their rights and be empowered to organise their interests privately. This position finds resonance in Akhtar, who has argued that the law should not be amended to treat nikah as marriage, as this would amount to Islamic exceptionalism and restrict Muslims from entering cohabitations while those in other religious communities are free to do so (Akhtar 2018). However, the pursuit of equality in the private arena is argued to be hollow in a social context that is patriarchal and depends on the marriage market and economic inequalities. Women's reproductive labour makes them dependent upon marital relations for financial security, a dependency that is aggravated by the labour market challenges that returning-to-work mothers face despite their formal equality in law (Blumberg 1981, 2001; Stolzenberg 2018). Thus, not surprisingly, there is a growing recognition around the world of the need to protect the rights of women in cohabiting relationships. In countries such as Scotland, these have been enshrined in statute (see Family Law [Scotland] Act 2006), whereas in neighbouring England, parties to such relations must make claims based on (a) their children's rights, (b) proving their financial contribution to the family life or (c) principles of trust law. Thus, there is merit in opting for the legal regulation of Islamic unions to protect Muslim women's rights in nikah unions.

The intervention runs another challenge: it attempts to manage multiculturalism from the top. Here, women's access to the law is conceived as monolithic. The purpose behind the way the women use the law is not queried. Such interventions thus run contrary to Mahmood's efforts to centre the diverse subjectivities of diversely situated women. While legal and Islamic feminist scholars have argued for the protection of Muslim women through recognition of their marital unions in some form through the law, such interventions should be informed by a greater understanding of the diversity within the women's interests and of how laws – religious and secular – are understood by the women in their lived contexts. Accordingly, in this chapter I demonstrate how women within British Muslim communities in England access the law. I show that women rely on their religious identity to advance their secular legal goals. Here, women not only rely on the religious norms to protect their interests but invest in developing religious identities and claiming religious knowledge to enhance their status in marital negotiations and disputes.

In this way, I attempt to go beyond the use of religion as an institutional system that offers resources such as an alternative forum for disputes or a means to secure access to lawyers. Instead, I conceptualise religiosity as capital that women can rely upon and accumulate to advance other interests. I show that apart from the state law, women rely on their religious knowledge, religious practice and piety to expand their agency and make claims in marital relations. This includes claims to marriage registration as well as the ability to exit these relations. While the law is an important means for rights-based ordering, I show that women's use of the law depends on their claim to religious identity and their understanding of religious rights. Such an examination of how women manoeuvre between the two legal orders shows that state policy prioritising legal awareness without protecting women's claims to social equality within the community is inadequate. To advance English Muslim women's claims within marital relations it is important to fortify their position within their religion and thus their community.

It should however be noted that efforts focusing on women's access to religion to protect their legal rights require women to be embedded within religious frameworks and to abide by the constraints imposed by religion. This may impose constraints different from and in addition to those experienced by men within the religion. Yet religious rights and solutions may be more suited to some who prefer working within the Islamic order: reaffirming religious membership without surrendering secular rights.

9.4 Methodology

The chapter draws on my doctoral fieldwork conducted during 2019–2020 in cities across England. It is based on 32 narrative interviews with South Asian Muslim women with Pakistani and Indian heritage from the regions of Punjab, Sindh-Gujarat and Mir Pur. A third of the participants had higher education qualifications. Participants were recruited through purposive snowballing techniques that allowed me to find participants with the required ethnic and religious backgrounds and educational qualifications. Initial forays for participant recruitment were made through imams who reached out to women whose nikah ceremonies they had helped organise or contacted families who relied on their counsel. To note, this did not imply that the women I recruited through the imams were very religious but that some members of their families relied on the imams for counsel. Participants were also recruited through local elected councillors, who shared my call for participants within their community. This technique was particularly useful in big cities.

Participant selection was independent of martial history and use of state/religious disputing forums. This kept with my focus on processes of marital negotiations instead of disputing. I examined how the participants made sense of and used state and religious laws. Notably, much research on Muslim women in England has focused on Shari'a Councils and is based on marital breakdown (Shah-Kazmi 2001; Bano 2012; Keshavjee 2013; Parveen 2017; Vora 2020). Other work that has located itself outside the councils has also focused on this aspect (Qureshi 2016; Uddin 2018). This chapter contributes to the nascent interest in the use of law and religion in the context of negotiations and social ordering (Akhtar 2013).

Unlike other work about nikah unions, in which scholars have problematised the non-use of secular law, seeking to understand what nikah means without marriage (Akhtar 2018; Vora 2020; Probert, Akhtar, and Blake 2021), I problematise both the use and non-use of either legal order in the development of intimate relations. I evidence the social meaning of marital statuses in either or both orders and the relevance of the absence of such statuses in avoiding a bias in favour of either system. As such, several participants in the study had been in nikah and/or secular marriages more than once. As a result, although there were 32 participants in the study, it was possible to examine the development and change in legal consciousness through their experiences in multiple relations of intimacy, which in total included 45 instances of marital negotiations.

The interviews were conducted in person and online to cope with the limitations of the pandemic. The median length of the interviews was 2 hours, and they were often conducted over two meetings over a few days. Participants often also allowed me to contact them subsequently. This helped me revisit the interviews and seek clarifications as my analysis developed. In two cases the marital story was developed by relying on accounts of family members. This helped me overcome barriers to accessing participants who did not wish to participate in the study because of the risk of feeling triggered. At the same time, these inputs are particularly relevant since parental involvement was key to the marriage negotiation in both these cases.

Throughout the chapter, I have maintained the anonymity of participants by changing their names and other identifiable attributes. For instance, I have only provided an approximation of their profession. During the interviews, the participants were not comfortable with voice recording. Thus, quick but copious notes were made at the time of the interview, and these were typed out on the same day to retain and reflect women's voices. This in fact turned out to be very useful as it required me to be extremely alert during the interviews, conscious of the cadence in the women's voices, their choice of words, the pauses and non-verbal communications (scoffs, snorts, laughs, sharp intakes of breath, exhales) that offered an opportunity for me to consider their words more deeply, pose questions and capture the dialectics they (and I) were mediating. The focus in this interviewing approach was to draw out women's subjectivities and learn how these influenced their legal consciousness.

9.5 Findings: the social relevance of women's religiosity

My research showed that British Muslim women garnered spiritual capital (Verter 2003) through religious practice and observing/rejecting the nikah ceremony as part of their intimate relations. Verter argues that spiritual dispositions may be regarded as a form of cultural capital (2003, 152). Individual piety within his Bourdieusian theoretical framework is a matter of taste and thus a product of social relations. Verter concludes it is 'a marker of status within struggles for domination in a variety of contexts, and that spiritual knowledge, competencies and preferences may be understood as valuable assets in the economy of symbolic goods' (2003, 152). Verter imagines spiritual capital as a 'more widely diffused commodity, governed by more complex patterns of production, distribution, exchange, and consumption' than religious capital, as conceived by Bourdieu, which is produced and accumulated within institutional contexts and is narrowly circumscribed to the field of religion (2003, 157). Religion is thus not only a means of salvation or a cultural production and consumption complex for the clergy, but it is also a means of developing and altering relationality – both socially and individually for the follower.

Verter's theory of spiritual capital helps us understand how women use religion and its objects to resist and participate in gendered power relations. By subjecting themselves to their religious ethic, participants developed pious identities claiming rights as Muslim women within religious and secular laws. The participants drew on embodied, objectified and institutionalised states of spiritual capital. They affirmed their religious upbringing (embodied state) or opted to study their religious texts and opted to wear the hijab and the Islamic dress, prioritising complete sex segregation outside the family, and rejection of music and dance, which some of them perceived as immoral, within their religious practice (objectified state). Finally, some pursued their faith with the aid of religious leaders, pirs and imams or, alternatively, participated in Muslim women's reading groups (institutionalised state).

Despite the differences in their practice, they made sense of their identities and rights claims in marital unions based on their religious practice. Through singular events such as nikah ceremonies and repeated daily rituals (*namaz* prayers), women honed their claim to an Islamic identity, which I argue advanced their access to secular law.

9.5.1 Nikah as a means to pious identity

The nikah was a means for women to perform their religiosity. Women across the sample noted the importance of the nikah for their spirituality and the progress of their relationship in their own eyes, those of the community and their faith. The ceremony abated issues of social stigmatisation and enabled women to initiate cohabiting relations within the community. Additionally, it acted as a means for women to practice piety and to situate piety within the marital relations. With their spiritual capital, religion became central to women's understanding of their relationships and marital problems.

To give an example, maintaining piety, women avoided a nikah if they sought to resist pressures for intimacy in dating relations. This is evidenced by quotes from other interviews where participants weighed the religious propriety of their actions and claimed their religiosity while living unorthodox Islamic lives, contrary to the practices espoused by some of their family.

Researcher: So, you mentioned you had relationships though you didn't marry. Did you have a nikah?

Saira: I have dated before. I was with a Pakistani man in my university. That didn't work. And later with a white man, that was very casual . . . But I know the difference (between *haram* and *halaal*). I know my limits!

Another participant explained that by undertaking a civil marriage without a nikah, she had avoided sexual relations and a hasty marriage. Within the community, a civil marriage was not considered a nikah and did not institute relationship obligations within the religion. In fact, for Humana, the civil ceremony was a means of prolonging her partner's stay in England and giving the couple a fighting chance at their relationship. The reconfiguration of the meaning of the civil marriage emerged through discussions with Humana's father and uncle, as well as the couple and the man's family. Within their understanding, nikah was a prerequisite for initiating married life. Yet the civil marriage prolonged the trial period. As for Humana, civil marriage also enabled the participant to live Islamically – that is, avoiding physical intimacy while dating. The secular law was a prop used by the couple to overcome immigration restrictions while piously dating. Additionally, Humana explained that a hasty nikah was a sin in Islam because it could lead to a divorce. It is an Islamic duty to carefully consider marriage, and parties should take their marital obligations seriously. Preferring a secular marriage without a nikah, Humana ensured that the couple avoided community pressure to marry and got to know her partner by dating before having a nikah.

In discussing the trends in marital practices within the South Asian Muslim communities in England, one participant explained that these days it is common to pursue one's own choice in partners. Scholars have observed that individuals abide by religious tenets when making their own choices (for instance by choosing a Muslim man, albeit from a different ethnicity), yet seek parental approval (Smart and Shipman 2004; Minganti 2016). In addition, Mohee (2011) notes that premarital relations were permissible when pursued with the aim of marriage. A participant explained that though Islam prohibited premarital sex, it was more likely to occur these days because of the freedom and independence afforded to younger individuals within the community and the possibility of such relations developing among couples:

> But this happens when there is an understanding that there will be a nikah. And not as one-night stands. It is a serious affair. They are planning to get married. You can't stop such things from happening – think about your own life Simran. What was it like – at that age. Would you tell your family if you had sex with your boyfriend before (marriage)? It is just unsaid. – Rabya

> No Muslim woman I know will have a *nikah* for sex. That would be an abuse of the nikah – Sabika

One participant, Azrah, began reading the Qur'ān when her relationship was deteriorating. She explained that since then it had become important to her to know and practise her religion. She explained that though she had been unable to claim rights in her first marriage because a secular legal marriage had never taken place, the Islamic ceremony continued to be important to her for reasons other than the communal validation of the relationship. For a period, she even took up the hijab to commit to her spirituality. Though she subsequently gave up the hijab, she continued to rely on Islam and desired an Islamic ceremony before initiating sexual relations.

> As a good Muslim, you need to have a *nikah.* Before we [Azrah and her new partner] had our nikah, we would meet in public places – coffee shops and diners. After my divorce, my religion was important to me. I began reading more and practising [Islam more]. I knew not to trust men easily again. I was clear, I wanted a nikah and not to sin if I was dating. – Azrah

The nikah was not just a prerequisite to sexual relations but a means to rely on religion as a touchstone in marital relations. Women's Islamic practice ensured spiritual protection and claims to morality. The women ascertained right from wrong, the permissible from the prohibited and their own identity as victims or wrong-doers within their intimate relations based on their religious rules. Religion had a significance that transcended issues of social propriety and contributed to their own self-perceptions and their worldview.

The cases discussed here along with the excerpts indicate the importance of religious rules and Islamic martial ceremony for women's identity within their relations and in their own perceptions as 'good Muslim women' who had practised sex segregation and knew the limits of sexual propriety outside marriage. Piety was thus honed through careful consideration of the religion when making decisions related to the nikah and sexual relations.

9.5.2 The importance of religiosity and religious knowledge

The women relied on more than their religious ceremonies as a means of claiming religious identity. Affirming an embodied experience of their religion through their upbringing, their knowledge of their religion – often through self-study and ostensible piety evidenced in their practice of Islamically appropriate attire, food and prayers – the participants claimed rights in the nikah and resisted obligations in the absence of the ceremony.

In my fieldwork, I noted among the participants an acute awareness of the need to affirm their spirituality within the community. This was evidenced in the interviews in numerous ways. The participants objectified their religious practice through verbal and material techniques. The women had developed a practice of making frequent references to their religion, making it a strongly visible part of their identity. This practice has in fact been noted by Mesarič (2017, 585) with reference to the Muslim community in Bosnia. Mesarič described the use of Islamic greetings and remembrance as an extension of personal religiosity and not just compliance with commonplace cultural etiquettes. Using verbal techniques, coupled with rules of sex segregation, he noted that individuals from the community converted cafés in busy, touristy areas of Bosnia into pious spaces for pursuing marriage prospects.

Similarly, within my research, I noted that by remembering God and their faith, participants not only expressed thankfulness and a desire for God's blessings; additionally, they sanctified their behaviour, claimed the propriety of their actions and thoughts and affirmed their morality. They thus created a space for religiosity within the precarious marriage market where gender power relations could work against them. They were acutely aware that their intimate and social lives were enmeshed; they needed to gain and retain equal status in the communal sphere to enjoy these in their intimate relations. Accordingly, navigating rights arrangements within intimate relations they relied on socially evident religiosity. Thus, one participant, Naman, observed how she and her partner often discussed Islam over their online and telephone dates.

> He kept a beard. Like a *hafiz* [a student of Islam]. He would talk about his religion, his faith. He would tell me that I should prioritise my son and care for him and would start reciting the Quran. He was so devoted. I felt, he will act religiously. He wouldn't be like this! – Naman

Naman explained that she talked about their lives in the context of religion. She had relied on her own religious knowledge to assess her partner and believed that if they had a dispute, they would settle it as per Islam. She believed that such conversations contributed to the establishment of a religious understanding between the couple and acted as a means to avoid a man who was abusive and restrictive, i.e., un-Islamic.

Another participant noted that it was important for her to know her religion in order to claim gender equality within social contexts. She explained that as a Muslim woman, she experienced unequal access to her religion as well as discrimination over her knowledge of her faith within the community.

> When I was growing up, . . . they bullied the culture as religion [into us]. But now I have read up. I have read the Quran and the Haddith, and I know – our religion gives us so many rights! . . . When [male] Muslim councillors challenge me, I recite the suras, and then they can see: I know. And that is a matter of pride you know. – Sabika

Gender inequality in the communal contexts was reproduced in the intimate sphere, where women experienced spiritual abuse, that is, abuse that resulted from a 'manipulation of religious texts' (Latif 2010). Here, perpetrators argued that behaviours that harmed the victims were religiously permissible and complaining about or resisting them itself constituted a sin. Some of my participants experienced this in the dismissal of their religious understandings and knowledge and the use of Islam to perpetuate sexual abuse and coercive behaviour. Such experiences were also shared by those who had attended university. The participants explained that their partners had claimed they knew Islam better and were religiously granted the right to control their wives. Women resisted inequality and abuse by relying on their pious identities and knowledge of their religion:

> Today, there is a lot more understanding (about Islam). Women know more about the religion, the internet has really changed that – anyone can learn. They know that you can divorce, remarry. You have a right to be provided for. You are protected. It's not just the man's will! – Lawyer 1

Azrah, who had started reading the Qur'ān when her relationship with her Islamic husband began deteriorating, explained that she became increasingly knowledgeable of her Islamic rights and began resisting the abuse within her relationship.

> There was this line in the Quran, that husbands and wives are supposed to be like each other's clothes. They should protect each other from indignity and ridicule. But he would himself disrespect me in public! He would call me a slag to his family. – Azrah

To rely on the theory on dispute transformation (Felstiner, Abel, and Sarat 1980), previously Azrah had felt emotionally distressed because her experiences were dismissed and denied by her husband who told her he knew her rights in Islam better. After reading up on her religion she was able to name her injury and blame her husband for being un-Islamic with her. This understanding emerged through her practice of reading up her religion and increasingly claiming her identity within it. Recognising her ex's behaviour of demanding sexual relations, calling her names, disrespecting her in social gatherings and not providing for her financially as religiously impermissible behaviours, Azrah resisted them and fought her husband, citing the Qur'ān and her religious right to respect as a spouse.

Prior to her engagement with the Qur'anic texts, Azrah was of the opinion that the secular law was not accessible to Muslim women in England, whose lives were governed by their community and their religion. Now she perceived these as acts of domestic abuse in secular law that were not permissible in Islam because they amounted to disrespect. Additionally, Azrah argued that Islam required rights in divorce under English law to be available in nikah unions. She relied on scripture to argue that Islam requires secular legal compliance (and thus nikahs should be accompanied with marriage) and that spouses treat each other with respect. To her, denying equal property in nikah amounted to disrespect to one's spouse and was un-Islamic. This case indicates how reading the two orders together helped women articulate claims that were otherwise considered inapplicable to their circumstances because of religious difference and the existence of a religious legal order.

Similarly, Sabika, who was earlier noted to have memorised Qur'anic texts to establish her knowledge of her faith as a woman within the community, also noted the importance of her religion to her intimate relations. In her marriage, her husband and in-laws had been controlling about her clothes and behaviour at home. She explained that they wanted a 'traditional' daughter-in-law who cooked, cleaned and cared for everyone. She observed,

> if that (controlling and coercive behaviours) was to happen to me now, I would think about it as a woman . . . That (sexism is) not in our religion.

9.5.3 Women's struggles for equal spiritual status in the community

Despite being aware of their Islamic rights, women still face inequality in making claims based on their religion. As Kalmbach has noted, women in many Muslim communities have not enjoyed a significant presence in mosques. This has had the effect of not only reducing their own knowledge but has also 'hampered their ability to obtain Islamic authority by building public reputations as teachers and transmitters of Islamic knowledge' (Kalmback 2012, 15).

This is evident in Sabika's effort to memorise the text. Religious knowledge had to be buttressed with religiosity and pious performance. While some participants took to wearing the hijab as a means of practising and performing their faith, others explained that they resisted external pressures to donning the hijab by vocally arguing that their religion did not require them to and relied upon their own embodied knowledge and practice and education to make such claims.

> They (the in-laws) told me to wear the hijab, so I would wear it when I visited them. Just as a show of respect. Not because I now believed that it was a required in my faith. I know my faith! I know my rights. I have been brought up to believe that your religion shouldn't be imposed on you. It should always come as a natural response. Not gonna happen. – Roshanyee

Roshanyee relied on her religious upbringing to resist the coercion to practise her religion in ways that her husband and in-laws desired. In this way, she insulated her faith from familial pressures and maintained an independent sense of what was right and wrong within her religion.

To advance their religious understanding, the women relied on online resources in addition to the Islamic texts, customs, familial practices, teachings and informal fatwas from their local imams and muftis. Through these combined resources they developed their religious practice, made life choices and justified their actions.

> Today, you can learn about Islam by just going online. Just google. There is so much out there. If you are Muslim, you can't say you don't know because you don't know where to look. You don't even need to go to a Hafiz. – Hazra

The means of accessing religious knowledge have evolved. As noted in Parveen Akhtar's work, early immigrants from Pakistan relied on their cultural knowledge of Islam from their families and hometowns. This was supplemented with religious knowledge they gained from satellite television, which aired Islamic teaching programmes (Akhtar 2014, 235). In that work, Akhtar observes that subsequent generations have had the benefit of religion education online. They have access to information from diverse sources. Additionally, through online forums, they can engage in lively debates on their religion and spirituality. This is unlike previous generations, where women depended on television shows and Arabic classes and where education on Islam was top-down and unilateral. Without access to social forums for educational discussions on Islam, women experienced it as a system of instruction from maulvis and imams on television. In contrast, the subsequent generations engage with Islam as a practice based on their reading of the texts, and multiple interpretations of these texts have emerged with the democratisation of access to the religion.

Despite growing online access to religious knowledge and the changing social context, participants observed limitations. Some explained that in their towns, mosques were accessible only to men. Women's religious practice thus took place outside the mosque and mostly at home. Samee argued for mosques to make more spaces for women so that they might enjoy equal access to the religion.

> The Mosques are not open to women! . . . They used to have specific hours when women could visit . . . so many rules . . . it is hard. We need more spaces for women for our faith to be ours! It is because we are not a part of the religion, we are not equal parts of the society.

To note, though Samee's complaints indicate that women could use the mosque during specific hours, the building had been undergoing repairs for several years, and, consequently, the management had decided to close the mosque during the visitation hours that were set aside for women. The inequality in women's access to mosques impacts Muslim women's capacity to engage with their peers on their religion, which in turn affects their ability to be seen as equal to their male counterparts in such discussions. To explain, a participant noted that women were not able to organise themselves and their interests within the community. While the men met during prayers and discussed social problems and concerns, women were mostly engaged in family chores.

> I tell the women, they must participate. Especially the young ones, but I don't think they want to. – Adaya

Adaya's comments sit in contrast to that of Samee, who urged that women didn't have enough resources allocated to them to develop their spiritual practice and social commitment to the community. Though they are able to educate themselves in Islam, there is limited communal recognition of their Islamic knowledge. For instance, female Islamic jurists remain a rarity on Shari'a council panels even though a key task for the councils is to resolve matrimonial disputes, which are predominantly raised by women (Khaleeli 2017). Additionally, research notes social resistance to the notion of a female imam (Kalmback 2012; Nyhagen 2019, 11). In this way, the importance of a male leader for the congregation is retained, even though Nyhagen notes the social permissibility of female Islamic teachers for women and children. Thus, while online forums, resources and self-education practices had enabled women's claims to rights protection within the private sphere, women still struggle to participate in the community on equals terms with men.

Consequently, women face challenges to their religious knowledge and struggle to socially validate their knowledge and practice of Islam. As noted earlier, some participants memorised religious texts by heart and recited these at will to challenge condescension by men they encountered within the community. The presumption of women's lack of religious knowledge coupled with the bias in favour of men's religious knowledge has had repercussions on women's ability to protect their rights within their intimate relations. For instance, some women claimed that it was only after significantly long experiences of abuse that they found support in their religion. Lacking a community network, women were left to their own devices.

Of my 32 participants, 17 had experienced spiritual abuse within their intimate relations, and one more participant noted that her daughter (not a part of the sample) had experienced such abuse as well. These statistics cannot be generalised to the rest of the community. However, it is relevant to note that of the 17 who had experienced such abuse, five sought to educate themselves about their religion in order to claim rights within it; another two relied on religious leaders to reinterpret their religion and ascertain the validity of their spouses' behaviour. Another six relied on their upbringing to understand their religion and their own status and rights within it. The women claimed their own interpretation of their religion, even if they faced resistance from their partners, families and in-laws, and they relied on their identities as devout women who had either studied the scripture or had grown up within its discipline and thus knew its law. Yet such claims required either that women invest in their own education on Islam or that they are brought up within a progressive understanding of the religion. Alternatively, women's adoption of subversive interpretations of Islam requires the support of religious leaders within the community. Without local community access to mosques and the organic nature of community development that was accessible to men, women's experience of their religion was more individual and isolated, denying them the resources of community knowledge and social support that were readily available to men within the community.

9.6 Legal awareness as a limited solution

This analysis indicates that though the women were able to seek rights in their intimate relations by relying on their Islamic practice, in fact they experienced difficulties accessing religious knowledge and enjoying an equal status as Muslims within the community. Not only was religious knowledge traditionally imparted according to the patriarchal, religious practices of madrasas concerning access to mosques, the madrasas' requirements on leading prayer services also favoured men. Accordingly, though the women noted the importance of learning their legal rights in marriage, they lamented the limitations they experienced accessing their religion and claiming their rights within it. The limitations they experienced were twofold. First, as previously discussed, they observed that within the community men had historically enjoyed greater access to religious texts and spaces for community building. Secondly, as a result men had an advantage to claiming a better understanding of the religion that the women. These factors were aggravated by policies that focused excessively on women's awareness of secular law without similarly incentivising women's awareness of their Islamic rights. The participants explained that not only did their religion give them rights in marriage, but also that it was through these that legal rights were accessible.

> How can you have rights in law when you don't have rights in your religion? Do you get me? – Sabika

The women prioritised the need for religious awareness, which helped them perceive their own interests through both the legal and religious orders. Accessing their legal interests in having a registered marriage or avoiding it, they could depend on their religiosity and piety, which helped them make sense of men's behaviour and preference to avoid a legal marriage. In response to such behaviour, they could rely on their religion, to make an Islamically informed choice to remain in these relations or exit them based on their partners' transgressions. Here, it was not the law but their religion that acted as a means of meaning making. Additionally, it was their religious identity, carefully curated and honed, that helped them to develop their claims and make them with the confidence of their *deen* (religious practice).

A key take-away from this analysis is that religious identities were affirmed by the women through their daily practice and operationalised to protect their interests in secular law. Legal awareness itself, independent of religious education, was important but dependent on women's understanding of their religion. Accordingly, subsequent policy and reform efforts must also focus on expanding resources for women's rights groups within the community and on mosques so that they might create additional avenues for women to participate collectively in their religion.

References

Abu-Lughod, Lila. 2013. *Do Muslim Women Need Saving?* Cambridge, MA: Harvard University Press.

Afshar, Haleh. 1984. "Muslim Women and the Burden of Ideology." *Women's Studies International Forum* 7 (4): 247–50. https://doi.org/10.1016/0277-5395(84)90049-9.

Akhtar, Parveen. 2014. "'We Were Muslims but We Didn't Know Islam': Migration, Pakistani Muslim Women and Changing Religious Practices in the UK." *Women's Studies International Forum* 47 (November): 232–38. https://doi.org/10.1016/j.wsif.2014.06.010.

Akhtar, Rajnaara C. 2013. "British Muslim and Transformative Processes of the Islamic Legal Traditions: Negotiating Law, Culture and Religion with Specific Reference to Islamic Family Law and Faith Based Alternative Dispute Resolution." PhD diss., University of Warwick. https://wrap.warwick.ac.uk/57689/1/WRAP_THESIS_Akhtar_2013.pdf.

———. 2018. "Modern Traditions in Muslim Marriage Practices, Exploring English Narratives." *Oxford Journal of Law and Religion* 7 (3): 427–54.

———. 2020. "Religious-Only Marriages and Cohabitation: Deciphering Differences Cohabitation and Religious Marriage." In *Cohabitation and Religious Marriage: Status, Similarities and Solutions*, edited by Rajnaara C. Akhtar, Patrick Nash, and Rebecca Probert. Bristol: Bristol University Press.

Akhtar, Rajnaara C., Patrick Nash, and Rebecca Probert, eds. 2020. *Cohabitation and Religious Marriage: Status, Similarities and Solutions*. Bristol: Bristol University Press.

Auchmuty, Rosemary. 2012. "Law and the Power of Feminism: How Marriage Lost Its Power to Oppress Women." *Feminist Legal Studies* 20 (2): 71–87. https://doi.org/10.1007/s10691-012-9197-6.

Bano, Samia. 2012. *Muslim Women and Shari'ah Councils: Transcending the Boundaries of Community and Law*. London: Palgrave Macmillan.

Bhabha, Homi K. 1994. *The Location of Culture*. London; New York: Routledge.

Blumberg, Grace Ganz. 1981. "Cohabitation Without Marriage: A Different Perspective." *UCLA Law Review* 28 (6): 1125–80.

———. 2001. "The Regularization of Nonmarital Cohabitation: Rights and Responsibilities in the American Welfare State." *Notre Dame Law Review* 76 (5): 1265–310.

Bone, Amra. 2020. "Islamic Marriage and Divorce in the United Kingdom: The Case for a New Paradigm." *Journal of Muslim Minority Affairs* 40 (1): 162–78.

Chan, W. 2013. "Cohabitation, Civil Partnership, Marriage and the Equal Sharing Principle." *Legal Studies*, no. 33: 46.

Family Law (Scotland) Act. 2006.

Felstiner, William L. F., Richard L. Abel, and Austin Sarat. 1980. "The Emergence and Transformation of Disputes: Naming, Blaming, Claiming . . ." *Law and Society Review* 15 (3): 631–54.

Fisher, Miranda, Shabana Saleem, and Vishal Vora. 2018. "Islamic Marriages: Given the Independent Review into the Application of Sharia Law in England and Wales, What is the Way Forward?" *Family Law (Chichester)* 48 (5): 552–57.

Jónsson, Ari Klængur. 2021. "A Nation of Bastards? Registered Cohabitation, Childbearing, and First-Marriage Formation in Iceland, 1994–2013." *European Journal of Population* 37 (1): 65–95. https://doi.org/10.1007/s10680-020-09560-2.

Kalmback, Hillary. 2012. "Introduction: Islamic Authority and the Study of Female Religious Leaders". In *Women, Leadership, and Mosques: Changes in Contemporary Islamic Authority*, edited by Masooda Bano and Hilary Kalmbach. Leiden: Brill.

Keshavjee, M. 2013. *Islam, Sharia and Alternative Dispute Resolution: Mechanisms for Legal Redress in the Muslim Community*. London: I.B. Tauris. https://doi.org/10.1093/jis/etu071.

Khaleeli, H. "Inside Britain's Sharia Councils." *The Guardian*, March 1, 2017. www.theguardian.com/law/2017/mar/01/inside-britains-sharia-councils-hardline-and-anti-women-or-a-dignified-way-to-divorce.

Latif, Zahira. 2010. "The Silencing of Women from the Pakistani Muslim Mirpuri Community in Violent Relationships." In *Honour, Violence, Women and Islam*, edited by Mohammad Mazher Idriss and Tahir Abbas. London: Routledge-Cavendish.

Mahmood, Saba. 2005. *Politics of Piety: The Islamic Revival and the Feminist Subject*. Princeton: Princeton University Press. https://doi.org/10.1017/S0020743806352361.

Manea, Elham. 2019. *Islamic Law and Human Rights Between Theory and Reality: Britain as a Showcase. Women and Shari'a Law*. I.B. Tauris. https://doi.org/10.5040/9781350989825.ch-004.

Manning, W. D., S. L. Brown, and K. K. Payne. 2021. "Does Cohabitation Compensate for Marriage Decline?" *Contexts (Berkeley, California)* 20 (2): 68–69. https://doi.org/10.1177/15365042211012076.

Mesarič, Andreja. 2017. " 'Islamic Cafés' and 'Sharia Dating:' Muslim Youth, Spaces of Sociability, and Partner Relationships in Bosnia-Herzegovina." *Nationalities Papers* 45 (4): 581–97. https://doi.org/10.1080/00905992.2017.1298579.

Minganti, Pia Karlsson. 2016. "Introducing 'Fourth Space': Young Muslims Negotiating Marriage in Europe." *Ethnologia Europaea* 46 (1): 40–57. https://doi.org/10.16995/ee.1176.

Mohee, Samia. 2011. *Young British South Asian Muslim Women: Identities and Marriage*. London: Centre for Intercultural Studies, University College London.

Nash, Patrick S. 2017. "Sharia in England: The Marriage Law Solution." *Oxford Journal of Law and Religion* 6 (3): 523–43. https://doi.org/10.1093/ojlr/rwx052.

Nyhagen, Line. 2019. "Mosques as Gendered Spaces: The Complexity of Women's Compliance with, and Resistance to, Dominant Gender Norms, And the Importance of Male Allies." *Religions* 10 (5): 321. https://doi.org/10.3390/rel10050321.

Okin, Susan Moller. 1999. *Is Multiculturalism Bad for Women*. Edited by Joshua Cohen, Mathew Howard, and Martha C. Nussbaum. Princeton, NJ: Princeton University Press.

Parveen, Rehana. 2017. "Do Shari'a Councils Meet the Needs of Muslim Women." Birmingham: University of Birmingham.

Phillips, Anne. 2007 *Multiculturalism without Culture*. Princeton: Princeton University Press.

Probert, Rebecca, Rajnaara Akhtar, and Sharon Blake. 2021. "When is a Wedding Not a Marriage? Exploring Non-Legally Binding Ceremonies." Briefing Paper for the Law Commission, Nuffield Foundation.

Qureshi, Kaveri. 2016. *Marital Breakdown among British Asians*. Oxford: Palgrave Macmillan.

Shah-Kazmi, Sonia Nurin. 2001. *Untying the Knot: Muslim Women, Divorce and the Shariah*. London: Nuffield Foundation.

Siddiqi, Mona. 2018. *The Independent Review into the Application of Sharia Law in England and Wales*. London, UK: The Home Office.

Smart, Carol. 1984. *The Ties That Bind: Law, Marriage and the Reproduction of Patriarchal Relations*. NY: Routledge.

———. 1989. *Feminism and the Power of Law*. London: Routledge.

Smart, Carol, and Beccy Shipman. 2004. "Visions in Monochrome: Families, Marriage and the Individualisation Thesis." *The British Journal of Sociology* 55 (4): 491–509.

Stolzenberg, Emily J. 2018. "The New Family Freedom." *Boston College Law Review* 59 (6): 1983–2053.

Uddin, Islam. 2018 "Nikah-Only Marriages: Causes, Motivations, and Their Impact on Dispute Resolution and Islamic Divorce Proceedings in England and Wales." *Oxford Journal of Law and Religion* 7 (3): 401–26. https://doi.org/10.1093/ojlr/rwy051.

Verter, Bradford. 2003. "Spiritual Capital: Theorizing Religion with Bourdieu Against Bourdieu." *Sociological Theory* 21 (2): 150–74. https://doi.org/10.1111/1467-9558.00182.

Vora, Vishal. 2020. "The Continuing Muslim Marriage Conundrum: The Law of England and Wales on Religious Marriage and Non-Marriage in the United Kingdom." *Journal of Muslim Minority Affairs* 40 (1): 148–62. https://doi.org/10.1080/13602004.2020.1744839.

10 'Love' versus 'convenience'

Muslim-Christian couples before the Ceutan marriage registry

Ibtisam Sadegh

10.1 Introduction

'It wasn't very common, but it was relatively accepted that a Legionnaire would meet a girl from Morocco and marry her,' said Eduardo. Having spent most of his childhood in Western Sahara and then relocating from one Spanish colony to another, Eduardo, the son of a Spanish military family, found it 'only natural' to join the Spanish Legion and follow the footsteps of his older brother, father and grandfather. 'I was only 20 years old,' he bragged as he showed me photos of a younger version of himself, with a sage-green shirt open at the top, exposing his bare, hairy chest. In 1987, after several years of service in the Canary Islands, the Spanish Legion relocated Eduardo to its Ceutan bases. During that year, Spain enacted stricter border controls with Morocco in an effort to regulate its population to meet the European Union's (EU) accession demands. It was in Ceuta that Eduardo met his wife, Leila, a Moroccan divorcee and single mother of two young children, who worked day-in, day-out waitressing in a Ceutan café to financially support her mother and daughters, who lived over an hour's drive away on the Moroccan side of the border. Eventually, their conversations grew longer and more personal, and the two started meeting outside the confines of the café.

Eduardo used his military connections to obtain permission for Leila to travel with him to Granada to meet his family in mainland Spain. Unlike today, military personnel were, at that time, prohibited from crossing the Moroccan-Ceutan border as regular civilians, but this did not discourage Eduardo from covertly making his way to Tangier to meet Leila's mother and daughters, risking hefty consequences. The couple lived in constant fear of being separated. In order to be allowed to work in Ceuta, Leila had a Spanish work visa that needed to be renewed periodically. The renewal process was lengthy, bureaucratic and complex. 'Therefore, the solution was to get married,' explained Eduardo. 'Being married to a Spaniard, they gave her residency rights.' Once married, the couple had a baby, adding another member to the large household that already included Leila's daughters from her previous marriage.

DOI: 10.4324/9781003470786-14

'Let's say that those of my time are the last romantics!' exclaimed Eduardo with a smile stretching from ear to ear.

> In the sense that in the history of the Legion there were many mixed marriages, but today you don't see this anymore. At the time it was quite like the recurring tale of – to put it in colloquial words – 'The Legionnaire and the Moor,'

expanded Eduardo, referencing a well-known Spanish song about a Legionnaire who falls in love with a Moroccan woman in a brothel in Casablanca. Ironically, the Legionnaire, consumed by jealous anger, ends up killing the woman after he finds her in a cabaret. Today, however, the transnational interreligious marriages that in the past were framed as representations of romantic love for the very fact that they cut across socio-religious and political boundaries are for the very same reason described as marriages of convenience; that is, sham marriages where it is assumed the sole purpose of the Moroccan partner is to obtain residency and citizenship rights.

Drawing on 14 months of anthropological fieldwork between 2015 and 2016 in the Ceutan enclave, this chapter offers an ethnographic account of Muslim-Christian intimacies in a border space where interreligious encounters reflect and are shaped by the relationships between the parties' respective religious communities.[1] Despite Morocco's repeated irredentist demands, Ceuta is one of two populated enclaves located on the Northern Moroccan coast that remain under Spanish rule. The enclave's complicated geopolitical context, its minute size and dense population make the enclave a zone of intense confrontation but also a place of peaceful coexistence between Muslim, Christian, Hindu and Jewish Ceutans as well as Moroccans and Peninsulars (Spaniards from mainland Spain) who have made the enclave their home.

In this chapter, I focus on the trajectories and courtship narratives provided by Muslim-Christian transnational couples to highlight the discourse that frames these marriages as a 'love' marriage or a marriage of 'convenience.'[2] The residents of Ceuta reproduce a politically extolled discourse of '*convivencia*,' which accentuates the enclave's peaceful multicultural society. This pervasive discourse serves both as a medium for the political management of diversity as well as a template for imagining the enclave's idealised future. Within this discourse, interreligious couples are celebrated as the ultimate symbols of Ceuta's multicultural success (Sadegh 2023). Further investigation, however,

1 This research forms part of the European Research Council's project 'Problematizing Muslim Marriages: Contestations and Ambiguities' hosted at the University of Amsterdam (ERC Project 2013-AdG-324180).

2 My focus is on Muslim-Christian couples because Christians and Muslims are by far the largest religious groups. Sephardic Jews and Sindhi Hindus together account for less than 1.5% of the enclave's residents.

reveals that many interreligious couples residing in the enclave are Moroccan-Peninsular spouses with none of the spouses identifying as Ceutan. Often these couples compromise on living in Ceuta for work purposes or due to its geographical location, believing the premise that Ceuta is an idyllic place that bridges Europe and Africa and their interreligious backgrounds. Once in Ceuta however, these couples learn that Ceutans problematise their marriages as marriages of convenience.

The transformation of the discourse about transnational interreligious marriages introduced in the introductory vignette – no longer presenting these mixed marriages as quintessential love marriages but as marriages of convenience – is linked to the bordering process following Spain's EU accession. As a consequence of the re-bordering process (Suárez-Navaz 2004) by which Ceuta became the EU's external southern border, Spain increased its border controls, and Ceuta grew into its imagined role of gatekeeper to Fortress Europe (Rumford 2006). It is against this backdrop, and the growing suspicions that non-European migrants are duplicitous interlopers, that the motivations of interreligious transnational spouses and marriages are evaluated. By exploring transnational interreligious couples' narratives of courtship and marriage, I highlight how and by who these mixed couples are problematised, and how these couples themselves evaluate, challenge and reproduce the problematisation of their relationships. I explore transnational interreligious couples' attempts to navigate the additional legal and socio-political challenges that they face and their responses to the shifting discourse. In so doing, I investigate the tactics employed by the Ceutan marriage registrar to determine which marriages are to be considered authentic, love marriages and which are of convenience and demonstrate that the indicators employed by state actors about what is a legitimate intimacy and a good reason to marry reflect Ceutans' perceptions of what marriages and partner choices are considered desirable. Additionally, I show how the legalistic language of 'marriage of convenience' is vernacularised at the grassroots to not only mean marriages for the sole purpose of Spanish documentation and citizenship, but as an opposition to 'marriages of love.'

10.2 Research orientation and clarifications

This chapter heavily relies on participant observation during fieldwork in Ceuta and multiple semi-structured interviews conducted with 22 transnational interreligious couples. Inspired by Bertaux (1981), these interviews focused on the couples' topical life stories. I posed questions on their courtship experiences, marriage choices and expectations, as well as more generally on their lives in Ceuta. Apart from three couples – Belgian-Moroccan, Dutch-Moroccan and Irish-Moroccan – all the transnational interreligious couples were Moroccan-Spanish, and only two of these couples involved a Ceutan as the Spanish partner. With one exception, all the Moroccan-Spanish couples consisted of the wife identifying as Muslim and the husband as Christian when first meeting. As opposed to the academic literature on interreligious couples involving Muslims that suggests most interreligious couples involving Muslims are marriages between Muslim men and non-Muslim wives, most of the interreligious couples in Ceuta involve Muslim women marrying non-Muslim men. This stands out when the significantly larger presence of Moroccan wives and Peninsular men is juxtaposed with the smaller number of transnational interreligious relationships involving Ceutans. This reveals significant intersections between religion, gender and nationality. Notwithstanding *convivencia* discourse, interreligious intimacies are problematised, and Ceutans who marry outside their religious group prefer to marry other Ceutans or, at most, Spaniards from the peninsula, instead of Moroccans.

In line with Connolly (2009), I started my research at the micro-level, focusing on the agency and narratives of these interreligious couples; however, the study of discourses, collective identities and public debates was likewise important to fully contextualise the research (Bracke and Fadil 2012). I therefore also interviewed local scholars, religious community leaders and the Ceutan marriage registrar and had many informal conversations with Ceuta's residents from different backgrounds. In interviewing the marriage registrar, I investigate the involvement of the state in the most intimate affairs. The aim is not to assess the fairness of the bureaucratic process of marriage but to shed light on possible systemic discrepancies and distortions which reflect the pressure that the Ceutan marriage registrar is under to act as the gatekeeper to Europe. Similar to Graeber (2012), I am interested in the couples' and the marriage registrar's narratives to reveal what 'interpretative logic' both actors have developed as they try to make sense of the Ceutan marriage process and the discourses that celebrate interreligious marriages as an example of *convivencia*, while problematising others as marriages of convenience.

10.3 Marriage migration, or migration and marriage?

In the 1980s, a decade after General Francisco Franco's death, Spain's bid to enter the EU required a revision of Spain's border policy and regularisation of its residents, particularly in its North African territories. To satisfy the EU-membership requirements, Spain started replacing the previous temporary markers identifying its border with Morocco with more permanent fixtures, and the previously undocumented Muslim residents were granted Spanish citizenship upon proving 10 years of residency (Moffette 2010). Spain's accession to the EU in 1986 was unquestionably a major event in the history of Ceuta as the Spanish-Moroccan border acquired a dual geopolitical significance by which it also became EU's external border with Morocco.

Following the granting of autonomous status in 1995, the Ceutan public sector significantly expanded to allow the municipal government the exercise of its newfound powers and to redress the decline in trade-related jobs. Today, the public sector employs roughly half of the enclave's working population. These *funcionario* positions are greatly sought after as they are lifetime appointed civil servants with significant wages. In Ceuta, *funcionarios* additionally receive exceptional wage bonuses, generous tax-breaks and attractive pension plans, making Ceuta the crème de la crème platform for these functionaries. This has resulted in many Peninsulars migrating from mainland Spain to Ceuta after succeeding in locking various functionary positions ranging from Ceuta's townhall to its prison, including teachers, police officers and prison guards, among many other positions, and some end up settling, marrying, raising children and making Ceuta their home.

In marked contrast to the earlier interreligious marriages involving military men, from the 2000s onwards many interreligious marriages involve Moroccan women who married Peninsular men holding various *funcionario* positions. This reflects migration patterns in which the Peninsular male partner would originally have moved to Ceuta or Morocco for the military or Spanish Legion, while in recent decades this has been for functionary positions. Many of these latter couples, however, found it strikingly difficult to consider Ceuta as their permanent home.

Fatima and her Peninsular husband Antonio met in her hometown in Western Sahara when Antonio was there as a *funcionario* for a teaching position in the Spanish school that had first opened during Spanish colonial rule. Once married, they resided in Casablanca before resettling in Ceuta. The couple thought the enclave would be the perfect environment to start a family that would combine their mixed backgrounds, but both spouses were disheartened to learn that Ceuta was not really what they had imagined it to be. 'They think badly of us [Moroccans]. I think it's because they think all female Moors, especially those coming from Morocco married to older man, are bad girls, between inverted commas, whores!' Her husband, Antonio, comforting his wife, explains:

> The problem is that there are marriages of convenience . . . Moroccan women marrying Spaniards, just to have 'los papeles'. There are many people who do that and of course, they think, a young Moroccan girl with an older Spanish man like me, maybe it's a fake marriage.

While emphasising that they are an exception, Antonio reproduces the problematisation of couples who like them are transnational and have a large age gap. The couple nostalgically remember their time in Morocco where they had many friends, including other mixed couples like themselves who would regularly invite them to their homes and social events. In comparison they had no close Ceutan friends and found it difficult to fit in as they felt both Muslim and Christian Ceutans were prejudiced against them and their relationship. They had expectations of Ceuta being an intermediary place that could intertwine their two backgrounds. Similarly, 'I thought Ceuta is better so that she can remain somewhat closer to her [Moroccan] family, while still being in Spain,' said Miguel about his and his Moroccan wife's decision to move to Ceuta. But his wife ultimately disliked Ceuta because she felt that she was constantly treated as a second-class resident there and reminded her that while she is Moroccan, Ceuta is Spanish.

Anthropologists' interest in transnational families has intensified since the 1990s, when several anthropological texts re-conceptualised research on migration and introduced the concept of 'transnationalism' (Schiller, Nina Glick, Linda Basch, and Cristina Blanc-Szanton 1992; Vertovec and Cohen 1999; Basch, Schiller, and Blanc 2005), which impacted the study of migrant communities as well as migrant families (Hajdinjak, Nazarska, and Tosheva-Hajdinjak 2011). Marriage and movement have long been intertwined. The association between them has been documented across both space and time (Brettell 2017). Globalisation processes have often resulted in substantially longer distances being covered in order to create such families; yet transnational unions and marriage migration are not novel developments, albeit occurring with ever-increasing frequency (Charsley 2013). Anthropologists have studied the impacts of both immigration and emigration on the marriage market and matrimonial practices; however, migration research remains mostly focused on labour mobility (Constable 2009; Kaur 2012; Brettell 2018), which in the literature appears to be prioritised over marriage-motivated mobility, and this even though immigration policies often revolve around family formation and reunification. The trajectories of the transnational couples residing in Ceuta connect labour and marriage migration. The process of migration of Peninsular and Moroccan partners often starts prior to and without the explicit intention of marrying, yet it is not completely separate from the idea of starting afresh, seeking a partner and forming a new family.

'There are many circumstantial marriages,' explains the Ceutan marriage registrar when questioned about the occurrence of transnational marriages in Ceuta that are also religiously-mixed. He explains:

> As you know, Ceuta is a city of civil servants. There are many funcionarios . . . Therefore, maybe divorced people come here, and with the extra money they make, [they] have a better quality of life, they can maintain their family there [in mainland Spain] and start a new one here [in Ceuta] with a Moroccan citizen.

The trajectories presented by my interlocutors show that some transnational interreligious couples met and married elsewhere before moving as a married couple to Ceuta, while others moved to Ceuta separately before meeting, courting and subsequently marrying. This resonates with the research of Esteve and Bueno (2012), who found that a considerable proportion of immigrants have no partner when migrating to Spain, and therefore the probability of them subsequently finding one in the host society becomes very high.

Many transnational partners either have a large age gap or met when they were relatively older. The age difference between Antonio and Fatima is more than 30 years, while between Miguel and Lubna there is an age gap of 20 years. Both Miguel and Antonio had been married and divorced in mainland Spain before applying for *funcionario* positions in Africa. Moreover, there is a discernible social class difference between the spouses. All these factors are weaponised by Ceutans in order to disparage such marriages as scams. Although there are many Muslim-Ceutans married to Moroccan partners in Ceuta with large age gaps and social class differences, the differences between these Muslim spouses do not draw the same degree of attention as those between transnational partners who are also interreligious. Muslim marriages characterised by large age or class gaps between the spouses are not understood in terms of the same interpretative paradigms as those applied to interreligious transnational couples. While there are many cross-border marriages in Ceuta that are not interreligious, it is couples who, in addition to being transnational, have different religious backgrounds that are generally problematised as having marriages of convenience. The interreligious factor is therefore viewed as a greater indicator of this effect.

Furthermore, despite not featuring in the discursively evoked 'older Spanish functionary' and 'younger Moroccan wife' marriage of convenience, there are other transnational interreligious couples residing in Ceuta that do not involve a Spanish spouse, such as Moroccan men married to non-Spanish Europeans. These couples remain largely ignored in the local discourse that primarily problematises marriages involving Moroccan women. In the Ceutan geopolitical context, marriages that involve one Spanish and one Moroccan partner are considered the least desirable types of relationships. From this standpoint, if a Ceutan were to enter an interreligious intimate relationship, it would preferably be with another Ceutan from another religious community. In the local discourse that problematises Moroccan-Peninsular marriages as marriages of convenience, Ceutans portray Moroccan women in transnational interreligious marriages as opportunistic, fraudulent, seductive and often young and poor, while the Spanish men that marry them are framed as naïvely and foolishly in love.

10.4 Navigating legality

The requirements for transnational marriages may vary depending on the location where the marriage takes place. However, if the couple desires to be recognised by their home countries as married spouses, the marriage requirements are also subject to the laws established by their respective countries. The Spanish legal system has, over time, imposed stricter controls over marriages concluded between Spanish nationals and foreigners, even when such marriages are celebrated outside Spain.

In January 1995, the Spanish General Directorate of Registries and Notaries issued legal instructions urging intensive verifications by marriage registries prior to allowing the celebration of marriages in Spain in circumstances when one of the parties is foreign (Boletín Oficial del Estado 1995, 2316–17). According to these instructions, the partners must undergo separate and confidential interrogations to ascertain the existence of true matrimonial consent by both parties. In so doing, the interrogator could ask questions about the intentions of the spouses to live together and have children, and how they manage their cohabitation, among others.

By the late 1990s, Spain, following the EU's lead, grew ever more concerned about so-called marriages of convenience. In December 1997, in an attempt to deal with this phenomenon, the EU outlined a set of measures to be adopted to combat marriages of convenience, in which the latter were defined as marriages involving a third-country national with the sole aim of circumventing the rules on entry and residence in the EU (Council of the European Union 1997). The EU resolution identified some factors that could allow a marriage to be presumed to be fraudulent. These included, inter alia, cases where the spouses could not have met before the marriage, did not share a common life or language, were unaware of their respective partner's personal and professional details and where the circumstances in which the couple met seemed suspicious or where monetary payments had been made towards the marriage, with the exception of dowry in cases involving third-country nationals where this is a normal practice in their country (Council of the European Union 1997, Art. 2).

Pursuant to this EU resolution, the Spanish Prosecutor's office issued a notice on 'marriages of convenience,' defining it as marriages celebrated with the sole purpose of regularising the situation in Spain of one of the contracting parties (Fiscalía General del Estado 2002), and the Spanish marriage registrar was established as the competent authority to decide on the validity of the celebration or registration of a marriage. Throughout the late 1990s, the Spanish General Directorate of Registries and Notaries demanded better investigations and referred to specific cases and indications that could prove the existence of a 'complacent marriage,' including discrepancies between the partners' statements about their courtship, such as where and when they had met or the superficiality of the relationship as deduced from the couples' statements during their separate interviews. The irregular legal situation of the foreign spouse as well as a notable age difference between the partners were also mentioned.

By January 2006, further instructions and protocols were issued to provide criteria on the basis of which to assess marriages involving Spaniards (Boletín Oficial del Estado 2006, 6330–38). These protocols established that 'complacent marriages' are frequently celebrated in exchange for a price and that the Spanish partner agrees to marry the foreign partner on the condition that there will never be a 'genuine cohabitation' or the 'will to found and form a family.' Instead, after an agreed term, the parties will legally separate or divorce. The marriage registrar was entrusted with the role of deciding which partners' intimacies are authentic. With the aim of preventing marriages of convenience, the certificate establishing the couples' legal capacity to marry – the '*certificado de capacidad matrimonial*' that was first introduced in 1993 as mandatory only for Spanish couples who wished to obtain legal recognition for their Spanish Muslim, Jewish or Protestant marriage ceremonies[3] – was extended to transnational couples involving a Spanish partner, even when marrying outside

3 In 2015, this was also extended to marriages celebrated by religious communities recognised as having 'well-known roots' in Spain.

of Spain. Therefore, these protocols, still applicable in the present day, compel couples to obtain this certificate, even when marrying abroad, should they wish to later register their marriage in Spain for legal recognition; to obtain it, a transnational couple must undergo these investigations by the Spanish marriage registrar.

While the name of the certificate suggests it should be issued to anyone who satisfies the requirements of legal capacity to marry, that is, that the parties are not already in a legally binding marriage and have the mental capacity to consent and are of marriage age, in practice the certificate became a means for the Spanish state to exercise a broad discretionary power of allowing or restricting marriages with non-Spaniards. In fact, the marriage registrar may refuse to issue this certificate if there is any suspicion of a sham marriage, regardless of whether the criteria of validity stated in the protocols appear to have been satisfied. The process of implementing these laws and policies appears to give rise to discriminatory recognition depending on the nationality of the person whom the Spanish partner intends to marry. I argue that the development and implementation of these procedures for warding off marriages of convenience fuelled the change in the way interreligious transnational marriages were perceived from being lauded as representing the ultimate love matches to being heavily problematised as sham marriages for the non-European partner to obtain residency papers.

10.5 The accounts of transnational spouses: 'love' versus 'convenience'

'I got a heart attack because I still didn't know her,' Antonio explained to me, justifying his surprise and hesitancy when Fatima proposed marriage on their first romantic weekend together.

> I knew that in a month, without knowing each other, Moroccans got married. They might only know each other from sight, or through their families, without any intimacy when they marry. Yet, when she told me 'let's get married' I don't know, I was still surprised,

he explained. 'Well, I knew him already and I really liked him,' defended Fatima, well aware by then that Spaniards consider short courtships and lack of knowledge about each other as indicative of a sham marriage.

> If I were a Spanish or European woman, who could live with him, and cohabit, maybe I wouldn't have cared as much, but of course, I can't [cohabit]. Because of the [Moroccan] police, because of my family, because of everything, I just couldn't,

justified Fatima, giving various social and legal reasons why she wanted to marry Antonio as fast as possible. It was only when we were alone that she disclosed that she also had religion at the back of her mind and that marrying him was the only way for her to leave her family and start living with him. Many Moroccan female interlocutors shared similar concerns.

Many female Moroccan interlocutors, who were living with, or in close proximity to, their families when they courted their partners, held that formalising their interreligious courtships through marriage was important to them because it meant their families were acknowledging their right to marry. Drissia claimed that every woman wants to marry before having children: 'I wanted to become a mother, but also to have my own life,' she said. Among the many religious and social considerations that are advanced, transnational interreligious couples often adduce certain legal considerations for why they aspired to marry their partners. Samira explained,

> It was his idea to marry, since we were here [in Ceuta], and I was without any papers. I didn't have a residence permit and he saw that we always had problems going to the doctor. So, he realised this and said, 'Well, we must marry' and so we did. Basically, the government almost forced us to get married and I don't regret it. [It was a case of] either he came to Morocco, or we marry here. We married to be together.

The residence permit acquired by the non-Spanish partner, allowing regular residency in Ceuta, is an important consequence of marriage for transnational couples and a sufficient motivation for these couples to marry as it facilitates their ongoing intimate relationship. Most couples, however, were very hesitant in explaining that they were also interested in getting married to overcome immigration hurdles. Afraid of how they will be perceived, some Moroccan interlocutors, like Samira, emphasised that they only got married because their Spanish partners proposed to them. Contrastingly, Spanish partners were more open about this but always explained that this was never their only motivation. 'Apart from the fact that we loved each other, marrying was the solution for the situation that we were in,' said Ernesto.

> Because there was always the risk that she would one day go to renew her visa in Morocco and they wouldn't let her return [to Ceuta], and so we got married, and since she was married to me, a Spaniard, they allowed her to become a resident,

he explained, emphasising that both 'love' ***and*** practical considerations about his wife's immigration status contributed to their decision to marry as quickly as possible.

The story of Miriam and Sergio similarly highlighted the intertwining of love and practical considerations, such as security, for their reason to marry. 'It seemed truly like in a movie. We were in a café. She was looking at me, I was looking at her, and it was special,' recounted Sergio, a Peninsular, about his first meeting with Miriam, from Morocco. 'We both stayed looking at each other. I was impressed by how beautiful she was, and she was also fixating on me,' said Sergio timidly. The couple recounted a series of misfortunes and the severe hardships they had suffered before meeting one another. In the mid-2000s, when Sergio was 34, he moved to Ceuta to work as a *funcionario*, but he became very lonely because 'Ceutans don't like to mix.' Miriam was a single mother making a bare living by buying second-hand clothes from Ceuta and selling them across the border in Moroccan street markets. When I spoke to them, they had been raising their three daughters in Ceuta. Sergio gave Miriam security. 'A woman is attracted to a man that can give her security,' he claimed, and Miriam, sitting beside him, agreed. 'It's not about being Muslim or Christian, about having money or not. It's just normal. A biological thing. Undeniable. A woman needs security more than a man,' said Sergio.

The interactions of gender, marriage and migration are the subject of a burgeoning scholarly literature (Palriwala and Uberoi 2008; Williams 2010), demonstrating that gender, while often underestimated, is an important key to understanding migration. My interlocutors' individual and marital aspirations reveal a common trend that reflects the intersection between gender and class mobility. The spouses' marital aspirations and what they seek in their partners form part and parcel of their life goals. The exchange of a family environment for security (financial, legal and the provision of a safe residential environment in which to raise children) has often been the implicit trade-off between transnational interreligious spouses.

> A man, and also a woman, by nature cannot live alone . . . They are made to live together. And when a man is alone in a city, like what happened to me, he always looks for a partner,

conceded Miguel. 'I don't know how to stay alone,' Jorge put simply, explaining why he sought the company of a Moroccan domestic worker, who ended up being his wife. 'I always need a woman's company,' he concluded resignedly.

10.6 Marrying in Spain and the role of the marriage registrar

Soukaina met Juan in 2010 in the small Ceutan café where she was waitressing. 'He used to come everyday to buy a coffee. He didn't even like coffee, but he would still come and buy coffee just so that he would give me some tips,' chuckled Soukaina. Coming from a neighbouring Moroccan city, she worked in Ceuta irregularly and would often sleep there overnight, despite not having residency papers. Her father died when she was young, and her mother raised her and her siblings in poverty, but by her mid-teens, Soukaina was already doing everything possible to financially support her mother. When she met Juan, Soukaina was 22 and heartbroken after the breakup of a previous failed romantic relationship with a Spanish policeman her age. When we were alone, she confided in me that she had never really stopped loving her previous partner even if he had hurt her and would regularly use his police networks to arrest her and prohibit her from entering the enclave. Juan, on the other hand, was twice her age and good to her. He went to the café until 'a relationship was born,' explained Juan. Soukaina explained,

> [We were] friends for a while, and then he fell in love with me, and I liked him, in inverted commas. We started going out, and I got accustomed to him. He cared a lot for me. He was always there for me and so one day we decided to marry.

Soukaina admitted that it was she who first proposed marriage; 'I wanted to marry because I didn't want to lose time. I wanted stability,' she said. As her life teetered on the brink of illegality, Soukaina would often mention that her desire to marry was based on her need for stability: 'He was in love with me, and I wanted stability,' she said. 'I always wanted a son, but I always wanted one in [the context of] stability,' she added on a separate occasion. About a year after their first meeting, Soukaina and Juan started preparing all the required documents to marry.

> To get married isn't as easy as before. Before, a couple could meet and get married, but not anymore. Now, there are more investigations. There are interviews. They have a long process to know if a marriage is real or a lie and it takes at least a year,

explained Soukaina. 'Now if you have an age difference, they'll already reject the marriage, saying it's a marriage of convenience or for money.' The couple were interviewed separately as well as jointly by the Spanish authorities. 'They asked me about him. What he likes and what not, about his character, because if we're supposed to be a couple, I should know what he likes and what he doesn't,' she said.

The couple explained that due to their large age difference, they were under more scrutiny about whether their proposed union was a marriage of convenience. The fact that Soukaina spoke Spanish fluently helped, she said: 'They realised that I could speak Castilian, and therefore we have a means of communicating. The problem is those couples that speak different languages and have no clue what the other is saying.' Nonetheless, the couple's first attempt to marry was refused. 'My application was rejected at first, although I know him very well and he knows me very well,' revealed Soukaina once I got to know her more. A year later, when Soukaina became pregnant, the couple reapplied to marry, and this time their application was accepted. Soukaina recalled how in the second application, she went to her interview with the marriage registrar holding printed baby ultrasound images to show proof of their romantic relationship to the authorities.

The marriage registrar's prolonged delays in processing marriage applications is in itself a strategy to determine whether couples are genuine in their desire to marry. Those applicants that fail the test of time are not deemed worthy of marrying one another. According to the same logic, not abandoning the relationship when a marriage application is initially rejected is believed to demonstrate the couple's authenticity. Soukaina is not the only interlocutor whose application for a marriage permit was initially refused and subsequently granted once pregnant. As opposed to the stereotypical intimacy-free 'marriage of convenience,' pregnancy is a clear indication of a sexual, intimate relationship.

'Preparing the documents was very difficult. Such a headache. It was horrible . . .' complained Rocio, the only female Peninsular interlocutor married to a Moroccan man.

> During the interview, I was still pregnant. They caused so many problems and requested so many documents. In the end, they only gave us permission to marry because at that moment I was pregnant. It's because they try to avoid couples marrying for convenience,

she justified. Rocio explained that she and her husband had to overcome various hurdles imposed by the Spanish authorities as well as misinformation from Moroccan ones about where to get the required documents, such as proof that her Moroccan husband was not already married. By the date of their civil marriage, several months after their interview with the Spanish authorities, Rocio had miscarried, but by then their permit to marry had been issued and marriage permits are generally never revoked.

Moroccan-Spanish couples who had strong links to Ceuta often repeated the same *convivencia* discourse as Ceutan interreligious couples. They insisted on the importance of celebrating a civil marriage as a compromise, as a secular option that respected their religious differences. Samira was only 18 years old when she met Rubén, who is 10 years older. Samira moved to Ceuta from Morocco with her mother in her early teens after her mother married a Ceutan man. However, domestic violence in the marriage led to a difficult time, and they ended up in a Ceutan shelter. When Samira turned 18, she was left undocumented as she was no longer considered her mother's dependant. When their time at the shelter was about to expire, Rubén, who had only known Samira for a few months, offered to help rent an apartment so they could all live together. Samira was living at the margins of the law, encountering continuous problems accessing the healthcare system and regular employment, so the couple decided to marry. It was obvious to them that they would celebrate a civil marriage; 'It was more of a midway point [between the two religions],' she said. It took the couple 8 months to prepare all the documents to marry in Ceuta. As she was not a regular resident in Ceuta, for the purpose of marriage, Samira had to return to Morocco to have an interview in Tetuán with the Spanish Consulate, whereas Rubén was interviewed by the Ceutan marriage registrar.

10.7 The moral gatekeepers of Ceuta: judging couples' intimacy, safeguarding the nation

In Europe, marriages of convenience have become central to political debates about migration policy and under the assumption that they are widespread, many countries have taken various legal measures to prevent migration on this basis (De Hart 2015; Williams 2010; Eggebø 2013; Maskens 2015). As a result, the process of marriage registration for transnational couples involving a non-European migrant has transformed from being a celebration of a civil matter into a state security interrogation. The state actors that evaluate and determine the authenticity of the migrants' narratives start from the perspective that migration is a growing problem and tantamount to an invasive plague which must be stopped in its tracks before it engulfs Europe (Kagné 2000). The fight against marriages of convenience has thus become an effort to restrain migratory flows. Moreover, my interlocutors' narratives show that the political measures and arguments made to prevent marriage migration and marriages of convenience are also having a strong impact on 'genuine couples' and how they represent their relationships to possible critics.

From the perspective of civil law, the mandatory requirement that the certificate be issued establishing a couple's legal capacity to marry is meant to control in advance whether the parties have (validly) consented to marriage and serves to verify that each contracting party complies with the legally stipulated conditions of capacity. The extension of this requirement to apply to the celebration of all transnational marriages involving Spaniards, even those celebrated abroad, provides the Spanish state with a greater degree of control over which marriages are later recognised, allowing Spain to go beyond simply ascertaining the observance of clear prohibitions of polygamous or unauthorised marriages involving minors or legally incapacitated parties. The refusal by the marriage registrar to issue this certificate can, in fact, be based on an entirely different basis, having nothing to do with capacity. The protocols adopted by marriage registrars (both national and local) to determine which marriages are fraudulent have altered family law itself and introduced immigration policy considerations into its substantive norms (Sánchez Lorenzo 2008).

The role of the marriage registrar, as they themselves describe it, is to separate the wheat from the chaff. Through his 'investigations,' the Ceutan marriage registrar determines which marriages he considers genuine. While some reasons for refusing a marriage are presented by the marriage registrar as objective indications of sham marriages (such as clear contradictions between what the partners say about their relationship), others are purely subjective (such as noticeable age differences, a lack of knowledge between the partners about each other's personal circumstances and backgrounds or the lack of a common language). These reasons are clearly grounded in the marriage registrar's own conclusions and understanding of what constitutes an ideal marriage. Cultural and social homogeneity between the partners is the implicit norm against which any perceived heterogeneity of circumstances is understood to indicate fraudulent intentions on the part of the migrant partner.

'There is a protocol that we follow,' explained the Ceutan marriage registrar when I asked about the legal process of concluding a transnational marriage. In the protocols the Ceutan marriage registrar adopts, he highlighted short courtship periods, significant age differences and no mutual language between the intended spouses as possible indicators of a marriage of convenience. He is particularly concerned when couples are not only transnational but also interreligious. Among exclusively Muslim couples, short courtships or substantial age differences, for instance, are not unheard of. And while transnational couples, including mono-religious relationships between Muslim-Ceutans and Moroccans, would still be investigated by the authorities to determine the couple's good faith – or lack of it – transnational couples that are also interreligious are considered more suspicious and subjected to closer scrutiny by the Spanish authorities. This reflects Ceutans' fears and problematisations of such mixed couples and has the underlying assumptions that Christians would know better than to enter into relationships that simultaneously transgress both socio-religious and political boundaries, and Moroccans who traverse these boundaries must be motivated by something other than pure selfless love.

The practice by state agents to select 'good' couples, reinforcing social and racial hierarchies by excluding certain types of intimate relationships as less desirable, is not unique to Ceuta. Similar dynamics have been observed in other European countries (Maskens 2021) as well as beyond (Charsley 2013), reflecting the trend of moralising national borders in recent years (Fassin 2012). Bordering practices shape the kinds of interviews that take place at the office of the Ceutan marriage registrar and create between the couples and the state functionaries conducting these interviews what Maskens (2018) calls the 'game of authenticity.' In these interviews, the functionaries try to find clues and indications that a true romantic relationship – or its opposite – exists between the partners, while the interviewees attempt to respond to these expectations with what they consider to be appropriate responses for these functionaries. Those enjoying structurally powerful positions use bureaucracy to radically simplify complex situations, causing fear and harm to vulnerable individuals, while clients of the system are forced to navigate and make sense of the bureaucracy in order to justify themselves or try to understand the underlying logic of the system (Graeber 2012). This dynamic can be seen in the experiences of transnational interreligious couples attempting to navigate the bureaucratic Spanish marriage process, having to translate and explain their relationships to the state agents who are judging their intimacy.[4]

The couples' responses, justifying their relationships against the stereotypes that mark their relationships as marriages of convenience, are observed even

4 This is comparable to the experience of asylum seekers who attempt to navigate the bureaucratic asylum process and are interrogated by the authorities about their claim for protection (Sweeney 2009; Kalir 2017).

in their day-to-day lives as they anchor their love stories in defensive rhetoric. Fatima, for instance, insisted that she wanted to marry Antonio quickly because, notwithstanding their short courtship and the 30-year age difference between them, 'he looks younger than his age,' and 'I always found him attractive. I liked him. That is why, after the weekend [we spent together], I immediately told him, "Let's get married".' While Marwa recounts that 'there are couples that don't even share a language. We speak the same way and spend a lot of time together.' Miguel was also keen to emphasise the legitimacy of his marriage: 'We married after many months together, while there are many here that marry after two days.' While couples justify their decisions, defend their marriage choices and emphasise their uniqueness, they nonetheless reproduce the very discourse that problematises marriages like theirs. This notion of a genuine or love marriage as opposed to a marriage of convenience inevitably begs the question of what therefore makes a relationship legitimate.

10.8 Conclusion

The transformation of discourses about transnational couples, shifting from being viewed as 'marriages of love' to 'marriages of convenience,' happened in tandem with the growing scepticism about non-European migrants and their hidden intentions following Spain's accession to the EU. With the enclave's stringent and ever-increasing border controls accompanied by the prevalent essentialising discourse of Ceutan *convivencia*, the intimate space of transnational interreligious relationships is increasingly understood as having foundational geopolitical importance (Pain and Staeheli 2014). In the light of Michel Foucault's writings on the state's interest in governing sexuality ([1978] 1990), conceived as the node of the reproduction of the population, sexual intimacy comes to be conceived as critical to the life and death of a nation and integral to the reproduction of national and ethnic boundaries (Yuval-Davis 1997). There is, therefore, an overriding public interest in the governance of this private space, and the Ceutan marriage registrar's role within this context is that of being an assessor of sexual and emotional intimacy as a guardian of the nation, protecting it from the greedy Moroccan Other.

As Eggebø (2013) points out, matrimonial migration or migration for love, and the corresponding legal regulations that it triggers, represents a privileged place to study changes in the ideals and practices of contemporary intimate life. The act of marriage offers a chance to adjust the conventional institutional definition of a couple to align with intimate relationships that are validated through marriage. Couples often face scrutiny based on societal expectations that reflect a 'pure' and idealised version of relationships, as described by Giddens as 'a relationship of sexual and emotional equality' (1992, 15). Some transnational couples, such as those formed through marriages between Muslim-Ceutan and Moroccan partners, are somewhat accepted in Ceuta, perhaps because these partnerships are believed to reflect this idealised egalitarian ethos, which is not the same for the transnational couples that this chapter focuses on that are also interreligious.

According to the anthropological literature, intimacy, and its associated practices, as emphasised by Giddens (1991) are increasingly influencing a global ideal for modern marriage, which is viewed as the ultimate goal. Striving for intimacy means staking a claim to being a modern subject who marries exclusively for 'love' (Hirsch 2003; Hirsch et al. 2007), avoiding what are understood to be messy compromises and mixed motives. Nevertheless, there is no universal definition of intimacy. As Lynn Jamieson (2011) suggests, there are, instead, various culturally specific practices of intimacy which can be seen to characterise a 'true love marriage.' It is therefore quite difficult to differentiate a 'true' transnational marriage from a 'fake' one, especially as the stability and security generated through marriage do not conflict with love. While Ceutans might rhetorically argue in favour of an idealised version of intimacy, intimate relationships, including contemporary ones, are never totally free from entanglement in economic and social structures (Jamieson 1999).

The indicators used both by Ceutans at the grassroots and by the relevant Ceutan authorities to distinguish what constitutes a genuine marriage from a marriage of convenience have revealed ethnocentric ideas regarding what constitutes an acceptable intimacy and marriage. When studying the discourse surrounding mixed marriages, the intersection between implicit hierarchies based on socio-religious identification and national identity is exposed. In Ceuta, as in other contexts (Morgan 2009), shared marital intimacy is understood as having physical and sexual dimensions, as well as involving a deep knowledge of one's partner. However, in Ceuta, the couple is also expected to show that they enjoy the kind of intimacy defined by the rules of egalitarian endogamy: a sharing of backgrounds, religious beliefs and practices; nationality; ethnicity; age; social class; language and education. These are all markers of what constitutes an ideal marriage in Ceuta. For Ceutans and state agents alike, marriage without intimacy cannot be a true marriage; and intimacy, among partners with too many differences, is simply impossible to achieve. Differences of religion, when coupled with a difference of nationality, at the heart of the couple's intimate life, are perceived as particularly problematic – despite being brushed off as superficial in the propagated discourses of *convivencia*.

Finally, this chapter shows how the legalistic language of 'marriage of convenience' is vernacularised to not only mean marriages for the sole purpose of Spanish documents, but also as an opposition to 'marriages of love,' ignoring the complex way love and practical considerations intertwine. Along these lines, Ceuta has increasingly come to conform to its imagined role of a gatekeeper to Fortress Europe, providing the backdrop against which the motivations of transnational spouses entering interreligious marriages with Spaniards are evaluated. Short courtships, noticeable age gaps or socio-economic differences are perceived as proof of the rhetoric that when spouses have different nationalities and religions, they are marriages of convenience. In response, interreligious transnational couples stress the various legal and socio-religious reasons for getting married, but by emphasising that they are unique, they reproduce the problematisation of their relationships. The impact of political measures on these couples is evident. However, the accounts of these mixed couples and the complex, multiple considerations they made in deciding to marry, show a nuanced picture, in which 'love' and 'convenience' are not in opposition. This chapter shows that interreligious transnational couples acknowledge their wish for the stability and security that comes with obtaining Spanish documents after marrying as one of the many reasons for marrying; however, this is not incompatible with a sense of commitment or love towards their partners.

References

Basch, Linda, Nina Glick Schiller, and Cristina Szanton Blanc, eds. 2005. *Nations Unbound: Transnational Projects, Postcolonial Predicaments, and Deterritorialized Nation-States*. London: Routledge.

Bertaux, Daniel. 1981. "Introduction, Biography and Society: The Life History Approach in the Social Sciences." In *Biography and Society: The Life History Approach in the Social Sciences*, edited by Daniel Bertaux, 5–15. Beverly Hills: SAGE.

Boletín Oficial del Estado. 1995. "Instrucción de 9 de enero de 1995, de la Dirección General de los Registros y del Notariado, sobre el expediente previo al matrimonio cuando uno de los contrayentes está domiciliado en el extranjero." BOE-A-1995-1943, 2316–2317. https://www.boe.es/buscar/doc.php?id=BOE-A-1995-1943.

———. 2006. "Instrucción de 31 de enero de 2006, de la Dirección General de los Registros y del Notariado sobre matrimonios de complacencia." BOE-A-2006-2776, 6330–6338. https://www.boe.es/buscar/doc.php?id=BOE-A-2006-2776.

Bracke, Sarah, and Nadia Fadil. 2012. " 'Is the Headscarf Oppressive or Emancipatory?' Field Notes from the Multicultural Debate." *Religion and Gender* 2 (1): 36–56.

Brettell, Caroline B. 2017. "Marriage and Migration." *Annual Review of Anthropology*, 46: 81–97.

———. 2018. "Conceptualizing Migration and Mobility in Anthropology: A Historical Analysis." *Transitions: Journal of Transient Migration*, 2 (1): 7–25.

Charsley, Katharine, ed. 2013. *Transnational Marriage: New Perspectives from Europe and Beyond*. London: Routledge.

Connolly, Jennifer. 2009. "Forbidden Intimacies: Christian – Muslim Intermarriage in East Kalimantan, Indonesia." *American Ethnologist*, 36 (3): 492–506.

Constable, Nicole. 2009. "The Commodification of Intimacy: Marriage, Sex, and Reproductive Labor." *Annual Review of Anthropology* 38: 49–64.

Council of the European Union. 1997. "Council Resolution of 4 December 1997 on Measures to be Adopted on the Combating of Marriages of Convenience." 97/C 382/01.

De Hart, Betty. 2015. "Regulating Mixed Marriages Through Acquisition and Loss of Citizenship." *The Annals of the American Academy of Political and Social Science* 662 (1): 170–87.

Eggebø, Helga. 2013. "A Real Marriage? Applying for Marriage Migration to Norway." *Journal of Ethnic and Migration Studies* 39 (5): 773–89.

Esteve, Albert, and Xiana Bueno. 2012. "Marrying After Migration: Assortative Mating Among Moroccans in Spain." *Genus* 68 (1): 41–63.

Fassin, Didier, ed. 2012. *A Companion to Moral Anthropology*. Chichester: John Wiley & Sons.

Fiscalía General del Estado. 2002. "Circular 1/2002, de 19 de febrero, sobre aspectos civiles, penales y contencioso-administrativos de la intervención del Fiscal en materia de extranjería." FIS-C-2002-00001. https://www.boe.es/buscar/doc.php?id=FIS-C-2002-00001.

Foucault, Michel. 1990. *The History of Sexuality: An Introduction*. Vol. I. Translated by Robert Hurley. New York: Vintage 95.

Giddens, Anthony. 1991. *Modernity and Self-Identity: Self and Society in the Late Modern Age*. Palo Alto: Stanford University Press.

———. 1992. *The Transformation of Intimacy: Sexuality, Love, and Eroticism in Modern Societies*. Palo Alto: Stanford University Press.

Graeber, David. 2012. "Dead Zones of the Imagination: On Violence, Bureaucracy, and Interpretive Labor: The Malinowski Memorial Lecture, 2006." *HAU: Journal of Ethnographic Theory* 2 (2): 105–28.

Hajdinjak, Marko, Georgeta Nazarska, and Nevena Tosheva-Hajdinjak. 2011. *Migrations, Gender and Intercultural Interactions in Bulgaria*. Sofia: International Center for Minority Studies and Intercultural Relations.

Hirsch, Jennifer. 2003. *A Courtship After Marriage: Sexuality and Love in Mexican Transnational Families*. Berkeley: University of California Press.

Hirsch, Jennifer, Miguel Munoz-Laboy, Robert Sember, and Richard Parker, eds. 2007. *Love and Globalization: Transformations of Intimacy in the Contemporary World*. Nashville: Vanderbilt University Press.

Jamieson, Lynn. 1999. "Intimacy Transformed? A Critical Look at the Pure Relationship." *Sociology* 33 (3): 477–94.

———. 2011. "Intimacy as a Concept: Explaining Social Change in the Context of Globalisation or Another Form of Ethnocentricism?" *Sociological Research Online* 16 (4): 151–63.

Kagné, Bonaventure. 2000. *Easy Scapegoats: Undocumented Immigrants in Europe*. Center for Studies on Ethnicity and Migrations (CEDEM).

Kalir, Barak. 2017. "State Desertion and "Out-of-Procedure" Asylum Seekers in the Netherlands." *Focaal* 2017 (77): 63–75.

Kaur, Ravinder. 2012. "Marriage and Migration: Citizenship and Marital Experience in Cross-Border Marriages between Uttar Pradesh, West Bengal and Bangladesh." *Economic and Political Weekly* 47 (43): 78–89.

Sánchez Lorenzo, Sixto A. 2008. La mujer marroquí ante el matrimonio de conveniencia. In *La situación jurídico-familiar de la mujer marroquí*, edited by Carmen Ruiz Sutil and Ricardo Rueda Valdivia, 181–91. Sevilla: Instituto Andaluz de la Mujer.

Maskens, Maïté. 2015. "Bordering Intimacy: The Fight Against Marriages of Convenience in Brussels." *The Cambridge Journal of Anthropology* 33 (2): 42–58.

———. 2018. "Screening for Romance and Compatibility in the Brussels Civil Registrar Office." In *Intimate Mobilities: Sexual Economies, Marriage and Migration in a Disparate World*, edited by Christian Groes and Nadine T. Fernandez, 74–97. New York; Oxford: Berghahn.

———. 2021. " 'True Love' as a Bureaucratic Utopia: The Case of Bi-National Couples in Belgium." *Social Anthropology/Anthropologie sociale* 29 (1): 18–34.

Moffette, David. 2010. "Convivencia and Securitization: Ordering and Managing Migration in Ceuta (Spain)." *Journal of Legal Anthropology* 1 (2): 189–211.

Morgan, David. 2009. *Acquaintances: The Space Between Intimates and Strangers*. Buckingham: Open University Press.

Pain, Rachel, and Lynn Staeheli. 2014. "Introduction: Intimacy-Geopolitics and Violence." *Area* 46 (4): 344–47.

Palriwala, Rajni, and Patricia Uberoi, eds. 2008. *Marriage, Migration and Gender*. Thousand Oaks: SAGE Publications Ltd.

Rumford, Chris. 2006. "Theorizing Borders." *European Journal of Social Theory* 9 (2): 155–69.

Sadegh, Ibtisam. 2023. " 'We are an Example of Ceuta's Convivencia': Muslim – Christian Marriages at Europe's North-African Border." In *Muslim Marriage and*

Non-Marriage: Where Religion and Politics Meet Intimate Life, edited by Julie McBrien and Annelies Moors. Belgium: Leuven University Press.
Schiller, Nina Glick, Linda Basch, and Cristina Blanc-Szanton. 1992. "Towards a Definition of Transnationalism." *Annals of the New York Academy of Sciences* 645 (1): ix–xiv.
Suárez-Navaz, Liliana. 2004. *Rebordering the Mediterranean: Boundaries and Citizenship in Southern Europe*. New York; Oxford: Berghahn Books.
Sweeney, James A. 2009. "Credibility, Proof and Refugee Law." *International Journal of Refugee Law* 21 (4): 700–26.
Vertovec, Steven, and Robin Cohen. 1999. *Migration, Diasporas and Transnationalism*. Cheltenham: Edward Elgar Publishing.
Williams, Lucy. 2010. *Global Marriage: Cross-Border Marriage Migration in Global Context*. Basingstoke: Palgrave Macmillan.
Yuval-Davis, Nira. 1997. *Gender and Nation*. London: SAGE Publications.

11 Labour market position, acculturation orientation, and other factors influencing migrant women's choices of partners and marriage decisions

The case study of a Polish woman living in Madrid

Jan Bazyli Klakla and Paulina Szydłowska-Klakla

11.1 Introduction

This chapter aims to describe the experiences of Polish women living in Madrid concerning their labour market position and the acculturation process in relation to their choice of life partner which results in endo- and exogamous relationships, both formal and informal, including marriage. The empirical data were collected as part of a larger research project investigating the acculturation experiences of Polish families living in Spain, and the theme of partner choice and position in the labour market emerged from the data as part of an analysis of acculturation experiences in the sphere of family and work. The original study also involved children, and therefore the theme of motherhood and the functioning of the family was also present in the narratives. This chapter aims to answer the following questions: What is the role of labour market position and acculturation orientation in the life partner choice among Polish migrant women living in Spain? What other life experiences are related to this choice?

To do this, we will use the case study approach and present the story of Patrycja, a Polish woman living in Madrid (main case), complementing it with the experiences of other women participating in the study (supporting cases). We will use the theory of the dual labour market, as well as the concepts of acculturation (understood as in the Relative Acculturation Extended Model, RAEM [Navas et al. 2005]) for interpretation. RAEM (Navas and Rojas 2010) indicates that people may put into practice (real plane) and prefer (ideal plane) different acculturation orientations in different areas of their lives. It highlights life areas such as family, religion, values (ways of thinking), social relations, politics, work, economy, and social welfare. Dual labour market theory (Doeringer and Piore 1970; Pardos-Prado 2020) assumes that the labour market is divided into two categories: a primary one with formal, better-paid

DOI: 10.4324/9781003470786-15

occupations that provide workers with a sense of security and perspective for promotion, and a secondary one associated with informal, low-paid, and low-prestige occupations. We would like to point out that, due to the qualitative nature of the study, our reflections refer primarily to the experiences of the described group indicating possible directions for further research.

Marriage decision-making among migrants and minorities in Europe is often considered in the context of the migration of culturally and religiously distinct groups. Meanwhile, it is also a topic of importance and interest in the case of intra-European Union (EU) migration. Unfiltered by such a multitude of cultural differences, the dynamics of human relationships can then be analysed – as we do – in relation to the more covert factors that influence them – such as the acculturation process, the labour market, and related public policies.

11.2 State of the art

The subject of the impact of migrant women's position in the labour market on their decisions regarding life partners is not often addressed in the literature. However, it is possible to find studies that in some way touch on the topic we address in this text.

The impact of the relationship between the phenomenon of marriage and that of migration is about unseen factors that affect both migration and marriage, creating the appearance of a direct strong relationship (Jang, Casterline, and Snyder 2014). Marriage in migration studies is also considered, of course, as one of the reasons for the decision to migrate (see Sinke 1999).

This is more often the case with studies that focus on so-called family migration and what happens to these families (and therefore married couples) after they arrive in the host country. For example, Bailey and Cooke (1998) argue in their study that husbands are more likely than wives to be employed full-time and that being a parent decreases the employment opportunities among married women. For married women with children, the negative impact on employment was significant and persisted for many years (Cook 2001). On the other hand, Clark and Withers (2002) find that the negative effects are relatively short-lived for most households and that wives' labour force participation is a dynamic phenomenon that changes more strongly over time than for men. Yang's (2018) research in South Korea indicates that immigrant women are more vulnerable to discrimination than their native-born counterparts in obtaining secure work in the formal sector. In this context, it is worth noting that the division of women migrants into economic migrants and those who are part of family migration or migrating for marriage is strongly contested at the theoretical level (see Piper 2003), as both spheres of life sooner or later intersect in the host country.

One can find many large quantitative studies on marriage choices. Milewski and Hamel (2010) show that among the factors influencing the choice of an exo- or endogamous relationship of Turks who grew up in France, there are social factors such as education, city of residence, and cultural factors such as kinship rules in Türkiye and attachment to the norm of virginity at the time of marriage. In a similar study, Huschek, De Valk, and Lifbroer (2012) find that contextual variables such as migrant group size and the type of integration policy appear to play a role in the likelihood of having a first- or second-generation partner of Turkish origin but not for the likelihood of choosing an exogamous partner. Carol, Ersanilli, and Wagner (2014), in a study about partner choice, include religiosity among the relevant factors, as well as those very contextual factors, such as rural background and the country's existing family reunification policy. A broad study by Hannemann et al. (2018), based on data from seven European countries, shows a difference between migrants from non-EU countries, who are more likely to seek a partner within their ethnic group, and migrants from EU countries, who are statistically more open to mixed marriages. Also worth mentioning is Carol's (2016) study on partner choice among Muslim migrants and natives in Western Europe, in which attention is paid to factors such as the level of individual religiosity, conflicting ideas about family life and relationships, premarital sexuality, attitudes toward marriage, and, finally, the role of parents in the matchmaking process.

Regarding the Spanish context, several studies can be found in recent years on the marriage choices of migrants in that particular country. Sánchez-Domínguez's, De Valk's, and Reher's (2011) findings among migrants from five countries – Morocco, Romania, Ecuador, Colombia, and Argentina – and a group of other developing countries show that the level of endogamy is highest among migrants from Morocco and lowest for those coming from Colombia. Moreover, the likelihood of an endogamous relationship is higher for those who married before migration compared to those who married later and lower for those who are better educated and for women rather than men. Focusing on Moroccan migrants, Esteve and Bueno (2012) confirm that those with higher education are more likely to enter into exogamous unions.

As the brief overview shows, few studies focus on the relationship between a migrant's position in the labour market and their choice of life partner. Among the closest to this topic is a study by Mills (1998), which examines some of the tensions that arise during the labour migration of young Thai women from rural to urban areas. In this, marriage choices are shown to illustrate the attempt to manoeuvre within and against the constraints that women migrants face as members of a cheap, mobile labour force. Another study by González-Ferrer (2011) shows that the temporal sequence of migration and key events in the family life cycle can help explain the post-migration employment patterns of migrants, especially women.

11.3 Methodology

The research behind this chapter is a qualitative study using a field research strategy with observations and multiple case studies (Yin 2018). One case in this study involved a parent (predominantly mothers) and a child/children.

In this chapter, only the women's narratives are used, and therefore each of them constitutes a case. It is based on an analysis of 18 semi-structured interviews with women and one joint interview with both parents. The cases of women who were married to other Poles whose children attend Polish Saturday schools and who arrived in Spain before or shortly after it joined the EU predominated in the group. Women who chose a foreigner or Spaniard as partners remained in formal and informal relationships.

According to the data cited in an article by Mikołaj Stanek and Elżbieta Sobczak (2007) about the situation of the Polish community in Spain, the majority of Poles in the first decade of the 21st century were involved in either the domestic (women) or construction (men) sectors. The 2001 census data they cite shows that the majority of people, around 55%, had general and technical secondary education, 19% had vocational education, and only 17% had higher education. Similarly, those with secondary education dominated the study group.

A semi-structured interview was used as the method of data collection. The interviews were conducted in a way that allowed the participants to say what was important to them to ensure that they were heard and to develop those themes that were relevant to the research question, even if they were not anticipated in the interview script (Smith et al. 2009). The guide for each interview was based on the theoretical assumptions of the RAEM (Navas et al. 2010), indicating that people may undertake and prefer different acculturation orientations in different areas of their lives, and included areas of psychosocial functioning highlighted by the model (see Section 1.1 Introduction).

The respondents were informed about the purpose and confidentiality of the study, as well as the possibility of withdrawing from the study. The adults were informed about the duration of the interview (approximately two/two and a half hours). They signed an informed consent for their participation in the study, as well as for their child's participation and the recording and transcription of the interviews. The interviews usually took place in respondents' homes, parks, or cafés.

The collected data were analysed using the template analysis method (Langdridge 2007). The analysis template – similarly to an interview scenario – was constructed based on the RAEM. In the text, we use a generalised understanding of individual acculturation orientations (see Rudmin 2003a, 2003b) based on two dimensions: the relative importance of the first culture (the minority culture) and the contact culture (the dominant culture) (2003a, 6) or, in other words, accepting or rejecting each culture, or saying 'yes' or 'no' to a particular culture (2003b, 3). As a result, when we write about assimilation, we mean acceptance of the contact culture and rejection of the first culture; separation is rejection of the contact culture and acceptance of the first culture; in the case of integration, we are dealing with acceptance of both the contact culture and the first culture; and marginalisation is rejection of both cultures.

11.4 Results

The women in the study were in three types of relationships:

1. Polish–Spanish/foreign
2. Polish–Polish
3. as well as in relationships that changed over time during their stay in Spain from Polish–Polish to Polish–Spanish.

Next we describe the emerging characteristics of the relationship between these relationship patterns and the labour market and acculturation. The effect of the categorisation related to the distinction between the primary and secondary labour markets and being in a relationship with a Polish or Spanish partner can be found in Table 11.1, which presents a comparison between the dual labour market sector in which each woman found employment and the nationality of her life partner. In brackets after the first name, there is information on the country in which the couple met (PL – Poland, ES – Spain). The names of the women we refer to in further analysis are in bold. In the case of a change of partner or work between dual labour market sectors, the woman's name appears twice in the table.

Most women working in the secondary sector are in relationships with Polish men, while women with Spanish partners usually work in the primary sector. Nevertheless, the relationship between the two phenomena has evolved in different ways, as we will try to describe.

The first pattern of relationships mainly concerns women who came to Spain because of previous contact with their Spanish partner or they met their partner while working in a place that provided contact with the Spanish environment. Consequently, most of them function(ed) in the primary labour market due to their education and other life circumstances. Functioning in a Spanish environment and having a Spanish partner result in each of them having social relations with both Poles and Spaniards. However, in the sphere of family, they are often guided by the values they know from their family home

Table 11.1 Categorisation of respondents

	Polish partner	*Spanish/foreign partner*
Primary sector	Zofia (PL), Teodora (PL), **Amelia (PL)**	Mariola (ES), **Patrycja** (ES), Pola (PL), Wacława (PL), **Magda** (ES)
Secondary sector	Sandra (ES), Joanna (ES), **Ewa** (PL), Elwira (PL), Linda (ES), Miłka (PL), **Patrycja (ES), Amelia (PL)**, Sabina (PL), Karolina (ES)	**Magda** (ES), Krysia (ES), Iwona (PL), Kornelia (PL)

as well. Therefore, this involves acculturative orientations such as integration or even separation (in some aspects such as child-rearing).

The second pattern describes women who migrated for economic reasons and after arrival found themselves in a secondary labour market that limits contact with the host community, such as work in the care or cleaning sector. Therefore it is in the Polish community that they met their Polish partner. Some of them remain in the secondary labour market due to a choice of some kind – flexible working hours allow for childcare and the organisation of family life. In these families, a separation orientation in the sphere of family or social relationships is prevalent, but there are also themes related to putting in practice aspects of host culture such as the introduction of siesta or Spanish dishes.

The final, outlier case, which we treat as the main case in this chapter, is specifically related to one person who changed her partner during her stay in Spain, as well as the labour market sector. Patrycja is the only person with a Spanish partner who works in the primary labour market (for some time now, having previously worked in the secondary labour market) and who has a secondary education. Due to her life situation and job change, she has entered into a long-term relationship with a Spanish national, which is reflected in the more inclusive acculturation orientations she puts into practice. It is through the example of her story and her family case study that we will try to illustrate the possible relationship between position in the labour market, acculturation orientations and other life factors, and the choice of life partner.

11.5 Main case – the story of Patrycja

Patrycja came to Spain at the age of 20, shortly before Poland joined the EU in 2004 and before the outbreak of the economic crisis in Spain in 2007. In Poland, she completed her education at the level of a secondary school exam but did not have the resources to support herself through a full-time university degree. When she did not have the opportunity to take up her dream job as a police officer, as at the time only men were recruited for the job, she took up temporary part-time work to ensure she could study part-time. After some time she went to Spain with friends, intending to earn money, but also for entertainment purposes.

Despite the difficulties at the beginning of her stay (which she did not inform her family about in order not to worry them), she showed a positive attitude, was determined, and tried to concentrate on work and learning the language. Hence, it can be said that she showed an integrative or even sometimes assimilative orientation from the very beginning. At the same time, a combination of social and economic circumstances (including difficulties in finding a job) did not support these orientations, pushing her towards separation or even marginalisation.

A schematic overview of Patrycja's career, as well as her relationships, can be found in Figure 11.1.

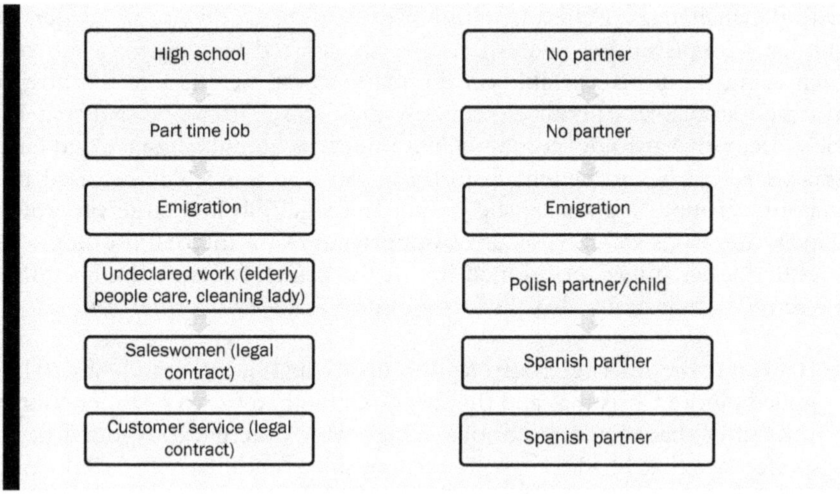

Figure 11.1 Schematic representation of Patrycja's career and relationships

With the help of Polish acquaintances, she found two jobs: as a caregiver for an elderly person and as a cleaner. In the context of acculturation theory, it can be noted here that she used informal mechanisms of a separative nature to find her way into the labour market, which was often the case for those women who migrated for economic reasons. The job – which, despite being a job in the secondary sector, supported Patrycja's ongoing process of adaptation to the new environment by providing the means necessary for basic existence which reduced stress, increased well-being, and enabled the basic process of cultural learning – was acquired through the minority social support networks used by migrants and in isolation from the host society. Based on the statements of the other women interviewed, popular networks used for informal job searches include Polish schools, Polish parishes and masses, and friends and family members who had previously arrived in Spain.

The attitude of Patrycja's employers in the secondary sector can be described as integrative to some extent and certainly supportive of the process of adaptation and finding her way in a new environment in terms of social and cultural skills. In her first job, she was given a dictionary and a book for learning Spanish, and in the house where she cleaned, the owner prepared a detailed list of activities for her to do. At the same time, the nature of the work – carried out in the domestic sector, but in the absence of real, in-depth contact with Spanish householders and members of the host society – prevented the full realisation of an inclusive acculturation orientation, especially in terms of social relations or family (including choice of life partner).

At the time, working in the secondary sector was one of the main barriers to integration (also in terms of choosing a life partner), and the acquisition of language skills was seen by Patrycja as one of the proactive forms of coping with the challenges of the adaptation process to break down this barrier. Once she had completed her Spanish course, she started looking for a job on her own using the tools available on the market that members of the host society use – available, of course, primarily in Spanish. It can be said that Patrycja's integrative attitude, combined with newly acquired language and cultural skills, enabled her to benefit from those job search mechanisms used by the majority group. As a result, she obtained a legal job in a large supermarket, which, due to its stability, security, opportunities for internal promotion, and slightly higher wages, positioned her in the primary sector. Importantly, her current working hours also allow her to personally care for her son.

> Through the internet I also signed up to such a job search site. They called before Christmas and they sent us straight away to a cashier course. And after that they offered jobs. There were different jobs, but I had a preference that I had to have a morning shift. A year later I started working here where I work (the mall).
>
> . . .
>
> In customer service, I am the only one from a foreign country because there are only Spanish women and me. But that's because the boss knows that I can handle anything, she knows she can rely on me. She never has a problem with me. All in all, it shows how you work. And later on, you find that it helps you.
>
> (Patrycja)

Internal promotion opportunities were quickly utilised by Patrycja. Patrycja attributed her success at work to the fact that she has a good connection with people but also to her integrative acculturation orientation based on exploiting the strengths of both cultural patterns, Spanish, and Polish. She says that at work she is guided by the values she has inherited from her family home related to respect for supervisors, diligence, and conscientiousness and that she is often praised for this.

> We were once at a dinner, such a Christmas dinner – 'the only one who will do what I say is Patrycja because the others will of course listen and do nothing and the only one who cares is Patrycja'. Because they taught us that way. For example, they taught us that way, that when someone of a higher position came in you stood up. And here [in Spain] no, it's not like that.
>
> (Patrycja)

Alongside developments in the professional field, there were changes in Patrycja's private life. After arriving in Spain, she entered into a relationship with a Polish man. From the point of view of acculturation orientations, the choice of a partner from her country of origin was a choice of separation in the sphere of family relations. Nevertheless, it should be noted that due to the difficulty in implementing an integration orientation – as we have already mentioned when writing about how few opportunities for contact with the host society were provided by Patrycja's work at the time – this choice was not entirely free.

Patrycja's preference for a more partner-like relationship, and consequently for a Spanish life partner, which manifested itself later in our protagonist's life, could not yet reveal itself due to her lack of immersion in Spanish society. Moreover, due to social contact being largely restricted to a group of Poles and other foreigners – which was also linked to her job in the secondary sector – perhaps this preference had not yet had the chance to emerge in Patrycja's consciousness as something that went beyond the familiar, hegemonic image of romantic relationships within her own cultural group.

In other words, to develop a preference for one or the other cultural pattern associated with romantic relationships – be it Polish or Spanish – it is necessary to come into contact (even indirectly) with both patterns and to believe that they fit into a conceivable image of the world.

After 2 years of the relationship, Patrycja gave birth to a son. Unfortunately, the relationship she was in did not turn out to be a happy one due to her partner's alcohol addiction. Shortly afterwards, Patrycja decided to separate from her partner. At that point, life circumstances – most notably the working conditions in the secondary sector – again came to the fore and prevented her from taking full control of her life and implementing the decisions she had made. Despite the breakup of the relationship, Patrycja was forced to cohabit with her ex-partner until her professional situation changed. Before that, she was simply unable to provide for herself and her son on her own. Thus, it can be said that over a long period, these circumstances forced Patrycja to persist with the separation situation (in terms of the acculturation process in the family sphere) despite her other desires and the decision she had already made.

With the change in her position in the labour market, which we have already described, and the transition to employment in the primary sector, an opportunity arose for Patrycja to fully implement the decision she had made earlier to leave her partner. Initially, she lived with a friend for a few months. It soon became apparent that the change in her employment situation not only enabled her to free herself from the consequences of her previous decision in choosing a life partner, but also to make a new one in this respect – Patrycja met Jesús, who was working in the same shop, but in a different position, and they soon moved in together. They continue to live together to this day.

It can be noted here that, on a theoretical level, it was the change of job and the opportunity to make a more integrative choice within the work sphere that, in Patrycja's case, allowed her to move on from the separation choice she had previously made regarding her life partner. It is also worth mentioning that when Patrycja separated from her first partner she received a lot of support from her Spanish work friends, who helped her with childcare at weekends when she had to go to work. The Spanish partner is like a father to the boy. They visit Jesús's mother and Patrycja's family in Poland together, they go to the cinema and do the shopping.

Visible here is integration as an acculturation orientation being put into practice, both within the family sphere and at work. It can be deduced from Patrycja's statements and the course of her post-migration biography that this was her preferred attitude from the outset, which, however, she was not able to fully realise at the very beginning due to life circumstances – including her position on the labour market in the secondary sector. It should also be noted that – as is evident even in Patrycja's example – the choice of a Spaniard as a life partner does not determine the abandonment of Polish cultural patterns and the adoption of an assimilative acculturation orientation.

> I mean she [her mother-in-law, Jesús's mother] is happy because she sees that Jesús is not complaining. She has four sons there and two of them are complaining that she won't cook. Then let him cook for himself. I'm always teasing her. We come to her house, and she says the table needs to be moved. She says: 'Patrycja, come and help me.' And I say, 'Really? That's why you had four sons, to help you with the hard work. Jesús, to the table.' At our house, it was always Dad, and Mum, everyone was doing stuff too. At our house, it was Mum who wore the trousers. What Mum said was sacred.
>
> (Patrycja)

This is how the relationship between the choice of life partner and the nature of the romantic relationship, the position in the labour market, the acculturative orientation, and the context accompanying migration is realised in the case in question. Significant factors influencing the labour market position were Patrycja's character traits, which made her study the language intensively; her life situation (related to raising her son on her own, dissatisfaction with her relationship and the need to work in the mornings); and also the sociocultural context (before the crisis it was not difficult to find a legal job without language skills). In addition to the position in the primary labour market, and an inclusive acculturative orientation, the failure of a previous unhappy relationship may also have been related to her choice of partner.

11.6 Supporting cases

The use of informal labour market mechanisms to seek work, primarily in the secondary sector, is something that emerges in the narratives of many of the women interviewed. This is particularly the case for women arriving before Poland's accession to the EU, for economic motivation and often with a Polish partner. They, in their search for work, mainly used the help of friends or family members who had previously arrived in Spain (Sabina, Amelia, Elwira, Linda). Then we can often observe the separation mechanisms that influence the persistence of previous relationships (be they spouses or informal life partners) in the new country of residence, and even the decisions to have a child and start a family despite theoretically unfavourable – unregulated and unstable – employment conditions. Often these individuals justify their preference for staying in the secondary sector of the dual labour market because of the flexibility of working hours and the fact that the partner is working in the secondary labour market as well.

A story worth mentioning in this context is that of Amelia. She came to Spain with the encouragement of her sister and found work in the care and domestic sector, like Patrycja. Both women also have a similar story of crossing the boundaries of the dual labour market and working in both the secondary and primary sectors. However, like some of the other women, what stopped Amelia from working on a formal contract was the flexibility of working in the domestic sector, which allowed her to care for her children. Here (but also in the stories of other women), the relationship between the labour market position and the acculturation process in the family sphere is being shaped interestingly; acculturation orientations related to the family sphere and the raising of children influence professional opportunities, and the realisation of these professional opportunities influences acculturation orientations in the family sphere and the choice of life partner.

> And I just preferred to clean, just to be at home with the child later in the afternoon and help her study. Especially since I didn't know how she was doing at school, I couldn't help her study, and so on. And later, when she was older, bigger, and I had the other one, well, then I just started working in my profession as a warehouse assistant in shops. I already knew the language well, so that was the next step, in terms of professional life.
> (Amelia)

On the other hand, she was a very ambitious person, and, like Patrycja, she quickly learnt the language, and as soon as she felt she could reconcile her parental responsibilities with her job, she went into the primary sector and into a job that allowed her to come into contact with the Spanish community – after a period as a nanny or waitress, she started working in a shop, where she was rewarded for high sales results. However, there were big sacrifices associated with this job regarding working hours, so eventually, despite her success, she gave it up.

From the point of view of decisions related to the choice of a life partner, Amelia's story is different to that of Patrycja. She had already arrived in Spain with her husband and their relationship was stable and had survived difficult beginnings in emigration as well as Amelia's change of job and transition from the secondary sector to the primary sector. As a result, even though in Amelia's case the influence of Spanish culture was so strong that Spanish was used as the language of communication at home, her approach has been largely separative, which is also reflected in the fact that she has decided to return to Poland to take care of her ageing parents. In Patrycja's case, on the other hand, the change of partner alongside work has pushed her towards a more integrative orientation.

This shows that the relationship we have described between the dual labour market sector in which women work after arriving in Spain and their decisions related to their choice of life partner is primarily related to a widening of choices and to an increasing degree of free will in marital and romantic decisions, rather than to the determination of one or the other. Both Patrycja and Amelia came into more intensive contact with Spaniards on a social and professional basis after changing jobs. The difference is that the former chose to turn one of these contacts into a long-term romantic relationship (which may have been influenced by, among other things, her integrative acculturative orientation), while the latter chose not to make such a decision. Undoubtedly, relationship satisfaction was relevant here. In Patrycja's case, we are dealing with the failure of the Polish–Polish relationship, while in Amelia's case, the relationship persisted.

Another woman interviewed, Magda, also started in the secondary sector, in a job without a contract in a restaurant, where she met her Spanish partner. She now works in a factory, as the only foreigner among the temporary Spanish workers who are mostly students. This example shows, however, that the secondary sector can also be a space in which one can meet a partner, but it is less likely and strongly depends on the nature of the work carried out (a restaurant vs the work in the domestic sector described in the case of Patrycja or Amelia).

Moreover, even if the respondent did not give such a reason explicitly, a hypothesis can be made, requiring verification in subsequent studies, regarding the impact of the position of a partner in the labour market. If the partner remains in the secondary labour market, the other half of the couple may also prefer work in the secondary labour market if work allows more family time or time to take care of children. This concerned mostly, but not only, stories of women who had endogamous relationships. Magda is in an exogamous relationship, married to a Spanish man who works as a cook, which requires long working hours and has less flexibility for being involved in taking care of the children. She had episodes of working in the primary sector. At first, she was able to work partly in line with her education. Then for personal reasons (a lack of satisfaction with the position offered), she decided not to continue to do so and started working in commerce and set up her own shop. This is also when she became pregnant. In the end, she chose a job incompatible with her education in a factory where she does not use her qualifications. She is satisfied with this job because it is close to home, not very mentally demanding, and gives space for childcare.

The third story we would like to recall is the story of Ewa, who, like Patrycja, once received a Spanish dictionary from her employer, whose child she was looking after. She – again like Patrycja – was highly motivated to learn the language. Her fate, however, turned out differently. In the interview, she admitted her career decisions were tied to the idea of starting a family and were primarily determined by a kind of convenience (she started working as a cook, which then ensured she could maintain her unemployment status and earn extra money informally). Her partner was also Polish and joined her 1.5 years after she arrived in Spain. As a result, she stopped learning the language further, as the level she had reached was 'enough' for the work she was doing. Ewa eventually returned to the secondary sector, but – like Amelia and Magda – she claimed this was her own decision, driven by her priorities related to the greater independence she believes this job provides. In the context of acculturative orientations, this attitude can be interpreted as separation, as those who choose this path choose to limit their contact with the Spanish community and focus largely on their Polish partner, family, and often a circle of friends of Polish or other foreign origins.

11.7 Conclusions

Concerning the research question posed at the beginning, Patrycja's story, as well as the experiences of the other women we cite in the text, suggest there may be a relationship between the position in the dual labour market, acculturative orientation, and the freedom to choose a life partner, in which this freedom of choice is to some extent limited by the aforementioned factors. This relationship manifests itself on several levels.

The first, and most tangible, is related to **the possibility of making contact**, which clearly must precede the decision to choose a life partner (or at least when we are not talking about arranged marriages). The sphere of work is the one to which adults often devote the greatest amount of time among the spheres highlighted in the RAEM. Working in the secondary sector, especially in those areas dominated by migrants and prone to the creation of 'bubbles' in which newcomers can function without contact with the host society, is not conducive to getting to know people from outside one's cultural circle. It is noteworthy that **knowledge of the language** is one of the most important factors which facilitate access to both the labour market and the Spanish community. It can be seen that it can provide support for the transition from the secondary to the primary labour market, as well as broaden the possibilities related to the free choice of a life partner.

In this context, there is no denying that the development of a relationship or the change of partner is undoubtedly also influenced by the **satisfaction of the previous relationship and the individual family situation** – if Patrycja's relationship had been a happy one, the issue of choice, both of a life partner and of a job, would not have been so important; she would not have been looking for a partner, nor would she have had to look for a stable job in order to raise her son alone. In this connection, **the individual history of experiences, as well as the life circumstances** accompanying migration or the **openness to an integrative acculturation orientation** that allows one to imagine a romantic relationship with a person of non-Polish origin is also important.

The second, complementing the former, concerns the **context in which this contact is made**. After all, it is not uncommon, for example, for women working in the domestic sector to come into contact with members of the host society in the guise of the people for whom they provide their services. It should be noted, however, that this contact – when established in the situation of, for example, a cleaner and the owner of a household – is then always marked by a relationship of power and inequality resulting from the relationship that exists between the person providing the work and the person for whom the work is provided. In the domestic sector, that is, in the case of work done behind closed doors, in the private sphere, this power relationship can sometimes be hidden on the one hand and extremely strong on the other, especially in the case of female migrant workers (see Kindler 2011). This can effectively hinder the establishment of partnerships and romantic relationships. Some other jobs in the secondary sector of the labour market can provide opportunities for intercultural contact on more equal terms – as it was in the analysed case of Magda working in a restaurant.

The third level is related to the **characteristics of the two sectors of the labour market**, which can differently support or discourage both the decision to enter into a partnership or romantic relationship and the further steps involved in potentially starting a family. The secondary sector, characterised by insecurity, instability, low wages, and often long, non-standard working hours, as well as a lack of visible prospects for improvement through internal promotion, does not leave those working in it with a particularly large amount of time or resources to devote to making all kinds of social contacts, including partnerships and romance, with people from the host country. The primary sector, offering greater stability, provides more of this freedom. In the group participating in the study, it was the stability of the job, rather than its location in the labour market, that was important for the interviewed women when starting a family. It is worth noting that the narratives of the interviewed women indicate that working in the secondary market – from the perspective of some people and at a certain life stage – may be seen as preferable. It sometimes offers the possibility of flexible working hours, which for many was an argument that enabled them to care for their children. The aforementioned conclusion leads us towards establishing the **links between work and family life and the relation between these two spheres.** From the point of view of acculturation theory based on the RAEM, the choice of a life partner is part of the family sphere of migrants' psychosocial functioning in the host society. It is therefore not an isolated choice – it is not only about the specific person we choose to engage with, but it is also a choice concerning our preferences concerning the position partners occupy in the family, the equality of roles, the tasks fulfilled within the family and others.

The relation between the sphere of work and the sphere of family, the possibility of which we present, might be a manifestation of an idea that has already emerged from our earlier research (see Klakla 2022) – the concept of 'leading areas' in the acculturation process. That is because it turns out that while it is not possible to state in general that any of the spheres is the most important in the acculturation process, within individual biographies it is possible to identify the sphere that sets the tone for the whole process. Depending on the individual circumstances of the migrant in question, the sphere that sets the tone for the acculturation process may be any of the spheres highlighted in the RAEM, including the sphere of work or family. It is not difficult to imagine the situation of a migrant who, upon arrival in the host country, finds themself in a friendly, open work environment in the primary sector, and it is this sphere – and the acculturation orientations preferred and pursued within it – that influences the nature of the acculturation process in the other spheres. By preferring an integrative orientation in the work sphere, also supported by the work environment, such a migrant can build bonds with co-workers that go far beyond work relations and in this way, the work sphere will influence the sphere of social relations.

It may so happen that among these co-workers – and then friends – there is a person with whom the migrant decides to create a family and thus the sphere of work influences the sphere of family relations. Legal work also gives access to social welfare – so there is a possible impact on this sphere as well – and also makes it possible to realise economic needs and often influences how these will be realised, which manifests itself in the impact of the labour sphere on the economic sphere. Of course, a similar relationship can also occur in a less optimistic context – when a discriminating, marginalising work environment triggers similar orientations in other spheres. A change in the work sphere – as was the case for Patrycja – leads to a change in other spheres in terms of the ongoing acculturation process.

As a result, **the law**, which is intended to be the law regulating migrants' access to the labour market and influencing this sphere among the spheres of psychosocial functioning of migrants in the new country, in fact often regulates the entire acculturation process, including influencing decisions related to the choice of a life partner. Even those women who were highly educated in Poland and had Spanish partners sometimes could not find work in the primary sector according to their qualifications because of systemic barriers (e.g., problems with diploma nostrification) and/or their needs related to childcare. By restricting choices – whether directly in the sphere of work or indirectly in the sphere of family and romantic relationships – the law influences the range of actions of individuals, which we can then interpret in terms of particular acculturation orientations. The question arises, however, whether, if the restriction is far-reaching, we can then speak of acculturation at all (at least in terms of preferences). If a given choice is the only possible choice, it is difficult to consider this in terms of a reference to maintaining or adopting the patterns of one or the other culture. The choice of spouse or life partner is often indicated – especially in the public discourse – as an expressive signpost of a particular orientation, and the number of mixed marriages functions as an indicator of the integration of a given group. However, given the aforementioned considerations, the validity of such an approach may be questioned.

11.8 Limitations and recommendations for further research

Our chapter is not free of limitations. This is because the earlier analyses deal with themes that only emerged from the data in the course of the analytic process. As such, there is a lack of in-depth information on the work or labour market position of the women's partners. This information would have allowed an in-depth assessment of the dynamics between the labour market positions of a woman and her partner. In addition, due to the purpose of the study, which was to explore acculturation experiences rather than relationship dynamics due to labour market position, equal subgroups were not recruited considering the composition of the relationships – most of the women in the study had a Polish partner. These were also relationships working to maintain their Polish culture by, among other things, sending their children to Polish schools, and thus were families in which a separation orientation was dominant, as manifested in the stories we described. This is not characteristic of the entire group of Polish couples living in Spain. Due to the existing gaps related to the small number of respondents and the limitations of the recruitment process, we cannot generalise the conclusions to the entire group of Polish women and their partners living in Spain, or even in Madrid.

Despite the limitations, the results indicate some trends regarding labour market position and the acculturation process, and the choice of partner among migrant women, that may be utilised in further research. The results confirm the data cited in the introduction about invisible factors influencing marriage and migration (Jang, Casterline, and Snyder 2014) – in the case of our study, such factors were acculturation orientations, socio-economic status (primarily education), motivation to learn the language and knowledge of Spanish, and life circumstances related to the family life cycle (satisfaction with a previous relationship). The women who came to Spain because of a Spanish partner (which may also be a motivation to migrate, see Sinke 1999), whom they met in Poland or within a professional context while working, were mostly educated, but some of them ended up in the secondary labour market. This should be taken into account in further qualitative research on the topic.

Both the position in the labour market may influence the choice of partner and, vice versa, the choice of partner may influence the position in the labour market once the woman arrives in Spain. Consequently, whether the partner is in the secondary or primary labour market may also be one of the factors sustaining the partner's labour market choice. Another factor keeping women in the secondary labour market has often been the appearance of children. Men, working large numbers of hours, most often in the construction sector, were not able to share childcare equally with mothers. Similar findings are indicated by Bailey and Cooke (1998) who argue in their study that husbands are more likely to be employed full-time than wives and that being a parent decreases employment opportunities among married women. This indicates the adoption of traditional gender roles associated with a woman taking on childcare in the first instance and then working in such a way as to make this childcare possible for herself. This may not be related solely and directly to women's needs but to the socio-cultural requirements of the country of origin or country of emigration, which impose certain expectations on women. These paths are worth exploring further.

Acknowledgments

The authors would like to thank Marisol Navas and Pablo Pumares (CEMyRI, University of Almeria, Spain) for their consultation in drafting this chapter.

References

Bailey, Adrian J., and Thomas J. Cooke. 1998. "Family Migration and Employment: The Importance of Migration History and Gender." *International Regional Science Review* 21 (2): 99–118.

Carol, Sarah. 2016. "Like Will to Like? Partner Choice among Muslim Migrants and Natives in Western Europe." *Journal of Ethnic and Migration Studies* 42 (2): 261–76.

Carol, Sarah, Evalyn Ersanilli, and Mareike Wagner. 2014. "Spousal Choice among the Children of Turkish and Moroccan Immigrants in Six European Countries: Transnational Spouse or Co-Ethnic Migrant?" *International Migration Review* 48 (2): 387–414.

Clark, William A. V., and Suzanne Davies Withers. 2002. "Disentangling the Interaction of Migration, Mobility, and Labor-Force Participation." *Environment and Planning A* 34 (5): 923–45.

Cooke, Thomas J. 2001. "'Trailing Wife' or 'Trailing Mother'? The Effect of Parental Status on the Relationship between Family Migration and the Labor-Market Participation of Married Women." *Environment and Planning A* 33 (3): 419–30.

Doeringer, Peter B., and Michael J. Piore. 1970. *Internal Labor Markets and Manpower Analysis.* Lexington, MA: Heath.

Esteve, Albert, and Xiana Bueno. 2012. "Marrying After Migration: Assortative Mating Among Moroccans in Spain." *Genus* 68 (1): 41–63.

González-Ferrer, Amparo. 2011. "Explaining the Labour Performance of Immigrant Women in Spain: The Interplay between Family, Migration and Legal Trajectories." *International Journal of Comparative Sociology* 52 (1–2): 63–78.

Hannemann, Tina, Hill Kulu, Leen Rahnu, Allan Puur, Mihaela Hărăguş, Ognjen Obućina, Amparo González-Ferrer, Karel Neels, Layla Van den Berg, Ariane Pailhé, Gina Potarca, and Laura Bernardi. 2018. "Co-Ethnic Marriage versus Intermarriage Among Immigrants and Their Descendants: A Comparison Across Seven European Countries Using Event-History Analysis." *Demographic Research* 39: 487–524.

Huschek, Doreen, Helga A. G. De Valk, and Aart C. Liefbroer. 2012. "Partner Choice Patterns among the Descendants of Turkish Immigrants in Europe." *European Journal of Population/Revue Europeenne De Demographie* 28 (3): 241–68.

Jang, Joy Bohyun, John B. Casterline, and Anastasia Snyder. 2014. "Migration and Marriage: Modeling the Joint Process." *Demographic Research* 30: 1339–66.

Kindler, Marta. 2011. *A Risky Business?: Ukrainian Migrant Women in Warsaw's Domestic Work Sector.* Amsterdam: Amsterdam University Press.

Klakla, Jan Bazyli. 2022. *Akulturacja migrantów z państw słowiańskich w Polsce. Studium socjologiczno-prawne.* Kraków: Jagiellonian University (unpublished PhD thesis).

Langdridge, Darren. 2007. *Phenomenological Psychology: Theory, Research and Method.* Glasgow: Pearson Education.

Milewski, Nadja, and Christelle Hamel. 2010. "Union Formation and Partner Choice in a Transnational Context: The Case of Descendants of Turkish Immigrants in France." *International Migration Review* 44 (3): 615–58.

Mills, Mary Beth. 1998. "Gendered Encounters with Modernity: Labor Migrants and Marriage Choices in Contemporary Thailand." *Identities Global Studies in Culture and Power* 5 (3): 301–34.

Navas, Marisol, María C. García, Juan Sánchez, Antonio J. Rojas, Pablo Pumares, and Juan S. Fernández. 2005. "Relative Acculturation Extended Model (RAEM): New Contributions with Regard to the Study of Acculturation." *International Journal of Intercultural Relations* 29 (1): s.21–37.

Navas, Marisol, and Antonio J. Rojas. 2010. *Aplicación del Modelo Ampliado de Aculturación Relativa (MAAR) a nuevos colectivos de inmigrantes en Andalucía: rumanos y ecuatorianos.* Sevilla: Consejería de Empleo (Junta de Andalucía).

Pardos-Prado, Sergi. 2020. "Labour Market Dualism and Immigration Policy Preferences." *Journal of European Public Policy* 27 (2): s.188–207.

Piper, Nicola. 2003. "Wife or Worker? Worker or Wife? Marriage and Cross-Border Migration in Contemporary Japan." *International Journal of Population Geography* 9 (6): 457–69.

Rudmin, Floyd W. 2003a. "Critical History of the Acculturation Psychology of Assimilation, Separation, Integration, and Marginalization." *Review of General Psychology* 7 (1): 3–37.

———. 2003b. "Catalogue of Acculturation Constructs: Descriptions of 126 Taxonomies, 1918–2003." *Catalogue of Acculturation Constructs* 6: 1–73.

Sánchez-Domínguez, Maria, Helga A. G. De Valk, and David Reher. 2011. "Marriage Strategies among Immigrants in Spain." *Revista Internacional de Sociología* 69 (M1): 139–66.

Sinke, Suzanne. 1999. "Migration for Labor, Migration for Love: Marriage and Family Formation Across Borders." *OAH Magazine of History* 14 (1): 17–21.

Smith, Jonathan, Paul Flower, Michael Larkin. 2009. *Interpretative Phenomenological Analysis: Theory, Method and Research.* London: Sage.

Stanek, Mikołaj, and Elżbieta Sobczak. 2007. "Polacy i Polonia w Hiszpanii na przełomie XX i XXI wieku." *Studia Polonijne* 28: 215–41.

Yang, Kyung-Eun. 2018. "Unequal Chance of Obtaining a Secure Job: Marriage Migrant Women in the Korean Labor Market." *Journal of International Migration and Integration* 19 (1): 91–110.

Yin, Robert K. 2018. *Case Study Research and Applications: Design and Methods.* New York: Sage.

INDEX

Legal Cases

For Product Safety Concerns and Information please contact our EU representative GPSR@taylorandfrancis.com
Taylor & Francis Verlag GmbH, Kaufingerstraße 24, 80331 München, Germany

www.ingramcontent.com/pod-product-compliance
Lightning Source LLC
LaVergne TN
LVHW021126300926
849160LV00010B/887
9781032747637